M1 6/87

A JOHN BOSWELL ASSOCIATES BOOK

WHAT EVERY EXECUTIVE BETTER KNOW ABOUT THE LAW

MICHAEL G. TRACHTMAN

SIMON AND SCHUSTER · NEW YORK

Manufactured in the United States of America

1   3   5   7   9   10   8   6   4   2

Library of Congress Cataloging-in-Publication Data

Trachtman, Michael G.
What every executive better know about the law.

"A John Boswell Associates book."
1.   Business law—United States.   2.   Contracts—
United States.   I.   Title.
KF889.3.T73   1987   346.73'07   86-24537

ISBN: 0-671-60046-X   347.3067

ACKNOWLEDGMENTS

I was able to practice law and write this book at the same time thanks to my partner, Paul Logan. He covered for me more than once, and for that I am most grateful.

Numerous clients have contributed both their insights and their experiences to this book, and I thank them for what they've taught me. I owe a special acknowledgment to Bill Algeo of Kappe Associates in Rockville, Maryland, whose encouragement and advice—before and after I started the book—have been of particular importance to me.

I am especially thankful to my editor at Simon and Schuster, Fred Hills. Lawyers always have trouble explaining the law to nonlawyers, and Fred's editorial skills were invaluable to me, most notably in the book's organization, and in the presentation of some of the law's more difficult concepts. In addition to giving me the opportunity to write the book, Fred's guidance made the book much more readable and comprehensible than it would otherwise have been.

Finally, from the time that this book was only a vague concept, John Boswell has been the perfect sounding board and constructive critic. John kept the book focused and on track, and his clear thinking sharpened my analysis of the business problems and solutions I've tried to confront. He was always precisely what I needed, whenever I needed him.

TO MY WIFE,
JENNIE,
WHO NEVER
COMPLAINED,
EVEN WHEN
I TOOK THE
MANUSCRIPT
ON OUR HONEYMOON

CONTENTS

INTRODUCTION

THE 90–10 RULE:
Approaching the Law on
a "Need to Know" Basis

The scene is painfully familiar to every business lawyer. It begins when a client learns that the other party to an agreement has decided to back out of the deal, torture the terms of a clear understanding, or file a million-dollar lawsuit for no apparent reason. Fueled by righteous indignation, the exasperated executive heads for his attorney's office.

"Here's a copy of the contract," he says. "It's right there in black and white. As far as I'm concerned, they don't have a leg to stand on."

After gathering the facts and scanning the fine print, the lawyer looks up apologetically. "I'm sorry," he says, "but I'm afraid it's not that clear-cut. If only you had . . ."—and the lawyer reluctantly fills in the blank, telling his client how the problem, which may take years and thousands of dollars to resolve, could easily have been prevented if only the client had written the right kind of letter, used some different words, or understood certain legal "technicalities."

The lawyer feels, well, almost guilty. It's no fun being the bearer of bad news, and he knows that the client views him as the gatekeeper to a system without apparent rhyme or reason.

The client feels both victimized and frustrated. He knows he's right, but he can't do anything about it. Like most executives, he wants to play by the rules. His problem is that no one ever tells him what they are until it's too late.

To avoid its pitfalls, the law requires you to master certain concepts, such as the nature of a contract, the difference between a negotiation and a binding deal, the way to handle oral and written agreements and to work with forms, what to say and do at the right time, and what to worry about if you're sued or if you find it necessary to sue someone yourself.

That, however, is often a lot easier said than done. Business law is an especially wide-ranging, often overwhelming body of knowledge. It intimidates many business people. They figure that no matter what they do, they'll never be able to learn it all, and they end up taking the "I may as well assume I'm right until somebody tells me I'm wrong" approach.

Others, having kept abreast of various laws and lawsuits, conjure up worlds of farfetched contingencies and legal hobgoblins, where no deal is worth doing. For them, knowing too much about the law can be just as troublesome as knowing too little.

Is there any hope, short of living with a lawyer (totally out of the question) or enrolling in law school (almost as bad)?

Fortunately, there is not only hope, but a solution. To keep clear of the danger of knowing too little and the confusion of knowing too much, business executives should approach the law on a strict "need to know" basis. You can't ignore the law, but don't bite off more than you can chew, either.

The "need to know" method works particularly well in the law, which, I've found, follows a kind of 90–10 rule: 10 percent of the law covers about 90 percent of the problems, and within that 10 percent is an enormous amount of practical, preventive, immediately applicable information. It's much more important to know some things than others, and once you cover what's most important, you quickly reach a point of diminishing returns.

I've placed my focus on that crucial 10 percent; and as a result, this isn't a book that's meant to solve all your legal problems. No book could; in truth, any absolute statement one might make about the law could be a setup for countless exceptions and complexities. You can't acquire a lawyer's expertise over a weekend. You'll still need legal counsel on a regular basis, no matter what.

But this is a book that can put you on the right track and keep you there. An executive needs to learn how to spot legal problems, and get the weight of the law on his side, while there's still time for a lawyer to do something about them. This book can help you do that. Properly applied, it can keep you out of the trouble that ensnares your competitors. It can show you previously unknown risks and chart your course around them. It can help you negotiate, by showing you the significance of what you are negotiating for. It can limit the number of times your lawyer will begin a sentence with, "If only you had . . ."

And when disputes arise, as they always will, it can give you the ammunition you need to win.

P A R T

ONE

LEARNING TO PLAY BY THE RULES

"If the law supposes that, the law is a ass, a idiot."
— *Mr. Bumble, in Dickens's* Oliver Twist

Most business executives assume that as long as they act in a way that's "fair," do what's "right," and use their "common sense," they won't run into legal trouble. But sooner or later, they all discover that what seemed so perfectly obvious to them is not so obvious in the eyes of the law. Mr. Bumble's sentiments find a lot of support in the business community.

In dealing with the law, the trick is to set aside your preconceptions. You need to accept the law for what it is, as opposed to what you think it is or what you think it should be. You have to learn to play by the rules, whether or not you agree with them.

Most of this book is designed to give you hard, utilitarian legal know-how, but Part One is different. It's very difficult to approach business problems by forgetting what you know, even temporarily, and yet that's exactly what the law requires. Part One is intended to help you over that hurdle. It's a matter of adjusting your perspective, how you look at things—and that's the first step in putting together the legal early-warning system that every executive needs.

1 THE PERILS OF COMMON SENSE

When I applied to law school, one part of the entrance exam required the applicant to accept as a given an outrageously bogus "rule of law," such as "To form a valid contract, one party must make misrepresentations to the other." The test then presented a hypothetical legal problem and instructed the applicant to choose the best advice, based on that rule, for his client. Among the multiple choices were various pearls of unassailable lawyerlike wisdom. They sounded right, but they were "wrong" —they didn't conform to the given "law." The correct answer, however, seemed like nonsense—the client had better lie if he wanted the contract to be binding, or the client should try to deceive the other party during negotiations.

It was very difficult to divorce oneself from what one knew to be "right," but according to the rules of the test, the seemingly "wrong" advice was the only "legal" advice there was.

The test focused on the prospective lawyer's ability to understand and apply the law regardless of his own opinions and beliefs, however strongly felt. It's a crucial, lawyerly aptitude. Every practicing attorney quickly learns that whether the law seems "right" or "wrong" makes for interesting cocktail-party conversation, and not much else. Being philosophically or even morally "right" doesn't do much for the client's bottom line; in the law, the only thing that really matters is "legal" or "illegal."

THINKING LIKE A LAWYER

This, as I later came to realize, is what law professors call "thinking like a lawyer." It's the skill of approaching a problem without preconceptions or passions, without regard to what seems right, wrong, fair, or unfair. The first thing every student learns in law school is that be it common sense or nonsense, the law is the law. You've got to focus on it and comply with it, or else.

In today's litigation climate, thinking like a lawyer can keep a business executive out of a lot of legal hot water. The question, however, is whether it's worth it. A primary asset of many executives is their business judgment, their intuition, their feel for what will fly and what won't. They've always relied on their common sense and gut reaction, and they always will.

I'm not suggesting that you let the tail wag the dog, ignoring your business savvy in order to stay out of court. Instead, I'm suggesting that you develop a sort of parallel awareness of the law. It can be kept in a separate mental compartment, to be used when you need it, in tandem with your conventional business acumen. Thinking like a lawyer merely adds a step to the way you make decisions: once you decide what makes sense from a business perspective, you should stop, take a step back, and measure it against the law's standards, which may be very different. That's what gives you the ability to stop your common sense from leading you astray, before it's too late.

Consider these examples:

• The Good Guys want their accounting records computerized before their next quarter begins. The Bad Guys say they can do it in two months, and on that basis, they get the job. Just to make sure, the Good Guys sign the Bad Guys to a contract that penalizes them $1,000 for every week the job is behind schedule.

Sure enough, the Bad Guys finish four weeks late, and pursuant to the contract, the Good Guys withhold $4,000 from their fee. Nevertheless, the Bad Guys sue for the money, plus interest. At the trial, everyone says that the Bad Guys agreed to be penalized for late completion. Can the Bad Guys recover the money anyway?

• The Bad Guys Construction Company calls up the Good Guys Equipment Company and places an order for five bulldozers. The next day, the Bad Guys get a better price from another company. So when the Good Guys deliver the bulldozers, the Bad Guys refuse them and deny ever having ordered them.

At the trial, the Good Guys show the judge their salesman's

order book, where the Bad Guys' order was dutifully and clearly logged. They even produce a witness who overheard the Bad Guys place the order. The Bad Guys say they simply don't remember. Can the Good Guys hold the Bad Guys to the deal?

• The Bad Guys Restaurant Chain orders one thousand crates of eggs from the Good Guys Dairy. The eggs are to be delivered one hundred crates each week, and the Bad Guys are to pay in installments, upon receipt of each shipment.

The first week's eggs are delivered, and no payment is made. The second week's eggs are delivered, and no payment is made. Finally, the Good Guys tell the Bad Guys that they can't deliver any more eggs until the account is brought up to date.

Inexplicably, the Bad Guys decide that's unreasonable, and they buy the eggs they need on the open market, at a higher price. And to add insult to injury, they sue the Good Guys for the difference. The Good Guys say they shouldn't have to keep delivering eggs they're not paid for. Did they do anything wrong?

In all three cases, I've telegraphed the outcome by using the Good Buy/Bad Guy nomenclature, and in all three cases you're right: the Good Guys lose and the Bad Guys win—despite, and sometimes defying, what's "right," what's "fair," and what makes "common sense."

The first example presents a clear, unambiguous, and undisputed contract clause in the Good Guys' favor—a deal's a deal, and this one says that they're entitled to the $4,000. But what the Good Guys didn't know is that the law will usually refuse to enforce a "penalty clause" like this one. They can collect the actual damages caused by the Bad Guys' late performance (of which there are none), but no more. And in the process, the Good Guys spent an additional $2,000 in legal fees.

In the case of the Bad Guys who ordered the bulldozers, the Good Guys' presentation goes unchallenged, but the Bad Guys still win. In most states, a contract like this one has to be documented by a written exchange between the parties. Here, the only document was a private order book kept by the Good Guys. If the Good Guys had mailed a simple confirmation, they would have won the case. But it's too late now.

The Good Guys Dairy abided by the "no tickee–no washee"

rule of doing business, and it seems logical that they shouldn't have to keep delivering what they're not being paid for. But they still lose. When goods are to be delivered in installments, the law often says that you can't cut off deliveries for nonpayment, unless you have good reason to believe your customer is going out of business or would refuse to pay eventually. You're supposed to sue for the money and, meanwhile, keep delivering.

These are not unusual situations chosen to make a point. They are the everyday grist for the business mill, the rules as opposed to the exceptions to the rules. The results seem "wrong," yet it's all "legal," and the failure to grasp that distinction—the failure to think like a lawyer before finalizing a course of action—is the stuff of which lawsuits and rude awakenings are made.

THE OMNISCIENCE PROBLEM

Let's assume that you're willing to accept the fact that common sense and intuition are unreliable, sometimes highly dangerous substitutes for legal know-how. You're ready to learn the law and think like a lawyer—whatever's necessary to avoid lawyers and lawsuits.

Unfortunately, your good intentions will carry you only so far. We live in a complex, convoluted society. Where once there were only the Ten Commandments, now there are law libraries with hundreds of thousands of volumes, supplemented by computerized legal research systems. Even the lawyers can't keep up. There's simply too much law to know.

Surely, you say, the "system" accommodates that predicament. Of course, it's said that "Ignorance of the law excuses no man," and that makes sense in some situations. A criminal, for instance, shouldn't be able to escape a robbery charge by contending that he didn't know robbery was illegal. But realistically, how could an executive's ignorance of, for example, boilerplate "legalese" and thousand-page business statutes be inexcusable? Wouldn't that amount to penalizing every executive just because he's not a lawyer?

Maybe, but even so, it happens every day—and there's the

rub. Business is governed by a system of law that is either widely unknown or consistently misapprehended, not because of negligence on the part of business people, but because of its breadth and complexity. And all the while, the law requires—in fact, demands—that you know what it is and how to use it. As a business executive, you're supposed to be virtually omniscient.

WHY THE LAW IS "UNFAIR"

That omniscience problem raises a serious question. Why doesn't the system concern itself with questions of fairness and reasonableness, instead of technicalities and legalities that require people to be nearly all-knowing?

It's a question that can't be answered without first posing another one: fairness and reasonableness according to whom?

Our society could have opted for a system of resolving disputes in which judges hear the evidence and use their sense of right and wrong to determine the winner and loser. Sounds good. But suppose the judge you draw happens to be your adversary's uncle? Or doesn't like the way you look? Or has a personal bias against your position? The result of the case would depend on the judge who happens to hear it. It comes out one way in one courtroom and the other way in another courtroom.

And when the dispute comes up again, you still won't know who's right and who's wrong without another trial. What you could or couldn't do would depend solely on who happened to be "the law" that day.

Rooted in revolution against monarchy, we took a different path. The system does not set out to produce technically correct results at the expense of fairness, although it happens. It does not seek to elevate clever gamesmanship over justice. But recognizing the tyranny of the other options, we chose to be a government of laws, not men. We operate out of a rule book. How "right" and "fair" you tried to be is largely irrelevant. There's too much room for disagreement about what's right and fair. It's in the eye of the beholder. What matters is whether you followed the rules.

That, stated simply, is both the benefit and the burden the

law imposes on the executive, the entrepreneur, the CEO, the consultant, the manufacturers' representative—and the average guy on the street.

On the positive side, theoretically, at least, the law is predictable and impartial, not subject to the whims and biases of individual judges. (It hasn't always worked that way, of course, especially among the poor, the minorities, and the unpopular.) It's not to be made up as we go along. As with a speed limit, you are told what the rules are in advance. You are notified how fast you're allowed to drive without running afoul of the law—and if you get a ticket because you didn't see the sign, it's your own fault.

On the negative side, as the world grew more complicated, so did the rules. The system, while well intentioned, seemingly expects you to be a law professor. If ignorance of the law isn't an excuse, maybe it ought to be. The speed-limit signs aren't always posted. And even when they are, they're often impossible to understand.

ADJUSTING YOUR ATTITUDES

There's no perfect fix for the omniscience problem, but the 90–10 rule-"need to know" approach works most of the time. What's important is mastering certain basics about the situations that recur most frequently, and if you couple that with the right kind of regular contact with your lawyer, you'll be able to circumvent the bulk of the law's disagreeability.

But to make the 90–10 rule work, you'll have to do more than just learn some rules. You'll also have to understand a bit about the law's ingrained perspectives and attitudes. The way most successful executives view the world just doesn't square with the way the law sees things, and the sooner you're able to swallow that and accept the law on its own terms, the more productive and less frustrating your legal experiences will be.

For instance, business executives are paid to focus on profits and efficiencies. In most cases, that's the way success is measured. Consequently, they have to make decisions in a pragmatic, one-sided, sometimes unsympathetic way. If a salesman consistently fails to produce, eventually he's got to go. The fact that he has an excuse for not producing usually doesn't matter. It's a numbers game. If a competitor is hurting you in the marketplace, you have to do what's necessary to beat him back, no matter what it takes. That's the nature of business. It requires a bottom-line approach to problem-solving.

The law, on the other hand, specializes in a larger, "what's best for society in general" point of view. As a result, your right to fire an unproductive employee might be severely limited, subordinated to a court's view of "broader social interests." Your efforts to dominate your competition might be restricted by a legislature's concern for "public policy." What's important to an executive is often unimportant, or even dangerous, from the law's standpoint, and the difference in perspectives often results in a headlong and confusing collision.

Or consider those times when, by any reasonable standard, you're right and they're wrong. They took the goods and didn't pay; they promised they'd finish in a week and it took them a month; the contract said one thing and they did another.

You'd expect that kind of situation to be wrapped up quickly and efficiently, but it rarely works that way. Nothing in the law is black and white. Nothing gets prejudged. Everybody gets his day in court, complete with every imaginable procedural safeguard, every benefit of the doubt, and every chance to tell his side of the story, no matter how long it takes. As much as a "let's cut out the bull and get to the heart of the matter" approach may be beneficial in business, it just gets in the way when you deal with the legal system.

It's often said that in dealing with those accused of a crime, our system would prefer to let a thousand guilty men go free than risk convicting one innocent man. It's not much different when it comes to the laws that apply to business. The system tries above everything else to be neutral, to adjust competing interests and to find a middle ground whenever possible. It's always looking at the other side of the coin, the other guy's point of view.

As a result, everybody, but everybody's got "rights." Buyers have rights, sellers have rights, consumers have rights, employees have rights—and thank goodness they do, but there are so many rights that one often contradicts another. That's why law-yers say "it depends" in response to almost every question their clients ask. It's tough to decipher all the variables, even in the seemingly "clear" cases.

The predictable result is a somewhat cumbersome, decidedly unbusinesslike mechanism, which is one of the prices we pay for a democratic society.

Those who are most successful in dealing with the law don't philosophize about it. They learn it, they accept it for what it is, and then—and by far, most important—they analyze how to take advantage of it. They know how the rules fit together, their underlying assumptions, where the holes are, where the short-cuts are, and what strategies work best. They employ the law's peculiarities as weapons. They learn to use the law on its own terms, as a tool, a means to get from point A to point B.

For most executives, dealing productively with the law means forgoing the temptation to rail at "the system"; it means adopt-ing the attitude that you can't beat it, so you may as well set aside the way you're used to doing things, at least for the time being, and join it. That's a cynical approach, to be sure, but there's no practical alternative.

Is the law "unfair"? During the business day, at least, it really doesn't matter. What's important is this: how can the unfairness of it all be imposed more on *them* than on *you*?

That's the focus of the remainder of the book.

2 LEGAL MYTHOLOGY

There's an additional roadblock that stands between most business executives and the pragmatic, preventive knowledge of the law they need.

The business community shares certain beliefs about the law that are so widespread and pervasive that they are presumed, without question, to *be* law. This "common wisdom" is a great example of the old maxim that if you repeat something often enough, people will eventually believe it's true. It amounts to a kind of deep-rooted legal mythology. And though it all seems right, it's all dead wrong.

THE CASE OF THE MISSING MONEY

An experience I had several years ago shows how ingrained and dangerous this mythology can be. Donald Dell, the well-known Washington sports attorney and television commentator, asked me to represent some of his tennis-player clients who were having trouble collecting their endorsement royalties from a tennis clothing company in Philadelphia. As the case unfolded, it became obvious that the executives who owned the clothing company were true believers in a variety of legal misassumptions, and it ended up costing them dearly.

The contracts Dell had negotiated for his clients required each of them to wear and promote the clothing company's tennis outfits. In exchange, the players were to get a cut of the sales. It seemed like an excellent deal, and the clothes sold well. But when it came time for the clothing company to pay up, its coffers were mysteriously empty, and its owners offered little in the way of explanation or regret. A brief investigation revealed that the clothing company had been newly incorporated just for this one venture, and the same executives owned an older, more established company with a surprisingly hefty bank account. It didn't take a Perry Mason to figure out that the proceeds from the clothing sales somehow got shifted from one account to the other, leaving my clients with a valid claim against a worthless company.

Dell told me he had known about the two companies right from the start of the negotiations. Recognizing the risks in that kind of setup, he had insisted both companies be on the hook for the money owed to the tennis players, just in case the executives were tempted to try some "creative accounting." According to Dell, the executives agreed, but for "tax reasons," they didn't want the obligation of the older, established company to be in the written contracts.

That was fine with Dell, but to protect his clients, he wrote a "confirming letter" to the executives—a typical lawyer's device designed to substantiate the terms of an oral deal. In so many words, Dell told the executives that in allowing his players to sign the written contracts with just the new clothing company, he was relying on their assurance that the older company would back up the obligation. He needed this security, he wrote, before the contracts could be finalized, and he concluded the letter by telling the executives to let him know in writing if there was any misunderstanding. He then waited a reasonable period of time, and when there was no response to his confirming letter, the contracts were signed.

The stage was set. When the executives refused to pay a nickel, I filed suit against both the tennis clothing company and the older, solvent company, and I also sued the executives themselves. Hoping to avoid a trial, I then contacted my opponents and attempted to negotiate a settlement.

The executives were, shall we say, less than receptive; they threatened to sue me for bringing a lawsuit against the company that had all the money. Dell's letter was just a typical, misleading lawyer's trick, they told me. It's the written contracts that count, they claimed, and everything else, especially a self-serving letter, is just "hearsay." As for my suit against them as individuals, that, they maintained, was "harassment," pure and simple. "Everything we did, we did through a corporation," they stressed.

The executives spoke with conviction. They were, without knowing it, parroting some of the most commonly held beliefs about law and business: when you have a written, signed contract, nothing else matters; when you do business through a corporation, you're always protected. And they were very wrong.

Under a legal doctrine known as "reliance," Dell's letter, combined with the executives' failure to respond to it, made the solvent company liable to the players, no matter what the written contract said. And under a legal doctrine known as "piercing the corporate veil," when money disappears from a corporate account under suspicious circumstances, the individuals behind the corporation can be held liable for its debts.

The executives had never heard of these doctrines. When they did what they did, they assumed the law was on their side. But during the trial, face to face with the law, they had an understandably hard time explaining how they ran the clothing company, where the money had gone, and why they had never answered Dell's letter. They never thought they'd have to answer those kinds of questions, and the more they tried to explain, the worse it got.

I asked the jury to award $900,000 to the players—about four times the amount I had asked the executives to pay during our pretrial negotiations. The jury deliberated for less than an hour —and awarded my clients more than $1.2 million.

THE SIX RED FLAGS

The clothing company executives were classic victims of their myths. Their problem was that they strictly subscribed to the rules as they understood them—an understanding not so much different from that held by a great many executives I've represented over the years. In so doing, they ignored the law.

According to the jury, at least, the executives got what was coming to them. Unfortunately, however, it usually works the other way—it's the well-meaning executives who normally get burned. Their legal misapprehensions make them easy targets. It's a tough way to get educated.

From my own experience, I've been able to categorize six of the most troublesome and widespread legal myths. Like anything else that produces a false sense of knowing what you're doing, they're all extremely dangerous. Treat them as "red flags"; if you normally rely on these assumptions, you could be heading in the wrong direction.

"I GOT IT IN WRITING"

The fact that it's in writing does not mean you win. As explained in the next several chapters, what is and is not a contract in the eyes of the law is not always so simple a question, and it usually doesn't matter whether the deal was made by a handshake, whether it was carved in granite, or whether it was written on the cuff of your shirt.

Moreover, not every writing that looks like a binding and enforceable contract is necessarily valid. Sometimes portions of an agreement will stand up, but the parts you want enforced will be nullified. There may be other documents in the deal which minimize the effect of your agreement—as the clothing executives found out. Or there may be language in the agreement that you don't understand, although you thought you did, making the agreement completely enforceable—against you.

"I DIDN'T SIGN ANYTHING"

This is a frequent companion to the "I got it in writing" myth. Many business executives believe that as long as it's not in writing, it's not binding. "I don't care what I said" goes the refrain. "I didn't sign anything, so there's no deal."

A contract is a contract—whether it's oral, written, or made in sign language. The fact that you didn't sign anything makes no difference. If you made the deal, and if it measures up to what the law calls a "contract," you're bound by it.

"FIND ME A LOOPHOLE"

I always know when I am about to lose a prospective client. He sits down, tosses a paper on my desk, and says, "You're a lawyer. Get me out of this." It is not said maliciously. There is a "logic" to it: every agreement has a loophole known by lawyers; you are a lawyer; therefore, you know the loophole. Any attempt to explain how and why this is not always so is construed as an effort to justify a higher fee.

The belief that there is always a loophole is usually born of hard experience, and it is understandable. Show me a practiced business executive who has never suffered the shock of having a seemingly ironclad agreement fall apart. Often, those who play the "find me a loophole" game had formerly fallen prey to the "I got it in writing" myth. Having once embraced the written agreement, and having been betrayed, they believe that no other agreement is to be trusted.

In truth, there often is a way to circumvent or minimize the effect of a written agreement. But that normally depends on someone's incompetence during the drafting or negotiation phase, and presuming that an adversary will always be careless or ignorant is most unwise. If the transaction was handled correctly—and there usually is a way to do it right—you're stuck. The facts and the law can form a prison from which there is no escape. Clarence Darrow on his best day could not change the effect of that simple fact.

"WHO READS THE FINE PRINT?"

In the law, ignorance is never bliss. Remember that purchase order you signed, the one that said it was "subject to the terms and conditions on the reverse side hereof"—the terms you never read? A lawyer drafted that "reverse side hereof" with someone like you in mind. And he did it because he wanted to protect his client, at your expense, whether or not you ever got around to reading it.

When people in business deal with each other at arm's length, there is a legal presumption that they have read the fine print, understood it, and agreed to be bound by it. Do not assume that it won't harm you just because it has never harmed you before, or because you never looked at it, or did not understand the mumbo jumbo, or because it was never discussed.

It is not that easy. There will be more about the fine print later in the book but, for now, just remember that someone paid a lawyer good money to make sure the "legalese" would leave you high and dry. And he did his best.

"LET THEM SUE ME. I'M PROTECTED"

Misplaced confidence generates the sort of bravado that leads to disaster. A perfect example is an executive who is willing to risk a lawsuit in the belief that his or his company's assets are protected.

Many investors and entrepreneurs know that the law treats a corporation like a separate person with separate assets. Corporate debts are not their debts. Corporate mistakes are not their mistakes. If the corporation goes under, it doesn't take them with it. Because of this basic principle of law, they look at a corporation as a shield which protects them against the consequences of their ill-advised actions.

But as usual, the law is not so cut-and-dried. As the clothing-company executives found out, there is a doctrine known as "piercing the corporate veil," discussed in more detail later in the book. It says that when a corporation is operated for the purpose of escaping obligations, the owners can be held responsible for the company's debts. Switching money among bank accounts, taking the money from one corporation and putting it in the name of another—you can't avoid your company's obligations that easily.

Some executives think they can dodge business creditors by putting their money and investments in their spouses' and children's names. But that doesn't work either. Most states have laws that prevent that sort of thing, known as "fraudulent conveyance acts."

Shrewd business planning can often limit losses and protect assets—but it doesn't work every time, and there is no cure-all. They've done away with debtors' prison, but once a court decides that you owe money, it gives your adversaries the resources they need to find it and take it, all the way into bankruptcy court, if necessary. If your reflex response is "So sue me," think twice.

"LET'S SUE THE BASTARDS!"

People in business need to weigh the spoils of victory against

the cost of victory. Unless there is a good, noneconomic justification for the effort, it makes no sense to pay a lawyer $5,000 to
collect $3,000.

I have found that one of the primary reasons some people are
so quick to sue is that they assume—erroneously—that if they
win, they can make the other side pay their legal fees. The
simple truth shocks many executives: even if you win, you can
lose, because it might cost you more to get what's coming to
you than you are able to recover.

In most jurisdictions, the loser does *not* pay the legal fees.
There are instances in which it does happen, but it is very much
the exception and not the rule. Other countries handle this
differently, and there is a movement afoot in this country to
follow that lead. But in most contexts, it has not happened yet.

So before commencing a lawsuit, remember that even if you
win the battle, the cost of victory may make it seem like a defeat.

These legal myths are very important in and of themselves,
but they also have a broader significance. Each is a "red flag" in
another sense: if you found yourself agreeing with any of them,
even a little, take it as a warning sign that you may be operating
on a variety of additional false legal assumptions. Some executives, for instance, have mistaken notions about the legal effect
of the written conditions that sometimes appear on the back of
checks—"this is a release of all claims," for instance. Others
misconstrue what can and cannot be used in court. Still others
harbor all sorts of misinformation about what they can do to
collect debts. And there are myths that are unique to particular
businesses.

What's important is to think about your legal preconceptions.
If you've been operating on a set of suppositions simply because
they seem perfectly obvious to you, run them past your lawyer.
They may not be so obvious to him.

P A R T

TWO

LET'S MAKE A DEAL:
The Nuts and Bolts of a Contract

In the winter of 1985, the case of Pennzoil versus Texaco went to trial in a Texas courtroom. Pennzoil claimed that it had an "agreement in principle" with Getty which gave it the right to purchase a controlling interest in Getty's stock. Texaco, Pennzoil argued, messed up the deal by offering Getty a higher price for the stock, causing Getty to back out.

If what Pennzoil claimed was true, Texaco would be liable for Pennzoil's damages. The law does not permit one corporation to interfere with the binding contracts of another. Texaco, however, had what it thought to be a clear defense against the charge. There was never any real "contract" between Pennzoil and Getty, said Texaco. There was just a lot of informal talk. At most, it was a "handshake deal"—the lawyers had not yet drafted the formal, written agreements. Nothing was final and binding, at least, not yet.

Texaco turned out to be wrong—the jury found that the Pennzoil–Getty "handshake deal" was, in fact, a legally binding contract, and hit Texaco with an $11-billion verdict, the largest damage award in history. Several months later, *The Wall Street Journal* reported that as a result of the "Texaco chill," some business executives were changing their way of doing business. As a general rule, no one had ever considered informal, conversational commitments to be legally binding, but now that wasn't so clear. Said the *Journal* in its April 15, 1986, issue: "Deal makers say the huge verdict, by undermining time honored assumptions on Wall Street about what constitutes an enforceable agreement and what doesn't, is forcing people to be much more cautious."

To my way of thinking, that caution is long overdue. Those "time honored assumptions" have always been wrong—they're all variants of the "I didn't sign anything" legal myth. That doesn't mean that deal makers should stop making deals. But it does mean that they should learn the difference between "just negotiating" and making a binding agreement.

That's why the study of contract law is so important. Essentially, it's the business world's operating manual. It's the chapter in the "rule book" that defines what's enforceable and what's not. Your attorney can't be with you every time you dictate a letter, talk on the telephone, or go to a meeting. By the time he gets involved, it's usually too late—the "crime" of unintentional or misconstrued obligations will already have been committed. And as a matter of economics, only the major or complicated deals get the red-carpet legal treatment. In the so-called "simple deals"—the ones that make up the bulk of what goes on in business—you're usually left to fend for yourself.

Without a functional understanding of contract law, you're an easy mark for the kind of lawsuit that devastates a company and destroys a career.

3 MAKING A CONTRACT: What You Don't Sign Can Still Hurt You

Business executives frequently talk about "making a deal" or "reaching an agreement" or "arriving at an understanding." At this stage of their negotiations, they want their attorneys to write it up in a "contract," which they perceive to be something very different from what they already have.

But more often than not, the "deal" or "agreement" or "understanding" is *already* a legally valid contract. It was made well before the ink hit the paper, and it stays binding whether or not a written version is ever prepared.

That's because lawyers and documents do not make contracts. People make contracts by what they say and do—in meetings, over the telephone, through correspondence. And a contract, once made, becomes immediately enforceable, whether or not it's in writing—that's the lesson of Pennzoil versus Texaco. In much the same way that you might point to a photograph and say "That's my mother," a contract and the form in which it is recorded are two wholly separate matters.

The business community has developed a litany of terms that contribute to the confusion. Each is understood to mean something other than "contract"—for example, "agreement," "agreement in principle," "understanding," "arrangement," "bargain," "handshake deal," "moral commitment." As a result, business executives get dangerously tangled up in terms they do not understand. They attach a label to their dealings, and although the label may have a meaning to them, it is often meaningless in the eyes of the law.

But a contract by any other name is still a contract. Your recent telephone call—the one in which you finalized the "understanding"—may indeed be a contract as enforceable as any your legal department ever drafted. That one-line letter you've just received confirming the "arrangement" may be evidence of a contract that is no less binding than a thousand-page merger agreement signed by the board of directors.

The failure to grasp this basic rudiment of contract law produces a dangerous misconception. It masks the existence of legal obligations, often with disastrous results. And it plagues the chief executive officer as much as the corner storekeeper.

A good example involves Leonard Tose, the former owner of my hometown Philadelphia Eagles. A few years ago, Mr. Tose got involved in complicated negotiations with some investors who wanted to buy the team. Eventually, an agreement was reached and the lawyers were told to start preparing the formal documents for signature. But before the papers were finalized, Mr. Tose reconsidered and decided not to sell.

The buyers maintained that the deal was beyond the backing-out stage, and they sued to get the team. In response, Mr. Tose confidently faced the media and assured Philadelphia that no deal had been finalized. There might have been an "understanding" or the outline of an "arrangement," he maintained, but there was no signed "contract," and whatever had happened around the conference table was not yet legally binding.

Like many executives, Mr. Tose apparently believed that a "contract" had to be in the form of a written, "legal" document. But when the case got to court, the judge disagreed. What was important, the judge said, was what had gone on between the people involved—not what they called it or whether they decided to have their lawyers write it down on paper.

It was a quick, but very expensive, lesson. Even without a document full of "whereases" and "wherefores," there was enough of a "contract" to cost Mr. Tose a seven-figure settlement.

Formal written contracts are important; make no mistake about it. A written contract draws together the meetings, telephone calls, and correspondence in one, final record. It remembers the details of the deal, no matter how much the parties forget. And if the transaction ever ends up in court, a written contract is the best evidence there is.

But the writing does not *create* the contract. The writing comes into being after the contract is born, as a means of clarifying and preserving it for future reference. Again, contracts are formed by what people say and do, not by what papers they sign. Once you understand and appreciate that bedrock concept, you've got the foundation on which to build an understanding of contract law.

THE NUT, THE BOLT, AND THE WASHER

So how is a contract formed? It happens when someone makes an "offer," which is then followed by an "acceptance," as long as there is "consideration." The courts term this process an "objective manifestation of mutual assent." The rest of us call it a deal.

An offer is an expressed willingness to make a binding agreement on certain terms. When you say, "I will buy your car for five hundred dollars," you have made an offer.

An acceptance is an unqualified and unconditional assent to the offer. As precisely as a nut must fit a bolt, it must match the offer, without deviating from it. You need only say "Okay," or "I agree to your offer," or "It's a deal" in order to communicate a proper acceptance.

Consideration means that each of the contracting parties must exchange something of value with the other. Like a washer that helps secure the nut to the bolt, consideration holds the deal together by giving each side something to gain if the deal is carried out. If you sell your car for $500, the consideration is the exchange of the car for the money. Instead of cash for the car, the consideration could be a different car, or a painting, or a promise to do something in the future. It need not even be a fair or even exchange. To eliminate questions about consideration, formal legal agreements often recite that they are made "in consideration of one dollar." Even that nominal sum is sufficient. All that matters is that something of value—almost anything—changes hands, both ways.

Consideration problems rarely come up in everyday business, and when they do, they generally produce a can of legal worms not worth opening here. In 99 percent of the situations you're likely to see, consideration will take care of itself.

At the precise instant that an offer is met by an acceptance, a legally enforceable agreement is formed. At that point, although they do not have to, the parties can express the deal in writing if they want, just in case there are any future disputes over who was supposed to do what. Any deal—from the simplest to the most complicated—can be memorialized in a written contract.

A proper written agreement is nothing more than a clearly stated recapitulation of the deal, signed by all parties to it. There are no magic words and there is no particular form that must be followed. The only "hard part" is to express the agreement accurately, precisely, and completely, so that there is no misunderstanding or room for misinterpretation. For example:

> *Seller is the owner of a DeLorean automobile that Buyer wishes to purchase. Seller agrees to sell it and Buyer agrees to buy it for the price of $500.*
>
> _____ *For Seller*
> _____ *For Buyer*

This is as valid and binding as any contract that ever was. The writing itself can be called "the contract" or "the agreement"—although it is really just an embodiment of the parties' deal in a tangible form. But no matter what you call it, either side could present it to a court and request damages or other legal remedies in the event of trouble.

And that's all there is to making contracts—which is, I realize, rather like saying that marketing is simply a matter of getting the customer to buy what you're selling, or that making a profit is simply a matter of spending less than you take in. Although the fundamentals of offer, acceptance, and consideration are easy enough to explain, it is no coincidence that in *The Paper Chase*, the demanding Professor Kingsfield was a professor of contract law. Conceptually, it can be a mind-wrenching topic, fraught with insidious complications.

Fortunately, however, you can learn to minimize, if not avoid, most of the complications that are likely to plague your everyday transactions without assimilating all of contract law's nuances and theory. In the next chapter, we begin discussing how.

4 THE COMPLICATIONS: "Loopholes" and "Legal Technicalities"

"Loopholes" and "legal technicalities"—that's what business executives derisively call the contract complications that affect them the most.

For example, after the DeLorean agreement described in Chapter 3 is signed, suppose the seller starts to take out the radio. "What did you expect for five hundred dollars?" he says. The buyer protests, but when he checks with his lawyer, he'll find that things aren't as clear as he thought, and the seller may be right—a typical loophole.

Or, as the buyer drives it away, a cloud of blue smoke fills the air, and he decides he wants out. But the contract doesn't say the seller's DeLorean has to be in good working order. A court may well make the buyer take the car, no matter how severe its problems—a vintage legal technicality.

Executives who get shafted as a result of loopholes or legal technicalities almost always have the same objection. "But that's not what I meant," they say. The general assumption seems to be that the law will bind a party only to what he really and truly meant in his heart of hearts, no matter what he said. After all, would the law sit back and allow someone's words to be twisted into a deal he never intended to make?

Indeed it would, and the mistaken notion that the law protects people from their own imprecise or incomplete agreements is what leads to the vast majority of loopholes and legal technicalities in the first place.

THE "REASONABLE PERSON" PROBLEM

Any effort to close the loopholes and avoid the legal technicalities has to begin with an understanding of one particularly

wide-ranging legal concept: contract law is more concerned with
how things look than with how they really are. What you really
meant is not important. What counts is how a "reasonable person" would *interpret* what you said and did. You are judged by
appearances.

For instance, suppose you tell your secretary to prepare a
letter offering to sell your company to me for $100,000. By mis-
take, however, she drops a zero and types the price as "$10,000,"
and you sign the letter without reading it. Can I buy the business for the price stated in the letter?

As long as your words sound like a genuine offer, I could
accept your offer and hold you to the deal. It makes no difference that you really didn't mean it. You could pass one hundred
lie-detector tests and it would not matter. If a reasonable person
would have understood what you said to be an offer to sell at
$10,000, then that's what it will be—period.

Often, this principle produces some truly "unfair" results.
It ties some people into deals and cheats others out of deals,
no matter what the parties to the transaction actually intended.

For example, a famous Virginia case arose from a night in
1952 when Mr. Zehmer and Mr. Lucy sat drinking and talking.
Lucy offered Zehmer $50,000 cash for his farm. Selling out was
the last thing Zehmer wanted to do, and he assumed that Lucy
was joking. But he also wanted to prove that Lucy was just a big
talker who didn't really have $50,000 cash. So he purported to
accept the offer, wrote up a memorandum of the sale, and
practically dared Lucy to follow through.

The next day, Lucy raised the money and declared that the
farm was rightfully his. When Zehmer refused to sell, Lucy
sued.

At the trial, Zehmer testified that he "was high as a Georgia
pine" and that the transaction "was just a bunch of two dog-
goned drunks bluffing to see who could talk the biggest and say
the most." But the court found that no matter what Zehmer
might have intended, it all looked real to Lucy. Zehmer might
not have *felt* serious, but he had *acted* serious. The court concluded: "So a person cannot set up that he was merely jesting
when his conduct and words would warrant a reasonable person

in believing that he intended a real agreement." Lucy, so to speak, had bought the farm, and the court ordered Zehmer to sell it to him.

When you think about it, the rule makes sense. If what people meant to say were more important than what they actually said, everyone would have to be a mind reader, and every party to a bad deal would have an instant escape hatch—"Maybe that's what I said, but it's not what I meant."

Still, although the rule may be sound, applying it is something else again. If there's an ambiguity, a judge or jury has to decide how your words and deeds would strike a "reasonable person." How, you might ask, will they do that? By their gut reaction, sad to say, and that will vary from gut to gut. One judge or juror might conclude that because your business is obviously worth far more than $10,000, a reasonable person should have known that your offer was the product of a typographical error. But another might conclude that a reasonable person is entitled to take what you said at face value. One judge or juror might agree that Lucy was entitled to take Zehmer seriously. And another might see it differently.

As predictable and impartial as the law tries to be, determining what's "reasonable" is a fickle and subjective process. It's usually little more than a matter of personal opinion. There are no absolutes, and allowing a court to make that determination for you is the quickest and surest way to lose control of your business destiny.

SAY WHAT YOU MEAN

There is a universal antidote to being caught between what you meant and what you said: say what you mean. It's a two-step process. First, be clear on your intent. Second, carefully choose the words that precisely convey that intent.

Suppose, for instance, you have perfected and patented a vastly improved electronic typewriter. One day you receive a letter from IBM asking your price for all rights to your invention. You really don't know what it's worth, but you're willing to talk, so you mention an arbitrary round number. "I really couldn't accept less than $500,000," you write, and you sit back to see what happens.

The next week, there are two letters in your mailbox. The first is from IBM: "We accept your offer. Enclosed is our check for $500,000." The second, from Xerox, offers to buy your type-writer for $1 million. You send IBM your regrets, and accept the Xerox deal.

Will IBM win when it goes to court to enforce its "contract"? Maybe. Maybe not. It will depend on how a court interprets your letter. Would a reasonable person construe it as an offer to make a binding agreement? Or was it just a "feeler," tossed out to see what the market would bear? The decision could go either way, which means that the worth of your invention—$500,000 or $1 million—will be determined by someone other than your-self, and that's no way to do business.

Your first mistake was responding before you had a real un-derstanding of what you wanted to say. Vague thoughts produce vague words. If, in truth, you'd like to hear what the prospect has to offer before you make up your mind, that's okay. Just say it plainly: "I'd like to keep my options open. How much are you willing to pay?"

If, on the other hand, you've settled on a price you'd be willing to accept, say so, and expend the extra effort it takes to make it clear. "I would be willing to sell my rights for $500,000." Don't ad-lib. Decide what you want before you speak, or decide not to decide.

Some business executives like to play their cards close to their vest, and many savvy negotiators feel it wise to veil their true intent in mystery. In many contexts, that may be good bargain-ing strategy. But if the negotiation gets down to offers and ac-ceptances—or words that might be interpreted as offers and acceptances—it's time to stop being cute or clever and reveal what you really mean.

Words are most of what the law has to deal with, and words are inherently imprecise. Nevertheless, courts ruthlessly punish loose language. You have to know what you want, and you have to make what you want known. It takes caution and fore-thought. In contract law, there's no such thing as a successful hip shooter.

Two Important Tiebreakers

Even when you are careful to say what you mean, the words you choose can still mean different things to different people. To you, "net profit" might mean the difference between what you made and what you spent—not the kind of thing you have to worry about defining. Yet some movie contracts take ten pages to explain and clarify the same two words. What happens when you use the right words and there are still problems?

Fortunately, contract law has produced some guidelines that help to predict how the ever-present reasonable person might react in such cases. Two of these guidelines are particularly important. In effect, they are the rules by which courts choose one side of the "here's what we really meant" story over the other.

INDUSTRY PRACTICE AND CUSTOM

Most executives have a vague sense that for one reason or another, the standard operating practices in a particular industry are important. But they're not really sure why or how.

On this point, the law is anything but vague: industry practice and custom are more than important—they are crucial. When in Rome, you are expected to think, act and talk like the Romans. Your words and deeds will be construed accordingly.

Suppose you are invited to an ultraexclusive art auction, where the bidding is done by signal—a slight nod, the touch of an ear, the flick of a finger—in order to conceal the identity of the bidder. Unfortunately, on the day of the auction you have an attack of hay fever, and as an unusually ugly (and expensive) vase goes on the block, you feel the need to dab your nose.

Suddenly, the auctioneer's gavel comes down. "Sold!" he says, as his eyes meet yours, "for one thousand dollars."

The next day, when you ask your lawyer to get you out of the "deal," there won't be much he can do. It will not make the slightest difference that you did not know the significance of what you did. You were there; you signaled; you're stuck. (The major auction houses, in fact, have prearranged signals with the major dealers precisely to avoid this sort of complication.) As long as a reasonable auctiongoer would have interpreted your nose wiping as a bid, the law will not disagree.

This principle has broad significance in the business community. In deciding how a particular act or choice of words should be interpreted, courts are especially influenced by the way things are usually done in the industry or business in question. In some fields, for example, it is understood by everyone that an offer is not meant to be serious until it is put in writing. Despite the usual precepts of contract law, courts generally defer. In other settings, like an auction, a finger to the nose is sufficient. The terms "gross" and "net" and "immediate delivery" mean different things in banking, in sales, and in engineering. Courts will assume that you know and use the peculiar meanings that apply in the context in which you do business, whether or not the dictionary agrees.

If you venture into unfamiliar territory, make sure you know the culture and the language. Even if you take particular care to say what you mean, it might be subject to interpretations you never heard of and don't understand.

PAST PRACTICES

Be very much aware of the past practices that have governed dealings between you and the party with whom you are now dealing. When a court tries to determine what "reasonable impressions" your words conveyed, past often becomes prologue.

I once represented a jewelry broker who had an opportunity to make a large profit if he could deliver a certain number of precious stones to one of his customers by a certain date. Upon receiving an assurance that the gems would be delivered in plenty of time, my client placed the order with one of his regular suppliers. Unfortunately, the supplier did not make the delivery by the specified date. My client lost the sale, and with it several hundreds of thousands of dollars in profit.

We sued, and the supplier defended on the ground that his catalogue, from which my client had ordered, clearly required a deposit, which my client had not made. Therefore, the supplier contended, he had not been obligated to ship the merchandise.

We won the suit because my client was able to show that the supplier had accepted his orders from the catalogue for a decade without requiring a deposit. The parties' past actions and practices demonstrated that the deposit requirement was to be ignored. On the basis of history, the court found that my client's supplier really did not mean what the catalogue clearly said.

Courts will always interpret your words and actions through the lens of your past practices. American law relies on precedent, and that predilection spills over into how courts think businesses ought to deal with each other. If "net 30 days" has always meant to you and your customer 10 percent interest after thirty days, a court will respect that tradition absent a very specific understanding to the contrary. If you and your customer have always had a practice that no deal is final until approved by the home office, courts will find that it remains in effect unless you can show a specific agreement to change it.

FILL IN AS MANY BLANKS AS YOU CAN

To really say what you mean, you must do one more thing: you must make sure your words tell the whole story about the deal you think you're making.

Take a situation in which you offer to buy a fleet of company cars for $250,000 and the seller accepts. The deal is clear, as far as it goes, but when are the cars to be delivered? What happens if they're delivered late? Is payment to be made by cash on the barrelhead, or would installment payments be acceptable? If so, would interest be owing? At what rate?

Practicality prevents business people from turning every deal into a book-length document that encompasses all possible contingencies, and the law knows it. Therefore, says the law, an offer with holes, once accepted, can still be the basis for a contract. It only has to cover a bare minimum of central questions. Typically, courts phrase the rule this way: if the offer is so indefinite and imprecise that a court would have no idea what to do if called upon to enforce a contract arising from the offer, then the offer is not valid; otherwise, it is sufficiently detailed.

That can be good news and bad news. The good news is that

business executives can form binding contracts without first
having to retain lawyers to answer every "what if" question that
might conceivably arise from the deal. Even with all the open
questions, your fleet-purchase offer specifies what's being pur-
chased, for what price, which is more than enough. When it's
accepted, a contract is formed.

But what happens if there's a dispute about delivery dates or
payment terms or any of the other details that are left out of the
deal? How do you answer the open questions?

That's the bad news. Like it or not, a court will take it upon
itself to answer the open questions for you, playing "fill in the
blanks" with your contract. It will do that by presuming you
would have acted like a—you guessed it—"reasonable person"
during the negotiations, had you thought to discuss the matter
now causing the problems. The court's concept of custom in
the industry and any prior dealings between the parties will be
very influential factors as it "assists" you in determining the
details of your deal—creating loopholes and legal technicalities
along the way.

To avoid situations in which a court makes your deal for you,
make it for yourself. The only way you can be sure that certain
terms are included in the deal is to put them in. The only way
you can be sure that other terms are not included in the deal is
to specify that they're out.

How Does It Look?

Ultimately, your best defense against the "reasonable person"
problem is continually asking yourself one, basic question:
"How is what's being done or said now going to look later on?"

Remember that no matter what the truth is, you may not be
able to prove what was really meant once you get to court. An
appreciation of this fact is drilled into the head of every lawyer
from the first day of law school. It is another element of "thinking like a lawyer": the only things that count are the things you
can prove.

Be careful, for instance, when the other party to your deal, a
person whom you trust, tells you that he's never going to use

the promissory note he wants you to sign. It's just that he needs it for his boss. Even if it's true, he may no longer be working for that company when his successor files suit, and your argument that it was all "just a formality" will be tough to prove. The documents make it look as if you meant it, and a neutral, reasonable judge would probably conclude that if it had happened the way you say it did, something would have been written down somewhere. You'll be done in by how things look, no matter how they really were.

And watch for opportunities to build language into the contract, and into the transaction generally, so that a disinterested observer, looking at it at some later point in time, would understand it as it really happened. Dell didn't write his confirming letter for the purpose of educating the clothing executives. He wrote it to be able to document his version of the facts in the event of a dispute. Being aware of the importance of appearances, he created something that backed up his side of the story.

How it looks, and not how it was *supposed* to look, is always what matters the most in the world of contracts.

5 OFFERS AND ACCEPTANCES:
Getting—and Keeping—the Upper Hand

As important as it is to carefully say what you mean, fill in the blanks, and be aware of how things look, it's not quite enough. The law itself creates some additional complications—contractual rules and requirements that don't always make sense and are not widely known, although they determine who's in control of every negotiation and, ultimately, success and failure. You can't avoid these complications unless you know about them, no matter how careful you are.

To get the weight of this law on your side, you'll need a solid understanding of how to make an offer, and how to avoid making one unintentionally. In addition, you'll need to know how to accept an offer, and how to avoid accepting one unintentionally.

And you'll need to know how to do all that in the real world, which is the tough part. Many business schools (and, for that matter, law schools) forget that knowing the law and knowing how to *use* the law are two vastly different things. It takes more than the ability to memorize and mouth the correct Business Law 101 terminology.

MAKING AN OFFER
(AND KNOWING ONE WHEN YOU SEE ONE)

You cannot form a contract unless someone makes an offer. No matter what else happens during the negotiations, until someone puts a valid offer on the table, it's all just talk. An offer, and only an offer, is what makes it possible to create an enforceable agreement.

But is it better to be the one who makes the offer or the one who receives the offer? Most executives intuitively feel that it's better to be the "offeror"—the law's word for the party who makes the offer. And in most cases, they're right.

The offeror possesses a tremendous, practical power: he controls the terms of the contract. Although the recipient of an offer gets to choose whether or not there will be a contract, the act of accepting or rejecting (except in "The Battle of the Forms," discussed in Chapter 13) can add nothing to the deal. It's strictly a take-it-or-leave-it capability. The offer gives the deal its substance. It literally *becomes* the contract.

And the offeror's power extends even further. An offer can also alter many of the rules that contract law imposes on the parties, and that can be of great importance. For example, although contract law says that an offer can be accepted orally or in writing, an offer can override that principle and specify how it is to be accepted: "This offer can be accepted only by signing and returning the enclosed form."

Worried about ambiguities? The offer can define its own terms, or dictate a procedure, such as arbitration, to be followed in case of a dispute.

There's a saying in the law: "The offeror is king." He determines what the contract shall be. If there's something you need that's not included in an offer, you have to assume the offeror's throne. Respond to the offer with your own counteroffer, and keep responding that way until you either get an acceptance or decide not to pursue it further. In business, you rarely get what you don't ask for, and the only effective way to ask for anything in a contract negotiation is by making an offer.

To do it, you have to say or write something that would strike a reasonable person as 1) a desire to make a binding deal, 2) without further haggling, 3) according to specified terms and conditions. An offer is an expressed willingness to wrap things up. The key is to carefully and deliberately pick and choose what you say to meet the criteria. You can do it informally, in ordinary language. Just make it plain that you are ready to strike a binding agreement.

For example: "Let's go on and finalize things. I'm proposing that we make the deal on the following terms." That shows a willingness to make a contract, now, and without any more bargaining.

Another version: "I think we ought to have an agreement so we both know what our obligations are. I offer to pay you a thousand dollars per day for your work. Is that acceptable?" Or, "I'm prepared to pay you a hundred thousand dollars a year for the rights to your product. Do we have a deal?"

Each time, you've shown your willingness to enter into an agreement on set terms. The idea is to convey your desire to finalize things in the way you'll both have to live with. Keep in mind what an offer is, and aim at the target with your words.

Knowing how to make an offer also helps you know one when you see one, and that can be just as crucial. An offer puts the ball in your court. Whether or not there is a contract is determined by your response to the offer you receive. Responding without knowing the legal significance of what you're responding to is like playing tennis blindfolded. You'll be taking uncertain verbal swings, not knowing when you might hit the ball or where it will go if you do.

And if you're not sure what you're dealing with, don't be afraid to ask before you act: "Was your letter intended as an offer?"

AVOIDING ACCIDENTAL OFFERS

Knowing how to make an offer is no more complicated than its basic definition—a stated willingness to make a binding deal, now, according to certain terms. And knowing when to make an offer is hardly a secret of the Pharaohs. As negotiations proceed, the possibility of an agreement begins to emerge in telltale ways. The parties get serious, the gaps start to close, and the time for deal-making begins.

The greater problem for business executives—that is, the one more likely to end up in court—is *accidentally* making an offer. It can happen anytime during the negotiations, or even as you attempt to get discussions started. You might say or do something that the other party reasonably construes as an offer (although you never would have made it intentionally in a million years), and if he accepts it, you have put yourself in a major predicament.

Suppose you are in the market to buy a business, and you hear about a local company that makes a revolutionary product. You don't know anything else about the company—including whether or not it's for sale—but you'd like to know if the owner is interested in talking. So you write to him: "Would you consider selling your business?"

"The business is not for sale, but I might consider an offer in excess of $500,000," he responds.

You assume that to be a bargaining position, and hoping to get negotiations going, you write back: "I'd pay $50,000 for the company. Are you willing to talk?"

A telegram is then delivered to your office: "YOUR OFFER OF $50,000 IS ACCEPTED. WE WILL EXPECT YOUR CHECK FORTHWITH."

That's the last thing you expected to happen. "I didn't intend to make any offer," you'll tell the owner. "I just wanted to find out more about the business and see how firm your asking price was."

"That's not how I took it," he'll say.

Then you see the headline in the afternoon newspaper: "LOCAL COMPANY SUED FOR PATENT INFRINGEMENT." The product you found so revolutionary is also illegal, and the company you may now own is effectively defunct.

Did you make an offer? Forget your inner thoughts. What matters, as always, is the reasonable impression your words conveyed. An unbiased observer reading your letter would see a rather clear offer—be it voluntary or involuntary—followed by an unequivocal acceptance. Litigation is the probable outcome, and you haven't given your lawyer much to work with.

Contractual havoc is the inevitable result of accidental offers. They make you buy what you don't want to buy and sell what you don't want to sell. Accidental offers lead to accidental contracts.

And far from being exceptions to the rule, accidental offers arise in the everyday and commonplace course of business as usual. Judicial "interpretations" can reveal them where you never dreamed they'd be, lurking between the lines of seemingly innocuous letters and conversations. (Or, for example, in the front-porch bragging of Messrs. Lucy and Zehmer.)

Like most accidents, accidental offers tend to sneak up on

you when you least expect them. You've got to take the proper precautions.

USE BUSINESS JARGON CAUTIOUSLY

A good place to start is by appreciating the fact that some of the business world's most useful negotiating lines can cause the most legal confusion.

For example: "What would you think about the following deal?" Or: "Here's what sounds good to me. Tell me if you'd consider something like this." How is a court to interpret what's meant by these approaches? Maybe they're offers. Or perhaps they're just negotiating techniques. Or mere inquiries. Or ideas intended to stimulate discussion. They can be interpreted in many ways, and that means trouble.

An especially popular bargaining technique is something like this: "If you'll give me the concession I need on this last point, I can make the deal." Are you locked in, without the right to further negotiating, if that final concession is made? You won't know until a judge tells you, and by then it will be too late. You've lost control.

You cannot—and should not—totally divorce yourself from the language of business. But you've got to realize and guard against its potential contract law consequences.

USE QUALIFIERS

One of the best ways to avoid an accidental offer is through the use of qualifiers. An offer is a clearly expressed desire to do a deal; if you sufficiently qualify that desire, you emasculate the offer, placing it in the "mere negotiation" category. A hedging, conditional or "iffy" desire to do a deal is not an offer.

For example, add qualifiers that make it clear that you are not ready to finalize things. "We might be able to make a deal as follows. . . ." Or "I would consider the following arrangement. . . ."

Insert language that plainly shows you are still negotiating. Say you'd be "interested in talking about" a deal, instead of saying you're ready to make a deal; mention how something "might be acceptable" instead of saying that it is. Use words that negate what an offer is.

And if you are dealing in writing, you can always include a sentence like this: "This letter is for discussion purposes only. It is not an offer to enter into a binding agreement."

THE DANGER OF LABELS

Some of the most disastrous accidental offers are made by executives who cautiously choose the right words to say the wrong things. They say exactly what they mean—and they make an accidental offer anyway. The usual cause of the problem is an overemphasis on labels.

I once had a client who attempted to sell his industrial building. He wrote to several prospective buyers: "My proposal is to sell the building for $2,000,000." A real estate developer immediately wrote back: "I accept your offer. Let's go to settlement as soon as possible." A week later, hearing of the first offer, an adjoining factory owner who needed my client's building for future expansion also responded: "I will pay $2,100,000, contingent on the sale being made within ten days."

Ecstatic, my client sold to the factory owner, and promptly got sued for breach of contract by the developer.

When I met with my client, he told me that he had anticipated the possibility of a bidding war for the property, and he'd carefully phrased his letter as a "proposal" for that very reason. He didn't want to get locked in before he got the highest price he could. I had to tell him what he didn't want to hear: most likely, a court would find that he had sold the same property to two different people. We were in trouble.

He was dumbstruck. "How could it be an offer if I specifically said it was a proposal?"

The law doesn't require that business executives think, talk, and write like lawyers. It respects the right of businessmen to deal according to their own protocol. Legally enforceable agreements can be made in a casual setting, using an informal and friendly vocabulary. Everyday language can be just as binding as the King's English. An executive can make a contract in the vernacular, without legalese, and without dotting every "i" and crossing every "t."

But many executives believe that the law is much more hypertechnical than it really is. They think that making or not making a contract is controlled by the use of legal "magic words." Call it an offer, and it's an offer. Call it something else, and it's not an offer. Saying what you mean becomes a matter of choosing the right name tag.

That's not how it works. Just as you can get misled by labels like "agreement," "understanding," and "arrangement," you can also get turned around by labels like "proposal," "quote," and "bid." Each may or may not be an offer, depending upon a reasonable interpretation of what's really being said. "I propose to do the deal for the price stated in my last letter" may be a "proposal," but it is also an offer, which, when accepted, forms a contract. But calling something an offer, on the other hand, doesn't make it one. "I offer to buy the building on terms to be negotiated" is no offer, despite the "offer" label. There is no present willingness to deal on specific terms.

Courts will look behind the label in the effort to derive the real meaning of what's being said. If you want to make an offer, it certainly doesn't hurt to call it an offer. And if you don't want what you say to be understood as an offer, it is best to call it something else. But either way, what you call it won't be determinative. Substance will triumph over form.

The Shelf Life of an Offer

What if you make an offer, and then you change your mind? How can you get it off the table before it's accepted?

The law says that an offer stays open for a "reasonable" period of time (whatever that is), or until you revoke it. And in order to revoke it, you must get word of the revocation to whoever might accept the offer before the acceptance becomes effective. Seems simple enough.

Suppose you offer to sell your rare coins to a dealer for $10,000, only to find out a few days later that you could get twice that amount from a second dealer. So before you hear anything, you drop the first dealer a note revoking the offer. Or, to play it even safer, you get him on the telephone, and personally tell him that the deal's off.

"But I already mailed you the money," he says. Your first

thought is relief. Thank goodness you called and revoked the offer before you got the money. You sell your collection for the higher price.

You've just committed a serious breach of contract. Believe it or not, you were legally bound to sell your coins to the first dealer, even though you revoked your offer before you received his acceptance.

This curious but common predicament results from the interplay of two rules of law that form an imposing trap for those who get caught between them.

First, the revocation of an offer is not effective until actually *received*. Until then, the offer is alive and well.

Second, unlike revocations, in most states (check with a local attorney) acceptances are effective from the moment they are dropped into a mailbox, properly stamped and addressed. This "mailbox rule," as it is known, moves up the moment when an acceptance forms a contract to the time the acceptance is *sent*, instead of when it is received.

This leads to some rude awakenings, usually involving situations in which the revocation and the acceptance cross in the mail. When that happens, the acceptance always wins. Even if the revocation is personally communicated, when the acceptance has already been mailed, a contract has been formed.

Especially if you are in a business in which markets are volatile and situations change unpredictably, these timing rules can make a big difference. It wouldn't hurt to have your lawyer double-check your procedures.

ACCEPTING AN OFFER—THE ULTIMATE DEAL CLOSER

An offer, however loosely phrased or lacking in detail, creates the potential for a contract. Whoever receives the offer can ignore it, reject it, or make a counteroffer. But that person also has the momentous power to accept the offer, turning a harmless dialogue into a binding contract backed by all the strength of the judicial system. That's why an acceptance has to fit an offer the way a nut fits a bolt. Contracts are not trifling matters, and the law won't create one on the basis of a wishy-washy, hedging response. To form something as extraordinary as a contract, you must respond to the offer with an unqualified and unconditional assent.

In short, if you want to form a contract, say "yes"—or words to that effect—and avoid adulterating the "yes" with added qualifications or conditions. If you want to reject it, say "no" or its equivalent, and make it clear. And make sure you'll be able to prove exactly what you said, just in case there's a subsequent disagreement—a topic dealt with in more detail in Chapters 7 and 8.

Saying what you mean is one thing. Saying it in a way that minimizes the risk that a court will misconstrue it can often be quite another.

Most acceptance complications tend toward four areas: saying "no" in a way that sounds like "yes"; saying "yes" in a way that sounds like "no"; saying something that might be either "yes" or "no"; and saying nothing at all.

WHEN A "NO" SOUNDS LIKE A "YES"

The law is not out to trap you or cheat you. It is somewhat forgiving of executives who do not sound like lawyers, and it attempts to focus on substance and not form. But despite the law's good intentions, there are certain exceptional times when it does attribute certain legal meanings to particular words and phrases, and nonlawyers are not always aware of these distinctions. As a result, a business executive's unknowing choice of terminology can result in a vastly different legal effect from the one he intended—like accidentally accepting an offer when he means to reject it, and vice versa.

When an executive is not quite satisfied with an offer, he might say something like this: "I'll make that deal, provided that certain other conditions are met." Or, perhaps, "That's acceptable, as long as we work out the other details."

Sometimes executives use this kind of phraseology: "Fine, but can we also finalize an agreement on the remaining questions?" Another example is something like: "Okay, but I'd also like to work out a deal on these other issues."

At first glance, each of these responses might seem like the functional equivalent of the others. There are differences in wording, but they all sound pretty much the same.

In fact, however, the law classifies them as virtual opposites —the first two responses are rejections and the next two are acceptances, and you can't do business safely or predictably unless you understand and appreciate the difference.

Suppose you run an advertising agency, and you make an offer to a prospective client to supply certain services at specific hourly rates, with everything to be billed and paid monthly. There is to be a minimum monthly charge of $1,000.

You receive the following response: "It's a deal, as long as you cut the hourly rates an additional 5 percent." Or: "We accept your proposal, but we will accept bills no more frequently than every quarter."

Is there a contract? In both cases, there was an affirmative response, with only a relatively minor objection to a portion of the proposal. At the least, shouldn't there be a contract on what was agreed to, with the other areas still up for more negotiation, or determination by a court?

In both instances, there has been no acceptance and there is no deal. Why? Remember the definition of a valid acceptance: unqualified and unconditional surrender to the terms of the offer—no "ifs," "ands," "buts," "provided thats," or "as long ases." Neither one of these responses passed the test, and in that crucial respect, they are the same as the first two examples discussed above. Each one is the equivalent of saying yes, *provided* that something else is added to the package.

The law says that such responses—which I call "yes, provided that" responses for shorthand purposes—as positive and upbeat as they sound, are outright rejections of the offer. Yes, in this instance, means no.

WHEN A "YES" SOUNDS LIKE A "NO"

Now suppose this is the response you receive: "Okay. It's a deal. But would it be all right if we delayed the monthly minimum charge for six months, until we get to know each other better?" Or: "We accept the proposal. But can you meet our next deadline?"

Is there a contract this time? There is. Though the responses do not seem unqualified and unconditional, the law says that your client accepted your offer. A contract is formed, on your terms, even if you decide not to delay the monthly charge, and even if you can't meet the client's next deadline.

The legal difference between this kind of response and the "yes, provided that" response is very important. If your client responds to your offer by saying that he agrees, *provided* his conditions are met, he has not really agreed at all. He is still bargaining. That's the "yes, provided that" response. It's like saying, "No, I won't do that. But here's what I will do."

But when your client says he agrees, and then asks a question or suggests a companion agreement—see the second set of examples above—the law draws a distinction. Unless he clearly says that his acceptance is contingent on a favorable response to his question or suggestion, the law says that he has assented in an unqualified and unconditional way.

I call this kind of response a "yes, but can we also?" acceptance, as in "yes, but can we also" add something else to the bargain? He might as well have said, "I accept your offer. Now I'd like to make an offer of my own." You are free to accept or reject his offer, as you see fit. But no matter what your response is, his acceptance stands.

As usual, the speaker's true intention does not matter. Even if he is not willing to go along with the offer until his questions are resolved, if a reasonable person would interpret his words, whatever they may be, as evidencing a "yes, but can we also?" intention, and not a "yes, provided that" ultimatum, he is stuck. No, in this case, means yes.

RESPONSES THAT CAN GO EITHER WAY

Business jargon and loose talk are the bane of the acceptance as well as the offer. They lead to unplanned and unwanted deals. For instance:

"That's a great offer, and we'll take it, but I'm worried about some of the language in the last paragraph of your letter."

"The terms you propose are fine with us, except we'd like a volume price break. What do you say?"

"We'll go along with what you propose, but we'd like to see it in writing and have our lawyer look at it too."

As typical as these responses are, none fits neatly into an acceptance or rejection cubbyhole. They all have the potential to go either way, depending on the context and the personal predisposition of the judge who hears the case.

Too many executives labor under the illusion that offers can be accepted only with unequivocally affirmative words and gestures, perhaps coupled with document-signing ceremonies and congratulatory cocktail parties, and it's just not so. Sooner or later, this kind of fuzzy language will have you explaining to your board of directors or your partner or your bank how it came to be that you accidentally accepted an offer you were supposed to reject.

If you think it through, it's easy to add a few words or make a few adjustments that will make your intent clear. If, for example, you want to reject an offer while maintaining an upbeat tone, you could rephrase the above responses like this:

"That's a great offer and we'll take it, provided that we can change some of the language in the last paragraph of your letter."

"The terms you propose are fine with us, except we'll need a volume price break before we can make the deal. What do you say?"

"We'll go along with what you propose, as long as we get it in writing and our lawyer approves it too."

As a result of these minor changes in phraseology, each response is now a definitive "yes, provided that" rejection. Unless you take such steps to clear away legal ambiguities, you relinquish responsibility for your business destiny to the courts. You take your fate out of your hands. Whatever your intention—accepting or rejecting—don't leave anything to the imagination.

In contract law, words are like weapons. Make sure you know which way the gun is pointed before you decide to pull the trigger.

THE SILENT ACCEPTANCE

One of my clients recently had a problem with an employment agency "headhunter." My client asked for some résumés to fill an executive-level vacancy. The headhunter sent them, along with a letter: "Our commission is payable if you hire any of these individuals, even if the employee is subsequently terminated for any reason, at any time." The letter concluded: "If we do not hear from you to the contrary, we will assume that these terms are accepted by you."

My client disregarded the letter and hired one of the referrals, who was promptly fired for incompetence. The headhunter then billed my client for the full commission—about $20,000—even though the employee lasted less than a month. "We had a contract," said the headhunter. "You took my referral subject to my terms and conditions. There's no discount for early termination. That was the deal."

"I didn't agree to anything," said my client. "It's your fault if you sent me the résumés before we had any agreement on what you would be paid if I hired one of your people."

When my client asked me what I thought would happen if he got sued, I gave him a typically lawyerlike answer: "It depends." Because it does.

Ordinarily, you cannot accept an offer by silence. This is especially true in the case of unsolicited offers—an offer out of the blue that says "We will assume that you accept our offer unless we hear from you to the contrary."

But there are exceptions. For example, suppose the headhunter and my client had done some previous business, and in the past my client had paid the commission without any questions. This kind of past practice could be very important. On this basis, a court could conclude that the headhunter and my client had agreed between themselves to change the usual rule and that my client was liable for the fee.

Many times, cases of this sort arise when someone silently accepts services or goods in a situation in which he ought to know that he's expected to pay for what he's getting. For instance, suppose you need a new roof on your house, so you contact some roofers. One responds like this: "We'll do the job for two thousand dollars. Unless we hear from you, we'll assume that's acceptable and we'll begin next Tuesday." When Tuesday rolls around, you spend it on your front porch, watching the roofers do the work, not uttering a sound. When they hand you the bill, you say, "Sorry. We have no contract. I'm not paying anything."

The law frowns on blatant tricks or ploys. There's a difference between not responding to an offer and gagging yourself. When it is just as easy for you to say something, you cannot sit back and accept the fruits of someone else's labors.

Don't take chances. No lawyer can accurately predict how cases of this kind will come out in court. The safest course is action, not inaction. Take the bull by the horns, and make your response clear. There will be enough uncertainty that the law will inject into your business life without your knowledge. When you have an opportunity to make your intentions known, do it.

COUNTEROFFERS

A "counteroffer"—that is, an offer made in response to an offer—has the dual legal effect of rejecting the offer that's on the table while substituting a new one in its place, to be accepted, rejected, or greeted with another counteroffer. Counteroffers are the vehicles by which business deals evolve—back and forth, inch by inch, through compromise and argument. In a typical business negotiation, the first offer is rarely accepted. The offer that ends up forming the contract is far more likely to be a counteroffer—or even a counter-counter-counteroffer.

Counteroffers are particularly apt to be made or accepted accidentally. By their nature, they usually arise during negotiations, and they can be tough to spot. Depending on how heated or involved the bargaining gets, you might not realize the legal significance of what you're saying or what's being said to you.

Every "yes, provided that" rejection, for example, is also a counteroffer, capable of becoming a contract upon acceptance: "I couldn't make that deal unless you lowered the price ten percent." You might have intended only to reject your adversary's offer while keeping the bargaining alive, but the law— through the reasonable person—translates your response as follows: "I reject your offer. I, however, offer to make the deal if you lower your price ten percent." If the other side recognizes your slip-up, you're trapped.

It's an easy mistake to make during a tough negotiation, but you can never lose sight of the importance of saying precisely what you mean, in a way that complies with the law. If you mean to reject without also making an offer, qualify your willingness to finalize things: "I can't accept that. However, I might be willing to make the deal if you cut the price ten percent."

As always, you've got to ask yourself contract law questions as you go along, and you've got to weigh what's said and done for its contract law content.

FACTORING IN THE REAL WORLD

How can contract law help a business executive? How does it apply in the real world?

Imagine an executive who, armed with his knowledge of contract law, interrupts a complex and difficult negotiating session to announce, "At this time, I'd like to make an offer." He then communicates a clearly phrased offer, in perfect compliance with the law. When he finishes, he sits down and awaits the acceptance or rejection.

In an actual negotiation, needless to say, that's an impractical, even silly tactic, and it won't generate much more than a quizzical look. Legal theory aside, that's not how businessmen bargain with each other. In the heat of battle, they don't exchange carefully worded offers and acceptances; they ask questions, they argue, they say things for effect, they haggle, and they compromise. Their focus is on the deal, not the law. Words are chosen to persuade, not to meet contract law requirements. First you build a consensus. Then you worry about a contract.

Most executives understand the gap between theory and practice only too well, and using "the way things are in the real world" as their excuse, they rationalize that contract law "just gets in the way." On that logic, they simply ignore it, or, at best, leave it on the back burner, until there's a "deal."

The problem is that by then, of course, it's too late. The law will already have worked its magic, carving in stone its loopholes, legal technicalities, and other complications, and negating for all time any opportunity for planning and prevention.

No successful business executive can treat contract law as an encumbrance, to be avoided in favor of "getting the deal done" or "avoiding technicalities." A functional, as opposed to a purely textbook knowledge of contract law is what allows you to start the negotiations in the direction you choose, bargain for what you want, and close every deal you make—staying out of trouble all the while. Paying attention to the reasonable person, saying what you mean, being sensitive to industry custom and past practice, avoiding accidental offers and acceptances, and understanding how contracts are and are not formed—it's all part of deal-making with an intelligent sense of prevention, an ability to keep the horse in the barn until *you* decide to let him out.

You don't have to think or talk like a contract lawyer to reap these benefits. But you do need an ever-present awareness of the law. What you say and do and what they say and do has to be continually assessed in contract law terms. It's not something you can keep in the closet and save until later, just in case you need it. It affects everything you do, as you do it, and you've got to use it as you go along.

GETTING THE NEGOTIATIONS GOING

For example, suppose you are in a situation in which you need to do something to get negotiations going. Sometimes, you can't just sit back and wait for people to come to you. But how do you do it without accidentally binding yourself to a deal you're not yet ready to make?

Without an understanding of contract law, it is virtually impossible. You might not even know that you are treading on dangerous ground. But if you know that it takes an offer to make a contract, and if you know what an offer is and isn't, you have the ability to protect yourself; you can hedge and condition your desire to make a deal to the point at which it's no longer anything close to a valid, contract law offer ("I'd consider making a deal if we could work out the payment terms"). Contract law shows you the problem and guides you around it.

KEEPING THE NEGOTIATIONS GOING

Skillful negotiators pride themselves on their ability to keep negotiations going in the right direction; the idea is to keep up the other side's optimism while at the same time avoiding a commitment to a deal that's not quite right.

But that can be dangerous. The difference between an acceptance and a rejection is not nearly so great as an executive without a solid foundation in contract law might suspect. There is a fine line between words that a reasonable person could interpret as a "yes, provided that"–type response—which is a rejection—and a "yes, but can we also?"–type response—which is an acceptance. An unforeseen ambiguity could be disastrous.

Contract law alerts you to the trap, and shows you how to keep the carrot in front of—but a safe distance from—your adversary's nose.

GETTING INTO THE DRIVER'S SEAT

And as important as these protective and preventive techniques may be, contract law is more than just a means to avoid business difficulties. It also gives you the resources to take control of a negotiation. It's the offense as well as the defense.

Sometimes, for instance, you receive an offer, and you like some parts of it, but hate the rest. As long as you have the ability to recognize the communication as an offer, you can often grab what you like, make it a contract, and leave the rest for further negotiation or determination by a court.

When you receive an offer with good parts and bad parts, make a counteroffer, composed of the good parts only. Present it in a way that increases the chance it will be accepted, such as "I'd like to finalize these details before we try to reach agreement on the other issues we have been discussing." A good tactic is the "we're going to get confused unless we start resolving what we can resolve" approach.

Your adversary may not be as steeped in the law as you are, and not appreciating the power of an offer, he might assume that the discussions are still only tentative—but he may well be wrong. Our friend the reasonable person will eventually have to decide whether yours was the kind of deal that could be agreed to in parts, or whether it was an all-or-nothing affair. You will be surprised how often it works.

THE REAL WORLD CHECKLIST

In applying your knowledge of contract law to the "real world," you'll find it most valuable as a precautionary device. It doesn't give you all the answers, but it teaches you the right questions, and that's generally all you'll need. For example:

• Do I want to make an offer? Am I really willing to be bound by what I'm about to say?
• If not, what *do* I want to say? Do I want to provoke an offer, or just start discussions and see what happens?
• Does what I'm about to say accurately and precisely set forth what I *mean* to say—be it an offer, or something else? Would a reasonable person understand it the way I mean it? Are there ambiguities?
• Is what I'm about to say complete? Have I left anything out that might be important to me?
• Is there anything I can do to make things look the way I need them to look, just to make sure the deal won't be misinterpreted later on?
• How about what's been said to me? Does it amount to an offer? Should I be careful about saying something—or not saying something—that might be construed as an acceptance?
• If it is an offer, what do I want? Do I want to accept it? Do I want to reject it? Do I want to make a counteroffer? Do I want to stimulate optimism or take a hard-nosed position, and how can I accurately convey what I mean to say without running afoul of the law?
• Do I want to keep the negotiations going, or bring them to a close one way or the other? What should I say to generate the legal effect I want?
• Do I want to make sure nothing is binding until it's in writing? If so, am I doing what's necessary to make sure I don't get stuck before I've signed anything?

To be sure, there will be times when you're not quite sure how to answer these questions, but the fact that you know enough about contract law to ask them gives you the ability to ask one more:
• Should I call my lawyer, just to make sure?

You will eventually pay the price if you lack a real, working understanding of offers and acceptances. There are, of course, many other contract law complications, but offer and acceptance difficulties are by far the most common. And they are as avoidable as they are predictable. If you understand the offer–acceptance process, you understand most of the contract law you'll ever need to know.

But you're not done yet. Even after you get the deal you want, you are only halfway home. You still have to be able to *prove* it.

You have several alternatives. You can, for example, let a sleeping dog lie, take your chances that there will be no problems, and do nothing.

You can rely on notes or memos that you have accumulated in your file, showing your version of who promised to do what.

You can send a "confirming letter" on the major points you are worried about, hoping to trap your adversary, à la Donald Dell.

You can draft your own letter agreement or memo of understanding.

Or you can call your lawyer.

Each alternative carries its own composite of pros and cons. Different situations should lead you in different directions. But one thing is clear: an agreement that you cannot prove or enforce is the ultimate triumph of form over substance.

Part Three explores what you need to know to keep a deal once you get it.

THREE

SEEING IS BELIEVING:
How to Protect Yourself
with Documents

When I first began practicing law, I attended a seminar for trial lawyers conducted by psychologists. Most trials require witnesses to recall what they saw or heard months or years before, and as a neophyte trial lawyer, I wanted to learn more about the recollection process.

To prove a point, the psychologists showed a film of a collision between a red car and a green car to a group of people. Half the group were asked how fast the red car was traveling before the "impact." The average answer was 30 miles per hour. Then they asked the other half how fast the red car was traveling before the "smashup." The average answer was 50 miles per hour, even though they had witnessed the exact same film as the first group.

The message was obvious: people are not very good recording devices. Their recollections are subject to influence. They have malleable memories. A skillful lawyer can, for example, manipulate how a witness recalls events by the words used in questioning the witness. Want the witness to recollect something as larger than it actually may have been? Ask "How big was it?" instead of "What size was it?" Want to plant the seed of a dispute in the witness' memory? Ask what was said during the "argument" instead of what was said during the "conversation." It works.

Then the psychologists showed the group a photograph of people standing inside a subway car. In the photograph, a black man wore a three-piece suit, and a white man was holding a knife. Several other people were reading newspapers or looking out the window.

After viewing the picture for five or ten seconds, the group members were asked to answer several written questions about what they had seen. Among the questions were "Who wore the three-piece suit?" and "Who held the knife?" A large proportion of the group recollected a white man in the suit and a black man with the knife, revealing in a most embarrassing way prejudices that were vehemently denied.

Again, the lesson was quite clear. Witnesses are not blank slates. They recollect what they see and hear through the filter of their own biases, prejudices, and preferences. Just as people often see what they want to see, their recollections are shaded by their experiences, their hopes, their personalities, and their self-interest. Of course, people sometimes lie under oath in the effort to help their case. But the same phenomenon consistently applies to the scrupulously honest, disinterested passerby who has nothing to gain or lose by the outcome of the trial. And if you ask a witness to recall the details of an event months or years after it occurs, what you usually get is next to useless. Time works black magic on memories.

THE "MY WORD AGAINST YOUR WORD" PROBLEM

What does all of this have to do with what business executives had better know about the law? For those who deal in business agreements, everything.

Most business lawsuits involve disputes over who is supposed to do what, rife with charges and countercharges. There's the "That wasn't the deal!"-"It certainly was!" argument. Or the "I never agreed to that!"-"You most certainly did!" dispute. And, of course, the "You specifically said this wouldn't happen!"-"I don't know what you're talking about!" confrontation, to name a few.

Like any lawyer, when I get a case like that, I eventually have to confront my client with a basic question: "How are we going to prove that we're right and they're wrong?"

"Don't worry" is the frequent response. "I've got a witness."

That's where the psychologists come in. A witness's memory is no guarantee of success—far from it. The other party to the lawsuit usually has a witness, too. Often, the witness both sides are counting on turns out to be the same person, and he ends up remembering things differently than either of the combatants.

Even when several reliable, credible witnesses are available, their memories of the crucial facts are unfailingly at odds. I recently tried a case in which what had been said at a meeting became crucial to the outcome of the trial. The five reputable executives who had been in attendance all testified under oath, each outside the presence of the others, and each told a different story as to what had happened at the meeting. The attorneys were not surprised.

And when an agreement is concluded on a one-to-one basis, as it often is, it gets even stickier. When a dispute develops, each side "remembers" the deal in a different way, often quite honestly, and both attorneys inevitably hear this: "Well, it's my word against his." The result is that neither party can prove that one version of the facts is the truth and the other is a lie. A "Yes, it is"-"No, it isn't" fight results, most often producing a "split the difference" settlement.

DOCUMENTS—THE ULTIMATE WEAPON

Is there a way out?

It is not easy to be a lie detector, and when judges or juries are pressed to choose between your version of an agreement and someone else's, they look for anything they can find to help them make a decision. Documents are what usually make the difference, tipping the scales to one side or the other. Memories are seen as fleeting and changeable, while documents are viewed as concrete and trustworthy. Documents give you credibility.

Moreover, the right documents often win the case before the trial starts, and sometimes before the lawsuit is even filed. No one wants to incur the expense of a no-win litigation. If a lawyer finds himself battling a convincing body of documentation with his client's or witness' unverified memory, he must advise his client what he is getting for the money—a chance to fight a tank with a bow and arrow. That is when the settlement negotiations get fruitful.

It has been proved in courtroom after courtroom: in the inevitable battle of recollections, documents are the ultimate weapon.

6 GETTING IT IN WRITING

If a contract is formed by what people say and do, and not necessarily by what they sign, why go through the often tedious process of drafting and executing a written agreement?

There are at least three excellent reasons for getting it in writing.

First and most important, a written agreement is the best ammunition there is in the battle of recollections. When there is a dispute over delivery dates or option terms or anything else, nothing nips it in the bud like a written agreement that clearly defines everyone's rights and responsibilities. Your adversary may "remember" the deal differently than you do. A clear, complete, and properly drafted writing cuts him off at the pass.

Second, litigation is often unavoidable, and when you're in a courtroom you need a way to prove your side of the story. A written agreement is excellent evidence. In a lawsuit involving an automobile accident, for example, the issue often turns on the condition of a road or the damage to a car. The parties frequently disagree with each other about how things looked— until someone pulls out a photograph. All of a sudden, the debate stops. A written agreement affects a lawsuit over a contract in precisely the same way. Without a document, it's up to the parties to argue about the details of their deal. But when the agreement is in writing, it can speak for itself—and that's usually enough for any judge or jury.

Third, even when everything about a deal seems "simple and clear-cut," getting it in writing can still be vital. Most of the deals that end up in court seem "simple and clear-cut" when they start out. That's because most executives don't spend their time looking for problems, and almost any transaction seems trouble-free as long as nobody focuses on the things that might go wrong. But when you try to put it on paper, you quickly discover an additional benefit of preparing a writing: it makes you think. Drafting a document for your adversary's review helps you see the problem areas that become obvious only when you deliberate and analyze. It is great preventive medicine.

MAKING THE "WRITE" DECISION: IS A WRITTEN CONTRACT ALWAYS BEST?

Does this mean that you should always push for a written contract? It is not that easy. Sometimes, getting it in writing is not the best route. Other times, it is foolish to do business in any other way.

ASSESS THE RISKS

The first thing you have to think about is whether the risks involved in the deal justify the time and effort it takes to prepare a writing. Be practical. You wouldn't prepare a written agreement with the kid who mows your lawn. Even if he does a bad job, the worst that happens is you're out a few dollars and you get someone else to do it the next week. The same analysis applies at the office. What's at stake? Will it really make that much difference to you, even if there is a disagreement? Focus on the deals that are significant enough to deserve some extra protection.

LOOK FOR THE DANGER SIGNS

If you hang up the telephone and you do not have a clear understanding of the agreement, chances are far greater that there will be disputes later on. If you don't quite trust the people you are dealing with, you should anticipate an escape attempt. Be on guard for such obvious danger signs.

When a deal looks particularly good, be extra-cautious. Emotionally, it is often overwhelmingly tempting to jump at it while pushing the doubts and the gray areas to the back of your mind. This cross-that-bridge-when-I-come-to-it philosophy can be a terrible mistake, akin to passing up a vaccination in favor of trying to cure the disease when you get it. It is easier and cheaper to clarify doubt and solidify obligations up front, in writing.

And don't be fooled just because the deal appears uncomplicated. That doesn't make it risk-free. When the complications crop up, as they usually do, you can spend a lot of time kicking yourself for not anticipating the risks and pitfalls that would have been apparent if you had taken the time to think about it.

Optimism is a fine quality, but you've got to temper it with realism when you're dealing with contracts. You don't have to assume, as many lawyers do, that everything will go wrong. But don't assume that everything will go right, either.

LOOK AT THE BIG PICTURE

Although a written agreement might seem like the best option at first glance, take a step back and look at the big picture. It is often wise to let a sleeping dog lie. Not only does the act of preparing a writing make *you* think, it also makes *them* think, and it often brings to the forefront issues you would rather leave in the background. If things seem to be going smoothly, perhaps the old adage about not fixing it if it's not broken applies. If there are other documents that you can use to prove what's important to you (for instance, letters sent by the other party during negotiations), maybe you ought to leave well enough alone. As in so many business matters, you have to balance the benefits against the risks.

More than anything else, deciding whether to get it in writing requires common sense, experience, informed business judgment, and, often, competent professional advice. There are no formulas or tricks. But if you want it in writing, you face two more decisions that are just as important: Who should write it, and what should it say?

THE BORDERLINE DEALS

When it comes to written agreements, business executives have to be concerned with the "borderline deals."

Some deals are too insignificant or routine to worry about.

They are rarely the subject of written contracts. Other deals are too complex, risky, or expensive to handle without counsel. They get referred to the law firm or legal department. But the borderline deals fall into a no-man's-land—important enough to be legally worrisome, but not big enough or complicated enough to warrant the delay and expense you incur when the lawyers take over.

When executives confront a borderline deal, they are expected to handle it correctly—but they are also supposed to do it cheaply and quickly. It is the corporate version of "Don't walk him, but don't give him anything good to hit."

To pull it off, you are going to need the help of an attorney who knows you and your business—but you are not going to need it as much as you think.

Over and over again, experienced business attorneys see the deals that lead to problems. They get a feel for a particular industry or business, and they know what ought to be included in an agreement to prevent trouble later on. They can spot the holes in contract documents—the things that might go wrong and the protections that have been left out.

If you don't have that kind of background, you are bound to have doubts and uncertainties when it comes to deciding whether a deal ought to be in writing and, if so, what ought to be in it. That understandable insecurity leads many executives to one extreme or the other. Either they turn over total responsibility for the transaction to a lawyer—buying peace of mind, but for a price—or, in an attempt to minimize legal fees and delay, they opt for no legal involvement at all—losing sleep, and usually a lot more.

It is an unnecessary overreaction. The borderline deals can be handled on a middle ground. You already know what you need to know about offers, acceptances, and their complications. Once you combine that knowledge with what you need to know about written agreements, you, with your lawyer's fine-tuning and troubleshooting, will be able to draft most of your own borderline-deal contracts.

Don't try to be your own lawyer. The result will almost certainly be disastrous. But on the other hand, learn to use your lawyer as a resource, and not a crutch. Take a shot at writing up your own borderline-deal agreements, and have your lawyer critique them before they're signed. After some practice and experience, you will be surprised how often the addition of a couple of sentences or the rewording of a paragraph is all your lawyer will have to do. And even if there are major problems, as long as you keep your attorney advised, you can usually find out about them in a brief telephone call, before you get in over your head.

You can handle the borderline deals economically and successfully, as long as you do not try to do too little or too much by yourself.

WHEN TO USE A LETTER AGREEMENT

When you need a written contract in a borderline deal, one of the best ways to get it is to propose a "letter agreement." For example, suppose you have been negotiating to buy some real estate. When the time comes to try to wrap up the sale, you might write the following, double-check with your lawyer, and send it to the seller:

> As I told you in our recent discussions, I am interested in buying your land, known as the island of Manhattan. I am willing to pay $24 in beads and trinkets, within 30 days. Our lawyers can write up the rest of the details. If this is acceptable to you, please confirm our agreement by signing and returning the extra copy of this letter that I am enclosing.
>
> Very truly yours,

> I agree to the terms and
> conditions in this letter: _____

A proposed letter agreement is really a written offer that, in addition to everything else, tells the recipient how to accept it. To be effective, it, like any offer, has to state the proposed deal clearly, in terms that plainly state your desire to finalize a binding agreement, and it should tell the recipient that he can form a contract by a mere signature. It is like saying, "Here's the deal I'm willing to make. If you agree, all you have to do is sign on the dotted line."

A proposed letter agreement is also an excellent way to confirm an oral deal, as in: "Here's my understanding of our agreement. If this conforms with your understanding, please sign this letter and return it to me." Now either you have a concrete, written agreement, or you know you have a problem while there's still time to solve it.

Being an offer, a proposed letter agreement is subject to the complications that apply to offers in general. And the recipient of such a letter has the same options as anyone who receives an offer. He can ignore it, accept it, reject it, or send a counteroffer —if he does it right. For example:

> *In response to your recent letter, we will sell you the island of Manhattan for the price you describe, but only if you pay within 2 weeks and agree to allow us to live on the island for as long as we want. If this is acceptable, please sign and return a copy of this letter to me.*
>
> *Very truly yours,*

Agreed and accepted: ————————————————

That is a clear rejection, coupled with a "yes, provided that" counteroffer—an effective and typical tactic by a recipient who is not quite willing to settle, but would go through with the deal if he gets some additional concessions.

What often happens instead, however, is that an executive will sign and return the letter agreement, writing something like this next to his signature: "Subject to the condition that you pay within 2 weeks and let us live on the island for as long as we want." The complications follow close behind. Some courts find that to be a rejection and counteroffer, but other courts disagree. If it was meant as a rejection, they ask, why did the recipient sign on the acceptance line? As usual, it is a question of how things look, and that always depends on the eye of the beholder.

WHEN TO USE A MEMORANDUM OF UNDERSTANDING

As an alternative to a letter agreement, you and the other party to the deal can jointly prepare a written contract for both of you to sign, often called a "memorandum of understanding" or a "deal memo." (Because of the word "memorandum" or "memo," many executives mistakenly think that these terms refer to a document prepared by only one of the parties. But they usually refer to a document prepared by and agreed to by everyone in the deal.) This kind of mutual effort generally works best when it is obvious that unilaterally sending a proposed letter agreement will be fruitless, usually because of the complexities that remain to be thought out. When you get involved in drafting a memorandum of understanding, you acknowledge that you need the input of each party to the proposed contract. The process entails further exchanges, until you both get language you can live with.

For example, when negotiations get to the point at which it is worthwhile to produce a draft version of the deal—perhaps after an unsuccessful exchange of proposed letter agreements followed by more discussions—one side might send the following to the other side for review and comment:

> Seller owns title to the island of Manhattan. Buyer has offered to purchase this land from the Seller for $24 in beads and trinkets.
>
> The price is acceptable to Seller, as long as payment is made within 30 days, and as long as Seller is permitted to live on the island indefinitely.
>
> It is, therefore, agreed that Buyer shall pay to Seller $24 in beads and trinkets within 30 days of this date. Seller shall then execute a deed for the island of Manhattan to Buyer.
>
> It is also agreed that even though Seller will own the land, Buyer will be allowed to live on the island indefinitely, without charge.

> *By signing this Memorandum of Understanding, the par-ties agree to be bound by the terms stated above.*
>
> For Seller: _____   Date: _____
> For Buyer: _____   Date: _____

If the Buyer sends this draft to the Seller, the Seller might be expected to respond with some concerns about the language. For example, the Seller might want to specify the types of beads and trinkets to be delivered, or he might want some assurances that he will not be disturbed in his continued residence on the island. The Seller might suggest that the Buyer take another crack at it, or he might redraft the document himself, including the language he wants. The Buyer would then take a look at it —hopefully, he would also call his attorney—and he would either approve it or suggest some language changes to protect his own interests. Eventually, the parties either give up or come up with something they are both willing to sign.

DEFENSIVE DRAFTSMANSHIP

A written agreement is only as good as the protection it provides. If it doesn't clearly say what you need it to say when trouble strikes, it was not worth the effort.

Each deal is unique, and there is no general prescription for successful draftsmanship. Nothing can substitute for creativity, knowledge, forethought, and clarity of expression. But when you sit down to analyze what your agreement ought to say, there are some reliable guideposts—the *why* and *what* questions.

THE WHY QUESTION

Courts construe contracts in light of their context. They begin by asking: "Why did these parties make a deal?" To the extent that the contract document itself includes an agreed statement of the deal's background and purpose, the likelihood that a court will understand and accurately interpret the transaction is dramatically increased.

Lengthy agreements drafted by lawyers accomplish this with

a series of introductory clauses, each of which typically begins with a "whereas." Each of these clauses says, in effect, "Here are some background facts that we both agree to." In letter agreements and memoranda of understanding, a simple introductory paragraph—in which the "whereases" are unwritten, but understood—does just as well.

If you buy a piece of used equipment, for example, you will gain valuable protection if the contract document signed by you and the seller includes a statement describing why you are buying it and what you are going to use it for, such as:

> *Buyer wishes to purchase Seller's crane to use for the purpose of loading steel on trucks at Buyer's plant. Seller is willing to sell the crane for the price and on the terms stated herein.*

You could have hired counsel to draft detailed and lengthy performance specifications for the crane, but you've served your purpose just as well with a background paragraph. If the crane cannot handle loading steel on trucks, you can persuasively argue that you didn't get what you paid for and you ought to get your money back—especially if you can show that the seller should have known it. Without the background paragraph, you would probably be in a "let the buyer beware" situation.

It can work the other way, too. If you sell equipment, push for some introductory language that says that the equipment is being sold "as is" or that the only promises made about it are the ones in the sales literature. In most business settings, this limits the claims that the buyer can make against you, even without all the technical disclaimers you've probably seen in commercial sales contracts.

You cannot anticipate and draft a solution for everything that might go wrong, but if the document describes the background of the deal and what each side expects from it, you have done the next-best thing.

THE WHAT QUESTION

The *what* question focuses on the specifics of what is to be done by each party, for what consideration.

Once a letter agreement or memorandum of understanding is

finalized, you are usually stuck with what it says—and doesn't say. If the protection you need is not in the agreement when you sign it, you probably won't be able to add it later on. During the drafting process, you've got to repeatedly ask yourself what is to be done by whom, and it always helps to run the final version past your lawyer, who can usually add a few additional "whats" you may not have thought about.

The *what* question is even more important when your agreement includes what lawyers call a "merger clause." In "legalese," it usually looks something like this:

> *This agreement includes all the promises, representations, agreements, and understandings that exist between the parties. There are no other such promises, representations, agreements, or understandings except as set forth herein.*

A merger clause cancels all prior agreements and understandings, unless they are written down in the contract document. The same legal effect can be obtained by more everyday language:

> *This letter includes our entire agreement. We agree that there are no other understandings or parts to the deal aside from those that we've written down at this time.*

A merger clause is often a good idea. It eliminates the past promises or statements that might be hiding in the closet, and this lends a certain level of certainty to the transaction. Without such a clause, for example, your adversary might contend that there was a prior oral deal (which you may not remember, assuming it ever existed) that is still valid. That supposed prior deal, as he describes it, might effectively emasculate the written agreement you were counting on. (That's precisely what happened to the clothing company executives described in Chapter 2. Their written agreement did not have a merger clause, and that allowed Dell's confirming letter to win the day.) It is then up to a court to decide whether or not the prior oral agreement is real, and if so, what effect it will have. The result is often chaotic and unpredictable.

But although a merger clause protects against such an eventuality, it exacts a price. Sometimes, there really *are* prior deals or promises or guarantees that you have depended on during a business relationship, and it is not always so easy to remember to put each unspoken understanding into the writing.

The best route to a sound agreement is to ask yourself the *what* question over and over again: what, specifically, are you supposed to do; what, specifically, are they supposed to do; and what, specifically, is to change hands in the process.

THE "WEASEL CLAUSE": HOW TO WRITE A "NONBINDING AGREEMENT"

There are times when you want to make sure that a document is *not* binding, even if your adversary thinks he's a party to an ironclad commitment. There are two good ways to get this done.

THE "AGREEMENT TO AGREE"

"Agreement to agree" letters are written all the time, for various purposes. Like an offer that is so qualified and conditioned that it is no longer an offer, these letters are peppered with "weasel clauses," making them so noncommittal that they lose any binding effect. For example:

> *"We agree to buy your product if it passes our testing."*

> *"You agree to ship at $100 per ton if we decide to order."*

> *"You will provide consulting services according to our needs."*

In each case, at least one side has agreed to do precisely nothing: there is no commitment to buy in the first example; there is no commitment to order any product, at whatever price, in the second example; and there is no commitment to retain anyone's consulting services in the third example. Remember that a valid contract needs an exchange of something valuable, both ways. "Agreement to agree" letters have "weasel clauses" that exclude this key component.

Even though they don't amount to contracts, however, "agreement to agree" letters can still be very useful. For instance, one of my clients was a tenant in an office building. He thought that he might need more space in about a year, and he approached the landlord about the possibilities. The landlord said that he couldn't guarantee the space without some sort of letter from my client, indicating his desire to lease it. My client wanted the space reserved, if possible, but he didn't want the letter to be binding, just in case he didn't need the space when the time came. So here's what we wrote to the landlord:

> *I believe that by next year, I will need the additional office space next to my present office. I am confident that we will be able to agree on a rental figure when the time comes. I understand you will keep the space open for me in the meantime. Thanks very much for your cooperation.*

The tip-off is that my client didn't agree to do anything, although he intimated that a deal *might* be cut in the future. As a result there was no binding deal, although the landlord didn't know it, and because he "got it in writing," he kept the space open.

Don't be too flip with "agreements to agree." It is easy to get ensnared in your own trap. Courts like to "imply" terms into commercial dealings, and it is not all that unusual for a court to decide, "by implication," that you agreed to lease the space or buy the goods or retain the consultant, even if your letter says you didn't. Moreover, as will be discussed in Chapter 9, you can sometimes get hooked into an obligation, even without a contract, if your letter misleads someone into relying on what you're saying. You should be aware of the fact that an "agreement to agree" tactic exists, but be careful.

THE "HOME OFFICE APPROVAL" CONTINGENCY

If you want to retain the right to back out of a written agreement, add a "weasel clause" like this: "This agreement is not final until it is approved in writing by our home office." If you don't have a home office, try this: "This agreement must be signed by an officer of our company before it is final." Or this: "This agreement is not final until my partner ('lawyer,' 'client,' 'bookie' . . . fill in the blank) agrees to these terms."

To most onlookers, this sort of condition seems like a lawyer's "technicality" without much significance. But it is much more than that. The "agreement" is still nonbinding because, according to its terms, you haven't agreed to go along with it yet. Until you do—by getting the approval or the signature or whatever other contingency you build in—there is no deal. The other side may think the deal is done, but you'll still have a way to weasel out.

WHEN YOU NEED IT IN WRITING: THE STATUTE OF FRAUDS

Although a contract does not have to be in writing to be valid, some varieties of contracts have to be evidenced by at least some paperwork, or there will be problems. This requirement springs from a seventeenth-century English statute known as the Statute of Frauds, which for reasons unknown was engrafted into the lawbooks of almost every state from the earliest times. (The statute got its name because it was hoped that a writing would prevent fraud—that is, purposeful misrepresentation—in certain kinds of agreements then thought to be prone to falsification. Today, however, the requirement that there be a writing is a historical anomaly that has virtually nothing to do with the prevention of fraud.)

A true dinosaur of the law, the Statute of Frauds makes little sense in most cases, and over the last century courts have tried to circumscribe and hamstring its effect through some of the most strained and twisted "interpretations" ever rendered. But nonetheless, the Statute of Frauds still exists in one form or another, with some differences from state to state, and it has to be dealt with.

The first thing you need to know about the Statute of Frauds is the kinds of transactions to which it applies. Basically, there are four categories of deals that it affects:

1. Promises to pay someone else's debt.

2. Agreements dealing with the sale of real estate or interests in real estate, like leases or mortgages.

3. Sales of goods worth at least $500.

4. Promises that cannot be performed within one year, like an employment contract for more than one year, or a promise to do something more than a year from now, or a promise not to compete for more than a year.

Each of these categories is construed as narrowly as possible. Courts will do almost anything to find that the Statute of Frauds does not apply. And even if it does apply, courts will do everything they can to find some way to make the deal work anyway. The point to remember is that if you are in a deal which might fall within any of these categories, you have no choice but to ask your lawyer whether the Statute of Frauds is a problem.

The second thing you need to know about the Statute of Frauds is how to satisfy it if it does apply. You do not need a written contract signed by both parties. All that is required is some document signed by the party who is trying to back out of the deal—perhaps a letter, or a note in his file, or a telegram. Almost anything will do. And the document does not have to describe the whole deal. As long as it refers to the essential terms, it will suffice.

You can handle whatever problems you might have with the Statute of Frauds by being sensitive to the kinds of deals it encompasses. If you have any suspicion at all that you might be governed by it, get legal confirmation. Your files can then be checked to see if you need any other documents, and if you do, they are usually easy to obtain.

WHEN YOU CAN'T GET IT IN WRITING: THE HIDDEN DANGERS

There are times when the parties to a deal try to put it in writing and fail. For one reason or another the disagreements are too great to overcome, and the language never gets finalized.

But to the surprise of all and the chagrin of some, there may still be a contract. Before a writing was attempted, there may have been an exchange of letters that included an offer and an acceptance. Or perhaps a contract was made over the telephone or in a meeting. In either event, a failed attempt to get a signed contract document does not automatically negate everything that preceded the effort. It has been said before, but it bears repeating. If there was a contract before the document drafting began, it continues to live, whether or not the document ever comes into being.

That can be dangerous. When you try but are unable to get it in writing, vulnerabilities get exposed, confidential information is often disclosed, and the relationship between the parties may be anything but cordial. If on top of that you are bound to each other in an enforceable oral agreement, someone, if not everyone, has some real problems.

If you are negotiating a deal that you want to get in writing, make sure there is no deal consummated before the writing is signed. Otherwise, you might not remember getting married, but you may still need a divorce.

7 CLINCHING IT WITH A CONFIRMING LETTER

Is an oral agreement (sometimes imprecisely called a "verbal agreement"—all agreements, including written ones, use words and are therefore "verbal") a binding agreement?

With few exceptions, such as contracts affected by the Statute of Frauds, oral agreements are just as valid in the eyes of the law as written agreements.

But when everything is done orally, how do you prove that an agreement was really reached? How do you prove it included the terms you remember? What do you do when the parties recall things differently?

Oral agreements lead to disagreements. It is virtually preordained by human nature. That doesn't mean you must avoid them. But it does require you to do what you can so that you are able to prove them once you make them. For that purpose, your recollections and those of your witnesses are not much of an insurance policy. You need documents, and next to a written, signed agreement, sending a confirming letter is the best way there is to get documents—and the law—on your side.

In one way or another, every confirming letter says the same thing: "I am assuming that the following is true: [It can be almost anything—a fact, a promise, or even the terms of a complicated agreement.] If I am wrong you'd better tell me, because I am relying on this and I am going to assume that I'm right." The concept of "reliance" is tremendously important in the law, as explained in Chapter 9. People are responsible for the actions they induce others to take or not take. Your reliance on what the recipient of the letter said or did—and his knowledge of your reliance—is what gives a confirming letter its teeth. The idea is to get the recipient to speak now or forever hold his peace.

If he doesn't, a proper confirming letter cuts off his escape routes. The recipient can't come back later and conveniently "forget" his promise or deny his statement. It's right there in black-and-white, as is the fact that you were counting on him to set you straight and not take advantage of your misunderstanding. If he does not respond to the letter, he is locked in.

A well-written confirming letter is probably an executive's most useful legal weapon. Even when it would be best to put the deal in writing, the press of time and the push of priorities often intervene. Confirming letters become serviceable halfway houses—not as good as a final, signed contract document, but far, far better than nothing at all.

SETTING THE TRAP

Should you decide to send a confirming letter, you must set the trap so that it holds the prey. But like any trap, it has to be disguised, and that presents a thorny problem of draftsmanship in which legal theory and business reality run headlong into each other.

On the one hand, the legal theory behind the confirming letter requires you to tell the recipient that you are relying on what he's said or done, so he'd better tell you if you're wrong. You've got to make whatever is being confirmed absolutely clear, and you've got to ask—almost beg—him to tell you if you are relying on an incorrect set of facts.

On the other hand, you really don't want the recipient to answer the letter. Your reason for confirming what you're confirming is that you want whatever's in the letter to be true. If the recipient responds, you have a problem. His silence means acquiescence, and that's what you're trying to promote. But the more you stress how important it all is, and how he's simply got to tell you if you're wrong—which the law says you should do—the more likely he's going to be to take a second look and figure that if it's that important to you, maybe it should be more important to him.

In effect, a confirming letter, being a kind of trap, needs a bit of camouflage to be truly effective. The law says: if there's too much camouflage, it won't work legally. Business reality says: if there's too little camouflage, it won't work practically.

THINK TWICE BEFORE YOU WRITE

Before you begin your efforts to resolve this dilemma, you ought to think about whether a confirming letter is appropriate for the particular situation you are facing.

In Chapter 2, I recalled a case in which Donald Dell decided to send a confirming letter to the clothing company executives, and it became the keystone of an important trial. But suppose Dell had received the following response:

> *Dear Mr. Dell:*
>
> *We acknowledge receipt of your recent letter. There seems to be a misunderstanding.*
>
> *At no time did we ever agree to allow our other company to back up the obligations of our new company. This would be unacceptable to us under any circumstance.*
>
> *Please let us know if you are still willing to go ahead with our deal.*

Sometimes the hunter gets captured by the game. This sort of reply was quite possible, and it would have backed Dell into a corner. Dell's letter—like any confirming letter—tipped off the clothing company executives to what he had up his sleeve, and it mapped out their escape route for them.

But Dell had analyzed the situation, and he was willing to take that risk. He knew that he could not make the deal without a solid assurance of payment from a solvent company, and he was willing to walk away if he could not get it. True, if there were problems, he could always testify about the promises he received, but that would just produce a "my word against yours" situation, with the inherent risk that a jury might find the other party more convincing than him when the battle of recollections commenced. So he opted for as much certainty as he could get in the circumstances, took the chance, and sent the letter.

That is the kind of strategic planning and deliberation which goes into the decision to send or not send a confirming letter. Is the issue so important that you cannot take a chance? Then try to get a signed agreement. If you can't, send a proper confirming letter—but understand the risks. Is the issue only tangentially important, and not worth jeopardizing the deal? Then let it alone. Is the point in question adequately documented in other ways? Then maybe it is not worth the risk. Might the receipt of the letter put your opponent on the defensive? As is the case when you try to get a written agreement, receipt of a confirming letter often gets the recipient thinking not only about the issue raised in the letter, but about all the other issues as well. Put that into the balance, and weigh it against the importance of the matters you seek to confirm.

MAKING IT WORK

Once you make the decision to send a confirming letter, you have to make it work—legally *and* practically. It has to meet specific legal requirements with clarity and precision. But while satisfying the law's agenda, the language has to be nonlegal and nonthreatening. The last thing you want to do is send the recipient scurrying to his lawyer. You have to balance the law against the reaction your letter is likely to provoke, and then you have to strike the appropriate balance. It's a judgment call, largely based upon the situation and the people with whom you're dealing.

Here are the law's prerequisites; the words, tone, and style you choose to meet them is, of necessity, up to you:

1) The letter should clearly request a response. Once you state your understanding of what you are trying to confirm, include language like: "If any of the above conflicts with your understanding, please let me know as soon as possible." Or, at the least: "Please advise me at your convenience if this is not so." Although a confirming letter depends on the recipient's inaction, it is useless unless you can show that you asked your adversary for a response.

It's usually best for the letter to specify that if the recipient does respond, he should do so in writing. Otherwise, when you get to trial, your adversary might claim that in a telephone call or a meeting that you don't remember, he told you that what you said in the confirming letter was all wrong. Stating that any response should be written helps to minimize that risk.

2) Give the recipient enough time to respond. Make sure that he doesn't have a "we did not have a chance to write back" excuse for his silence. Don't send the letter just a day or two before you need an answer. Don't write things like "Unless I

hear from you within three days, I will assume this letter meets with your approval." The key is to be able to show that by his inaction, the recipient assented to the contents of the letter. But if the recipient has a good reason for not responding—like the lack of time—the letter loses its clout.

3) Make sure you can prove that the recipient got the letter. In most jurisdictions, the law will presume that a letter was received if you can prove that you put it in a mailbox, properly stamped and addressed. Have the employee in your office who does the mailing keep a logbook with the details. Even better, get a receipt of mailing from the post office, which you can do without making it too obvious to the recipient that you consider this an important piece of mail.

Messenger services, telegrams, or mail that requires a return receipt will also work, though in a small office this could raise suspicions you want to avoid. Consider that possibility before you choose any of those alternatives.

4) Tell them you are relying on them. If it's not obvious from the context or the circumstances, a confirming letter has to advise the recipient that you are relying on the accuracy of whatever's in the letter. It has to be clear that you will be damaged or prejudiced in some way if your understanding is incorrect. For example: "This confirms that you will have the equipment available next week." That's not nearly as effective as: "This confirms that you will have the equipment available next week. I'm counting on this for a job I need to finish, so let me know if this is not the case."

The letter should have an "I'm depending on you" thread running through it. Remember that you are writing the letter in case something goes wrong. You'll want to be able to stand in a courtroom and tell the judge: "They knew I was relying on what they told me. I told them I was counting on them, right here in this letter."

Often, a confirming letter is used to memorialize an oral agreement, sometimes pending a more formal agreement and sometimes just to document what would otherwise be left to a battle of recollections. A typical confirming letter of this type begins: "I wanted to confirm the agreement that we reached during our meeting last week. As I understand it . . ." Although

the fact that you are relying on your letter as an accurate statement of the deal is almost always implicit, it still doesn't hurt to
allude to your reliance in a way that won't look suspicious or
provoke the kind of response you'd like to avoid: "I believe the
above to be accurate, but if I've misstated anything, I trust you
will let me know," for example.

WHEN THE SHOE'S ON THE OTHER FOOT

When you receive a confirming letter, immediately renew acquaintance with your lawyer. You will both feel a lot better. If
you choose to fly solo, respond to it in writing, promptly and
without fail. Point out any inaccuracies in clear and certain
terms, and even if the letter is substantially accurate, tell the
sender that although it properly expresses some of what happened, it is not all-inclusive, and it is somewhat misleading.
Suggest a meeting to produce a mutually acceptable document.

If the deal is going to be governed by a writing, it had better
be one that you had a hand in drafting.

8 "BUT WE HAD AN ORAL AGREEMENT!" —How to "Paper the File"

When there is no written agreement or confirming letter—and sometimes even when there is—you need to focus on what lawyers call "papering the file." This involves the preparation of "file documents"—handwritten notes or dictated memos that you write and save in your file, just in case you need them to prove a point later on.

Think of these notes and memos as the instant replays of oral agreements, promises, and other significant business communications. Like football fans who rely on the videotape to see what "really" happened, judges and juries, years after the deal is done, turn to the notes and memos that were prepared as the deal was unfolding. And like television directors, business executives have the power to decide what plays to record, what angles to use, and what to edit out. They can create the evidence that a judge and jury will use to determine their fate, making these documents one of business' most important and powerful tools.

A CASE STUDY

To understand the power of notes and memos and how they can be used, consider the following example, composed in part of excerpts from actual trial testimony.

A building contractor, whom we'll call Contractor Smith, was employed to work on a major office-building project. During the course of construction, Contractor Smith spotted a flaw in the architect's plans.

The architect, whom we'll call Architect Jones, was in charge of supervising the construction. He acknowledged the mistake and was thankful that Contractor Smith had caught it. The job already had its share of problems and was behind schedule. Architect Jones asked Contractor Smith how much it would cost to correct the problem, and when told that he could do it for $50,000, Architect Jones gave him the go-ahead. "Don't worry about the paperwork," he told Contractor Smith. "I'll have to get formal approvals, but we don't have time to wait for all that now. I'll take responsibility."

With that exchange, Contractor Smith and Architect Jones formed a garden-variety oral contract. But when the time came for Contractor Smith to get paid, Architect Jones claimed that he had never authorized the work. What he recalled saying was that he needed to get formal approvals and that Contractor Smith should wait for the paperwork before he started.

Perhaps Architect Jones truly did not remember what had happened—he was, after all, a busy, pressured man—or perhaps he was unable to get the extra work approved and was just protecting his pocketbook. Either way, Contractor Smith was out $50,000.

Contractor Smith sued Architect Jones for the money, and the case went to trial with all the potential of becoming a classic, "my word against yours," coin-flip kind of lawsuit. But it didn't turn out that way. Like many builders, Contractor Smith kept a "job log"—a notepad that he carried in his back pocket so he could jot down anything significant or out of the ordinary that occurred on the jobsite (material deliveries, problems with other contractors, start and finish times, and so on). Before Architect Jones's lawyer ever got to question him, Contractor Smith's lawyer had him explain how he used the job log.

Q: Mr. Smith, did you keep any log or diary on this job?
A: Yes. I kept a job log with me at all times.
Q: Why did you do that?
A: I do this on every job I work on. I use it to keep records of significant things that happen on the job—when materials are delivered, which of my men are absent, problems I might have, changes I'm told to make. Anything that comes up that I need to remember.
Q: How often do you write in it?
A: I make my notes every day, as things are happening. I

don't wait until the end of the day. I write the things down as they happen, so I know that I get it right and don't forget anything. That's why I carry it with me, in my back pocket.

Q: Did you make any notes about the promise the architect made to you?

A: Yes. Right here, on the day in question, it says: "Architect told me to do the work to correct design flaw. I told him it would cost fifty thousand dollars. He said he would take care of the paperwork later. Do the work. He would take responsibility."

Q: How long after the conversation did you write that down?

A: Less than a minute.

That took the wind out of Architect Jones's sails, right from the start of the case. What could his attorney do now? He might try to get Contractor Smith to say that his notes could be inaccurate, but Contractor Smith will remind him that he wrote down the conversation just after it happened, when it was freshest in his mind. He might imply that Contractor Smith could have made up the whole thing. It's possible, Contractor Smith will say. But he will also testify under oath that he wrote down the conversation at a time when he had no reason to believe that there would be any problems. There was no reason to lie. The log was not prepared for litigation, he will say. It is one of his basic business records that he keeps routinely.

Contractor Smith's lawyer then gets the opportunity to question Architect Jones.

Q: Mr. Jones, is it your testimony that you do not recall authorizing Mr. Smith to do the work?

A: Yes.

Q: How large was this job in terms of men and contractors?

A: Approximately five hundred men working for fifty different contractors.

Q: What were your responsibilities on the job?

A: Supervise all the work by all the contractors. Make sure everything was being done properly. Solve problems. I would have to get around to all facets of the job, inspect it, answer questions, and keep it moving.

Q: Did you run into any major problems on the job?

A: Yes. One of the contractors walked off the job and we had to replace him to stay on schedule. We had a fire that caused some damage. There was a cost overrun on the foundation work of several hundred thousand dollars.

Q: Do you have a perfect memory, Mr. Jones?

A: Of course not.

Q: Would it be safe for me to assume that, not having a perfect memory, you remember the things that are more important better and more completely than the things that are less important?

A: I guess.

Q: Were Mr. Smith's problems, in the scope of this job, as large and important as the other problems you dealt with?

A: I guess not.

Q: Do you ever take notes or keep records?

A: Yes.

Q: May I presume that you do that to help you remember things that you might otherwise forget?

A: True.

Q: Like the less important things, which you are more likely to forget, not having a perfect memory?

A: Okay.

Q: Show us your notes on your conversations with Mr. Smith.

A: I don't have any.

Q: Would you now tell the jury, Mr. Jones, why they should prefer your version of the facts, which you render without the notes that would help you remember things you might otherwise forget, over the version offered by Mr. Smith, who happens to have made such notes?

Contractor Smith's 79-cent job-log book just got him $50,000 —not an uncommon result when a document is matched against a memory. The human propensity for faulty recollection is a glaring weakness, easily exposed to a jury. And just as surely as mere memory makes the other side weak, it is documents that will give you strength.

ADMISSIBILITY AND CREDIBILITY

To do you any good, your handwritten notes and your memos to the file have to satisfy certain technical, legal requirements known as the "rules of evidence." That makes them "admissible," meaning you can use them in court. When lawyers shout "Objection" during the course of a trial, they are usually asserting that something someone has said, or a document someone proposes to rely on, violates the rules of evidence and ought to be disallowed. A judge decides what is and is not admissible, and that ruling determines what evidence can be used in reaching a verdict.

The rules of evidence are far too complex and convoluted to discuss here, but they mainly seek to ensure that your notes and memos are accurate and reliable. If a document is prepared under conditions that make it seem credible, that will usually be enough. The following guidelines will help you meet these criteria in the majority of situations you're likely to encounter.

GET IT DOWN AS IT HAPPENS

To be admissible and believable, a note or memo has to include as little recollection and as much observation as possible.

Notes taken during a meeting or while talking on the telephone pass the test. They are like a transcript of what happened, created while it was happening. They do not depend on your memory for accuracy. But a memo dictated a day after the meeting presents some problems. It is only slightly more reliable than your memory. Courts value the notes, but may find the memo inadmissible.

If you can, create the notes and memos as the event in question is taking place. If that is not feasible, do it as soon thereafter as you possibly can. The less the document depends on your recollection, the better.

DON'T RECOPY YOUR NOTES

Never recopy and discard your notes, even if you only intend to make them more legible or clear up ambiguities or inaccuracies. Recopying raises the possibility that you editorialized a bit in the process. Similarly, do not dictate a memo and then discard the original handwritten notes on which it was based. You need to be able to prove that the memo was faithful to the notes.

It is the document prepared while the event was happening, or immediately afterward, that law respects—not a sanitized copy or a reworded version prepared for courtroom purposes.

DON'T CHANGE YOUR NOTES OR MEMOS

For the same reason, never change or add to the original document. If, in reviewing your notes or memos, you remember a missing detail or you spot an inaccuracy, make that the subject of a separate document. Never alter the face of the original.

MAKE NOTES AND MEMOS A PART OF YOUR ROUTINE

Take notes and/or dictate memos to your file as a part of your regular business routine. Documents that are specially created for a particular event are not nearly so credible as documents prepared in the ordinary course of business.

In the case study example, suppose Contractor Smith did not routinely keep a job log. Instead, suspecting trouble, he had jotted down some notes of his conversation with Architect Jones and put them in his wallet. Think of the ammunition that gives Architect Jones's attorney. Why did you create a special document for this incident? Did you foresee trouble? If everything happened as clearly as you say, why would you expect difficulty? Is it just a coincidence that the only notes you ever took relate to a conversation that turned into a dispute? How can you prove that you did not create this document after the trouble developed, and not before?

If you routinely take notes, make relevant diary entries, or dictate memos to your file regarding important events—especially the ones that don't always end up in court—you escape this sort of inference. You can prove that you did not just happen to single out this one conversation for special treatment, and the argument that you might have fabricated the document is weakened.

MAKE IT LOOK CREDIBLE

Make sure your notes and memos appear complete and accurate. Remember Chapter 4's "How Does It Look?" admonition? The same thing applies to documents—especially those which you present to a judge in the hope that he will believe what they say. The notes and memos don't have to be neat and clean (sometimes a few coffee stains lend an air of authenticity), but they do have to look reliable. That means no "doodles"— they lead to the question of what was going on while you were sketching sailboats in the margins. And it means writing down a complete version of what happened, not just an edited rendition of the parts of the meeting you liked.

When you create documents, keep in mind the likelihood that someone is going to look at them later. They are not private records. The mere creation of the notes and memos does not guarantee success. Write with the assumption that they will be scrutinized by others for signs of weakness.

Making Documentation Company Policy

Making up your mind to be more diligent about documentation will help, but as with most resolutions, you're likely to be more successful over the long haul if you formulate specific, realistic goals. Try to develop a detailed documentation policy customized for the size and makeup of your company and the type of business you're in. Your lawyer can help you develop a strategy, but here are some generally applicable techniques and guidelines to keep in mind:

MAKE IT EASY ON YOURSELF

You won't be nearly so likely to document something if you have to go out of your way to do it. Make it convenient.

Some executives, particularly those who travel a lot, use portable dictating machines. The tapes accumulate until they return, and then a secretary transcribes them. Some larger companies have systems which permit their employees to call a special number and dictate a memo or confirming letter over the telephone into a dictating machine. Both techniques work very well. Just make sure that the memo bears the date when it was dictated, and not just the later date when it was typed.

Keep something to write on by the telephone, or at the least, get into the habit of dictating a memo to the file after every important call. Some business executives figure that they can get a more complete and accurate record if they record their telephone calls. That works, except for the fact that it's a crime. Never do it without checking with your lawyer. The same thing goes for secretly recording meetings or face-to-face conversations without the consent of all parties.

And of course, keeping a notepad or pocket diary with you— and using it—always works. The point is to avoid situations in which you have to fumble for a way to get an important point on paper.

For meetings, it's sometimes tough to think, speak, and take notes all at the same time. At especially important meetings, it's good to have a designated note taker.

Surprisingly, many executives take notes or dictate memos, which is wonderful—except they can't find them when they need them. If you're in the kind of business in which you have separate customer or account files, put a subfile labeled "NOTES" in each individual file and use it to accumulate these materials. If you don't have that kind of setup, keep a chronological file of your notes and memos. When you need the document, you'll probably have at least a general idea of when the conversation took place and you should be able to find it without much trouble.

Finally, be sure to save your calendars, appointment books, and similar logs. There have been many cases in which Mr. X claimed to have had a meeting with Mr. Y on a particular date. If Mr. Y can then show that he was out of town that day, he's got the upper hand.

USE OTHER BUSINESS RECORDS
AS MUCH AS YOU CAN

Even if you routinely take notes or write memos, it is difficult to overcome the inference that you do it to prove a point. Usually, there is no other reason for you to take the notes or write the memo. They have no other reason to be. Your bias—which cannot be credibly denied—tarnishes the evidence.

One way to combat this problem is to incorporate your notes and memos into other, routinely kept business records that have independent reasons to exist and be accurate.

For example, suppose that like many consultants, accountants, and engineers, you routinely keep time records which you use to construct your bills. You can use those records as your notes and memos. Instead of logging only "meeting 12/1/85," write something like "12/1/85, spoke to Smith; agreed that interest rate would float at 1 over prime."

Your time records are important to your business. They have to be accurate. Unlike documents created for the sole purpose of helping you in litigation, they have other purposes, and they're kept routinely. The notation gains credibility.

The same goes for expense logs, weekly activity reports, sales records, and all the rest of the documents you're required to maintain. These kinds of documents are supposed to report events truthfully and are not created solely for the purpose of making your lawyer's life easier. As a result, they are not so suspect as they might otherwise be.

DOCUMENT WHAT NEEDS DOCUMENTING

As a practical matter, you cannot write confirming letters, take notes, or dictate memos about everything that happens on every business day. You have to make pragmatic choices based on your judgment and discretion.

You'll know the important concessions, breakthroughs, and breaches when you see them. And no book can tell you whom to trust and whom to suspect. Here are some other instances in which documentation is especially important:

• *Promises, assurances, and representations.* In Chapter 6, we talked about the importance of putting a background paragraph in a written agreement. In an oral agreement, documenting the promises, assurances, and representations that induced you to make the agreement is just as crucial.

For example, if you hire a consultant because he tells you he'll be able to accomplish certain things for a certain price, document it. If you buy a certain product because of what the seller said it could do, write it down. The list could go on endlessly, but if it was important enough for you to have made a specific request for it, it's important enough for a document. And it works both ways. If it was important enough for them to have made a specific request of you, document what you told them.

• *Dealing with underlings.* When you negotiate a deal with a lower-level executive, you have to be especially careful to document whatever concessions you obtain. Lower-level executives have upper-level executives to whom they have to answer. Many times, I have seen an underling finalize an oral agreement and then, to save his job, attempt to squirm free as the agreement starts to yield criticism up the corporate ladder. Be sensitive to the bureaucracy that your opponent has to face. Try to find out how much independence and flexibility he really has.

• *The incomplete writing.* If you are a party to a written agreement that does not have a merger clause ("This document includes the entire agreement between the parties, and there are no other agreements or representations apart from those set forth herein," for example), be very careful to document any oral agreements, promises, or other communications that preceded the agreement. They survive your written agreement, and may be as big a part of your deal as the contract document itself.

Even if your written agreement has a merger clause, you may still need to concern yourself with confirming letters, notes, and memos. Many written agreements have a clause that requires all amendments or later agreements to be in writing. If you are a party to a written agreement without such a provision, you have to be on guard for oral deals made after the contract is signed. It is not at all unusual for a party to a written agreement to contend that it was changed by a later "handshake deal"— and the battle of recollections begins.

• *Offers and acceptances.* The fact that you said and did all the right things during the offer–acceptance stage is only as good as your ability to prove it. The subtleties of language that separate offers from nonoffers and acceptances from rejections are subject to differing recollections and, for that matter, outright fabrications. If they "remember" your rejection as an acceptance, or if they "remember" the offer as having different provisions than you do, you have a problem. They, and not you, may be believed at trial. You may be called upon to prove the content or existence of an offer, counteroffer, acceptance, or rejection, and you must approach the need for documentation with this risk in mind.

THE FLIP SIDE

When a lawsuit is commenced, the other side will have an almost unfettered right to probe your notes, memos, and correspondence. So when you create a document, it should say what you want it to say; it should be clear; and you should be willing to abide by it.

More than one major lawsuit has been turned upside-down by an embarrassing note or memo buried in a file. Trial lawyers are always on the prowl for documents that are a little ambiguous or unclear—a bit of contradiction or controversy is all it takes to throw your case off stride. Suppose, for example, you testify that Mr. Smith made an offer at a meeting; you remember it as if it were yesterday, you say. If you took notes during that meeting, they'd better reflect the offer just the way you described it. If they don't, you're in for an interesting cross-examination. Your notes and memos—the ones you created to protect yourself—can have an exactly opposite effect.

Aside from your own caution and forethought, you can minimize these difficulties if you take the time to talk to your attorney. Go over the kinds of documentation requirements that are unique to your business, and retool your "papering the file" habits as appropriate. Aim for a better understanding of what to stress in your notes and memos—and what to avoid. Keep in mind the fact that creating too many documents is sometimes worse than not creating enough. You lose control, and you raise the odds in favor of a slip-up.

The same goes for confirming letters. It is always an excellent idea to sit down with your lawyer and develop some standard language, again tailored to the particular problems that arise in your business. Choosing the right words often makes the difference between winning and losing, and your attorney can help. A "menu" of form paragraphs can be created, literally enabling you to construct future confirming letters from preapproved pieces.

Be aggressive in your documentation strategies, but be smart. Do not play fast-and-loose with a document. It is tough to deny you said it when you put it in writing.

FOUR

MASTERING THE EXCEPTIONS

Baseball was designed so that three strikes are an out and four balls are a walk. But it did not seem right to allow a pitcher to hit a batter and count that only as a ball. Fairness dictated an exception, so the batter was awarded first base when hit by a pitch. Foul balls counted as strikes, but it did not seem right to call a foul ball a third strike. That was different from missing the ball completely. Equity therefore wrote another exception into the rule book, and a foul ball was no longer a third strike (unless, of course, it was a bunt).

And so the game evolved—something of a hodgepodge of rules and exceptions to rules which become almost comedic when explained to someone who has never witnessed a game. But each exception has a history and a purpose which, on reflection, seems right.

The law is the same way. One of the problems in establishing rigid rules to govern human experience is the simple fact that life is not black-and-white. There are situations that cry out for an equitable exception. And these exceptions sometimes develop lives of their own, leaving the rules as inconsequential afterthoughts.

Nowhere is this more true than in the laws that apply to business, and a business executive without a knowledge of these equitable exceptions is fighting with one arm tied behind his back. Following the rules is important. But finding a legal way around the rules is often the difference between failure and success.

9 PUTTING THEIR MONEY WHERE THEIR MOUTH IS: The Doctrine of Reliance

A contract, whether written or oral, is what allows you to compel people to do what they promise to do. If you have a contract, you have an enforceable obligation. If you don't, the deal is not binding.

But under the right circumstances, the law provides a momentously important exception to this rule, known as "reliance." It allows you to hold someone to a promise, even without a contract.

From small acorns, large oak trees grow, and many legal historians trace the origins of the reliance doctrine to a promise made in 1891 by John Ricketts to his granddaughter, Katie Scothorn.

Out of generosity, Mr. Ricketts told Miss Scothorn that he would pay her a handsome yearly stipend, and Miss Scothorn promptly quit her $10-a-week job to commence a life of leisure. Unfortunately, Mr. Ricketts then ran out of cash and was unable to make the payments. When he died, Miss Scothorn thought she was still entitled to the money, and she sued his liquidated estate to get it. "I relied on his promise and I quit my job," she reasoned. "If he had not made the promise, I would have kept my job and at least I would have had my salary. Now I've got nothing."

In 1898, the case reached the Supreme Court of Nebraska—the highest court in the state. Clearly, there was no contract between Mr. Ricketts and Miss Scothorn. There had been no offer, no acceptance, and no consideration. As a result, the lawyers who represented the Ricketts estate convincingly argued that Miss Scothorn did not have a legal leg to stand on.

But the justices were moved by her plight. They thought she should get the money, although they couldn't think of a reason to give it to her under existing law. So they did what supreme courts usually do in such a circumstance: they made an exception. And when a supreme court makes an exception, it becomes law. Because of her *reliance* on Mr. Ricketts' promise, Miss Scothorn was awarded her stipend.

The doctrine of reliance is gut justice at its best; it makes sense and it rings true. You've got to honor your promises and statements when you should know that others will rely on them and be damaged if they're false—even if there's no contract. The law makes you put your money where your mouth is.

Applied to the business world, as it is on a daily basis, this simple principle of logic and reason is often a lifesaver, and sometimes a backbreaker.

PROVING A RELIANCE CASE

For the doctrine of reliance to come into play, you need to be able to prove certain things about the transaction. Obviously, you first have to show that the reliance actually occurred. That means proving that you substantially changed your position because of what you were told. But once you clear that hurdle, you also have to be able to prove three more things: you have to substantiate what was said; you have to show that whoever said it had reason to know that someone would rely on it; and you have to document that the reliance was reasonable.

PROVING WHAT WAS SAID

The battle of recollections is not fought solely over oral agreements. It also plagues reliance cases.

Suppose you are the marketing director of a company that is planning to launch a major new product. You've already produced television commercials that tie in to magazine ads ("Look for more information and a valuable coupon in the latest edition of *Newsmonth* magazine"). You're sure you're going to be first in the market—which is crucial—until you hear that your competitor is about to introduce the same product in just a few weeks.

A bit panicked, you call the *Newsmonth* advertising manager.

"I know it's past the deadline, but I need this ad in the next issue. Can you do it?"

"No problem," he says.

"I can't afford a foul-up," you say. "These ads tie into TV commercials. If you can't do it, tell me, and I'll wait a month if I have to."

"No problem," he says.

So you schedule the commercials to coincide with the next issue—at a cost of several hundred thousand dollars. But *Newsmonth* blows it. No ad. Incensed, you call the advertising manager. "I just wasted a ton of money based on what you told me. My company looks ridiculous, thanks to you. I expect *Newsmonth* to compensate us."

But he "recalls" the conversation differently. "All I said was that I'd do my best. No promises." Your blood starts to boil at the "my word against yours" fight you know you're facing.

A solid confirming letter sent right after your conversation would have made the difference: "Confirming our conversation of August 1, you told me that our advertisement will appear in the next issue. On the basis of your assurances, we will schedule expensive television advertising which refers to this ad. Please let me know immediately if any of the above does not agree with your understanding so that I can make the necessary changes in our plans."

It is now a case that will probably settle in your favor, long before trial.

PROVING KNOWLEDGE OF RELIANCE

In the example above, suppose the conversation went a little differently. You call the advertising manager and say: "I know it's past the deadline, but I need this ad in the next issue. Can you do it?" "No problem," he says. End of conversation.

When the ad fails to appear, you call up to complain about the hundreds of thousands of dollars you wasted on the commercials. He admits making the promise, but says it was an honest mistake. "Besides, how was I supposed to know it was that important to you?" he responds. "You should have told me."

He has a good point. Without a contract, the law won't hold someone to a promise made in good faith unless he *knows* that people are relying on him. He's got to be on notice that people will be damaged if the promise is not kept. But if there's no reason to know that anyone will be hurt, it's a different story.

In many settings, the fact that someone is relying on what's being said is obvious. When you describe your needs to a salesman, for instance, and he tells you that his product will meet those needs, the reliance becomes implicit. The salesman won't be able to argue later on that he was "surprised" that you were relying on his assurances.

PROVING THE RELIANCE IS REASONABLE

Suppose your company is considering a major expansion, for which it will have to borrow $10 million. The whole deal depends on the terms of the loan, and you're assigned to negotiate with the bank. You call up the loan officer and explain that you're looking for a fifteen-year note, at 1 over prime. You make sure he knows that you'll be relying on whatever he tells you, since if the terms are right you'll be signing construction agreements and reporting to stockholders. He says he'll send you a written commitment in a few days.

The next week, you get a letter from the loan officer: "We will be pleased to arrange financing at 1 over prime, payable over fifty years." Obviously, it was supposed to read "fifteen," not "fifty," but so what? You now have proof of the promise in writing, and the loan officer knows you are relying on him. Can you make it stick?

Absolutely not. If you have good reason to know that there is something fishy about the situation, as is the case here, you cannot rely blindly and then hope to collect damages when you get hurt. You cannot act inequitably and expect to benefit from an equitable exception.

Now, suppose the letter said what you hoped it would say: "We will be pleased to arrange financing at 1 over prime, payable over fifteen years." On the basis of that promise, you sign the construction deals and send notice to the stockholders, but a week later, you get a call from the loan officer, who sounds strangely troubled.

"There's been a slight mistake," he says. "I've been overruled on my recent letter. The terms will be one and one-half over prime. I'm sorry if I caused you any trouble."

You're the one who should be apologizing to him—for costing him his job. Your reliance on his letter was reasonable, and you have a good shot at holding the bank to the terms in his letter.

HOW THE RELIANCE DOCTRINE IS USED

Reliance cases arise in all kinds of circumstances. Anything that can be the subject of an agreement can be the subject of a case based on reliance. But there seem to be some fields where reliance cases grow like weeds.

THE QUALITY OF GOODS AND SERVICES
Reliance is often the refuge of the misled and disgruntled buyer of goods and services.

Suppose you're in the market for machinery. You want something that requires minimal maintenance. If the salesman falsely says that his machine needs maintenance only once a year, and if you rely on that when you decide to buy it, a court will help you out. If the sales brochure says the machine will do 10,000 RPM—which is what you require—but it does only 8,000 RPM, you have a good claim.

Or suppose you need a package designed, and your budget is $5,000. If the designer you hire says that he bills by the hour but agrees to stay within your budget, and if you relied on that in deciding to hire him, you will be able to contest any excess billings.

To avoid these kinds of consequences, sellers of goods and services often require you to sign a contract that negates your reliance rights. This is usually accomplished by sneaking in a merger clause: "This contract includes all the terms and conditions of the agreement, and there are no other promises or representations except those set forth herein." If you go along, you can no longer rely on any previous promises, claims, or assurances. You have, in effect, agreed to do the opposite: you've promised not to rely on anything unless it's in the written agreement.

But that kind of merger clause won't stop a reliance case based on things said *after* the written agreement is signed. It limits the impact of what's said to get you to go along with the deal, but it doesn't affect any later conversations.

For instance, a merger clause in your sales agreement might keep you from suing because the machine does only 8,000 RPM, although you were told before you signed the contract it would do 10,000. But if the salesman then orally promises to fix your machine if you buy another one, and if you do, you can probably make him honor the promise. Your claim would not be based on the contract with the merger clause; it would be based on your reliance on what he said thereafter, which isn't affected by that contract.

Because of that possibility, sellers often add a "no amendment" clause to the merger clause, as in: "This agreement may not be amended, and no other agreements between the parties shall be valid, unless in writing and signed by both parties." In most situations, that puts you on notice that you'd better not rely on anything unless it's in a written contract.

The combined effect of the "merger—no amendment" clauses can be very effective. It can get a little complicated, so you ought to check the details with a lawyer, but it's something to look out for if you're a buyer, and you might want to consider using it if you're a seller.

EMPLOYEE RELIANCE

Most executives know that they have a right to promote or fire employees as they please, as long as there's no employment contract that says they can't. But suppose the first page of your company's employee manual says something like this: "We value and reward competent work. Promotions are based upon merit only."

The company now has a potential reliance problem. Suppose the boss's nephew—who is marginally competent at best—gets promoted over another employee who has always received the highest job ratings. Or suppose the employee is fired because of economic conditions, but the nephew is kept on the payroll. On the basis of the manual, can the employee make a successful claim against the company?

If a court believes that he relied on the manual (for example, suppose he turned down other jobs in favor of your company's merit system), he most certainly can.

Lawsuits of this kind are becoming almost fashionable, and they have inspired a change in the way employee manuals are drafted. Now they say that the company reserves the right to ignore the manual, change it, or do away with it; they stress that employees may still be fired at management's discretion; and many of the manuals caution employees not to rely on them, since they are provided for "general information" or "guidance" only.

DISSEMINATING INFORMATION

Businesses that compile and disseminate information on which others depend are frequent targets of reliance cases.

For instance, when an investor is solicited to put money into a business, he'll ask to see a financial statement, and he'll make his decision on the basis of what it shows. If he then loses his investment, he'll want to recoup, and the first place many such investors look is at the accountant who prepared the financial statement.

If the financial statement didn't present a completely accurate picture of the business, they argue, the accountants ought to be held responsible. The accountants respond by saying that they prepared the financial statement for their client, not the investors. They've never even heard of the investors. Maybe so, say the investors, but we relied on it. And it's common for a business to show its financial statement to outsiders, like banks and anyone else who's interested. The accountants should have anticipated that others would rely on their work.

More and more, the courts agree with the investors—or anyone else who relied on the financial statement and was harmed. And the idea applies to many other fields. How about an engineer who prepares a report that says a particular process will work? If a company takes that report to a bank and gets a loan based on it, can the bank hold the engineer liable if the process does not work and the company goes out of business? It is quite possible. This is the reason financial statements and other reports often include something like this: "This report is for management information only and is not to be relied upon by any other person or entity." Sometimes that works, but talk to your lawyer.

10 TRICK PLAYS, END RUNS, AND ARTFUL DODGES

Aside from reliance, there are many other equitable exceptions that thread their way through business dealings, trying to bring sense to situations that fall through the cracks. You may be stuck, but then again, the law just might surprise you.

"If It Looks, Walks, and Quacks like a Duck . . ."

For example, suppose a salesman for Looter Computer calls for an appointment, and you agree to see him. When he arrives, he is carrying a Looter Computer briefcase, he shows you Looter Computer literature, and he hands you a Looter Computer card. The salesman analyzes your firm's business needs and tells you that the Looter 1000 will do the job. Looter Computer is a national company with a good reputation, and the salesman seems to know what he is talking about. You agree to buy the Looter 1000, and you sign the Looter Computer contract he hands you.

A month later, your accounting is in disarray. The Looter 1000 is wholly inadequate. So you contact Looter headquarters, and you tell them their salesman totally misrepresented what the Looter 1000 could do. You want your money back, and you threaten to sue them for all the damage their salesman caused.

"He's not our employee," they reply. "He is an independent contractor working on commission. He doesn't report to us, and we are not responsible for what he says." The Looter representative suggests you pursue the salesman, not Looter. "And let us know if you have any luck. He still has some of our sample equipment." Needless to say, the salesman is nowhere to be found.

Looter's tactic is one of the oldest corporate shell games in existence—the business version of "Now you see us, now you don't." Are you stuck? The general rule of law says you are. But the exception says you're not. Ordinarily, unless a person is a company's "agent," the company can't be held responsible for his actions. But "agency law," as it is called, is based on very specific and complex concepts, and it doesn't always square with common sense. You are not necessarily your company's agent, for example, even though it pays your salary, or because you work for it full time, or because you use its trade name.

From the days of the door-to-door salesman, companies learned how to take advantage of this loophole. They would sign up an employee to a carefully worded "You are not our agent" contract and send him on his way. When customers did business with the employee, they would *think* they were dealing directly with the company. But because the employee was not its agent, the company could escape responsibility for whatever he said or did. That gave the company the best of both worlds: its name and reputation could be used to attract business, but if something went wrong, it could still bail out. Many innocent bystanders got caught in the trap.

Eventually, the courts caught up with the scam. If it looks, walks, and quacks like a duck, they decided, it should be treated like a duck, and a doctrine called "apparent agency" was born. If a company is responsible for making it *look* as if a person were its agent—even if he's not—the law now provides that the person will be treated as the company's agent. Companies are responsible for the impressions they create.

Looter Computer says the salesman was not its agent, and despite the way it looked to you, Looter may well be correct. But it gave the salesman its briefcase, its literature, its cards, and its contracts. He was Looter's "apparent agent," if not actual agent, and he got that way because Looter let it happen. Looter knew that customers would be favorably influenced if they believed that the salesman was a Looter representative, not just a free-lancing commission seeker who might be here today and gone tomorrow. The exception will hold Looter responsible for the salesman's actions.

THE EXCEPTION TO THE EXCEPTION

If a customer has good reason to know that the salesman or other company representative is not really the company's agent, then the customer cannot use the "apparent agency" doctrine. The company is not permitted to mislead the customer, but the customer also has an obligation to look out for himself.

Companies sometimes take advantage of this exception to the exception by "telling" the customer the facts of life in an inconspicuous way. If there is a written contract, you'll often see fine print like this: "Representative is not the agent of Company and is not able to bind Company in any way." That tells the customer that no matter what's been said up to that point, it can't be held against the company.

The same holds if the disclaimer is tucked inside the sales literature, or on a business card, or anywhere else. The idea is to notify the customer that he's dealing with an independent contractor. The apparent agency then is no longer apparent, and the company is off the hook.

In a situation in which there is no contract, sales literature, or business card, a company can still give a customer the message. Have you ever seen a sign in a fast-food franchise or a gas station that says "INDEPENDENTLY OWNED AND OPERATED"? Now you know why it is there. It is tough for a customer to argue that he thought he was dealing with an agent when the sign tells him that he's dealing with an independent contractor.

At its core, however, the doctrine of apparent agency is a flexible concept, and it can hurt you or help you when you least expect it. Courts will look to see whether and to what extent the appearances were misleading. If you're a seller of goods or services, don't think that merely calling your sales force or servicemen or representatives or franchisees "independent contractors" automatically solves your problems. It doesn't. And if you find yourself the victim of a Looter Computer salesman, don't give up without a fight.

PIERCING THE CORPORATE VEIL

The law normally treats a corporation as a separate person. It is not the same as the people who own it or run it; a corporation is a distinct being, with its own rights and assets and responsibilities. That is one of the major benefits of operating through the corporate form, as opposed to partnerships or joint ventures or proprietorships. Its debts and liabilities are not your debts and liabilities, and if it gets sued and wiped out, the "corporate veil," as it is called in the law, protects you.

This concept was developed to encourage new and risky businesses, while limiting the consequences of failure. But as frequently occurs, the protections that the law provides to encourage honest dealings are often used as tools of fraud. Corporations became convenient devices to escape financial obligations. Once a corporation is created, the owners could do business behind the corporate veil, and when the time was right —lots of debts and lots of cash in the bank—they could take the money and run, perhaps to start up once again in the guise of a different corporation. That leaves the creditors with a lawsuit against a worthless company.

It worked, until the courts decided that despite the historical protections, there had to be times when creditors could "pierce the corporate veil," as the doctrine is called, right through to the stockholders who own the business. There now exists a significant and ever-growing body of law that defines the kinds of circumstances which make it possible.

Those who deal with corporations often treat them as if they were impenetrable sanctuaries, and those who deal through corporations often labor with a false sense of security. But anytime you can prove that the owners of a corporation consistently abused its protections in order to avoid their lawful obligations, a court will react.

Although the corporate schemes concocted over the years defy classification, there are some generally applicable legal principles at the foundation of almost any "piercing the corporate veil" situation.

FOLLOW THE MONEY TRAIL

First and foremost, courts look at the money trail. Corporate owners must treat the corporation as the separate entity it's supposed to be. If corporate funds are routinely shifted back and forth between corporate and personal bank accounts, the corporate veil is in trouble. The death knell for many corporations sounds when a court finds that the owners routinely treat the corporate funds as their own—for example, regularly paying personal expenses out of the corporate till.

If the corporation's stockholders don't respect the corporate veil, neither will a court. And the best way to measure the respect afforded the corporation is to see if the people who own it allow the corporation to keep its own money, or merely use it as another personal bank account.

THE "TWO CORPORATIONS" GAME

Sometimes, the same people form two corporations. That is perfectly legal, unless they play the "two corporations" game.

For example, suppose corporation A sells pencils that it buys from a pencil factory. Corporation B handles the books, the collections, the accounting, and the other administrative work for corporation A. As a result, corporation B charges an outrageous "management fee" for its services, which just happens to clean out corporation A's bank accounts every month.

When the pencil factory tries to collect the money it is owed, it will find an empty shell where corporation A used to be. Unless the pencil factory takes the trouble to search for corporation B, it will probably figure that the situation is hopeless, and after some "Why throw good money after bad?" reasoning, it will walk away—exactly what the corporate operators hoped would happen.

The "two corporations" game can be played in a variety of ways, but the same thing always happens: the money ends up in the "silent partner" corporation—the one the creditors never dealt with and usually never heard of. But it works only if the creditors let it work.

If there's enough money in question, follow through on your suspicions and probe just a little bit. See if the owner of the destitute corporation is still in business, although under a different corporate name. Find out if he's still driving the Rolls. If he seems relatively unharmed by his "business failure," that usually means that the money that started in corporation A and was paid to corporation B is now in either corporation C or his pocket. You may well find that your bad debt is not as bad as you thought.

LOOK AT THE OPERATIONS

Courts will look long and hard to see if the corporation was run like a corporation. Did it have separate books and records?

Were separate financial statements prepared for it? Did the officers and directors hold meetings, as called for in the corporate bylaws? Were there a corporate minute book and stock registration book that were kept up to date? Did it establish and maintain banking and credit relationships?

Real corporations that conduct real business have no trouble satisfying these criteria. In phony corporations set up to deceive creditors they will be conspicuously lacking, and courts know it.

IF AT FIRST YOU DON'T SUCCEED . . . TRY THE LAW OF TORTS

A "tort" is a civil (as opposed to a criminal) wrong. Aside from a breach of contract, it is what you do that causes you to be liable for damages to someone else. Committing negligence is a tort. Medical malpractice is a tort. Libel and slander are torts. If you buy a can of soup and it makes you sick when you eat it, chances are that someone committed a tort and will be held responsible for it.

Most business executives know that a company can be held liable for damages in the usual tort situations—for example, manufacturing a product that causes an injury. But tort law is often used to fill in the holes in the other laws that apply to business, and its scope and breadth can be startling. If a lawyer can't think of a lawsuit based on a contract, he'll try the law of torts, and he'll often succeed.

Consider, as examples, these common business situations.

THE INNOCENT MIDDLEMAN

Suppose you are a distributor of heating units. You sell one to a dealer, who sells it to a retail store, which sells it to an apartment house—and it explodes, destroying the building. The owner thinks you ought to pay the damages.

"I didn't do anything," you tell him. "All I did is order it from the manufacturer and sell it to someone else. Go after the company that made it or the store you bought it from." He tells you that the manufacturer is three thousand miles away, he can't find the guy who owned the store, and he thinks you should be the one who makes him whole.

You didn't manufacture it, you didn't design it, you didn't sell it to him, and you had no contract with him. How could you be responsible?

If the apartment house owner sues you for breach of contract, *you'll* win. But if his lawyer's thinking, he'll file a lawsuit based on the law of torts. And *he'll* win. According to the law of torts, everyone in the entire chain of distribution is liable to the apartment owner, from the manufacturer to the wholesaler to the distributor to the dealer to the dealer who bought from the dealer. Nobody has an excuse.

There is method in this madness. First, the law figures that the businesses in the chain can obtain insurance more economically than the consumer. They can spread the cost out and pass it on in the price of the product, as a cost of doing business.

And second, suppose the store from which the consumer bought the product goes out of business. Suppose the manufacturer declares bankruptcy. Should the consumer lose all rights? The law decided that rather than leave consumers high and dry, the risk of insolvency ought to be borne by all the businesses in the chain of distribution, again as a cost of doing business. The consumer can, therefore, pick and choose whom in the chain he wants to sue—a distributor, or a wholesaler, or everyone from the manufacturer to the retail seller. That way, he's more likely to find someone who will have the money to reimburse him.

But it doesn't end there. Fortunately, you have rights as well.

Suppose you had bought the heating unit from a larger distributor; he got it from a wholesaler; and the wholesaler got it from the manufacturer. When you get sued by the consumer, the law gives you the right to sue the distributor and the wholesaler and the manufacturer, right on up the chain. You may have to pay the consumer, but they've got to reimburse you. When you sue those above you in the chain, they have the same right to sue those above them, until it eventually gets to the manufacturer. The idea is that everyone eventually gets involved, no matter whom the consumer decides to begin with, and liability keeps working its way to the eventual source of wrongdoing.

What happens if you are an innocent middleman and everyone above you in the chain is out of business or uninsured? You didn't do anything wrong, but when you turn around to hand the ball to the next business in line, there's nobody there. The hard truth is that you are stuck with the responsibility. The buck has to stop somewhere, and the law of torts has made a conscious decision to put this kind of risk on those who sell rather than those who buy.

NO CONTRACT DOES NOT MEAN NO LAWSUIT

Suppose your doctor tells you that you should have your tonsils taken out, and you agree. In the eyes of the law, there's a contract between you and your doctor—he'll take out your tonsils, and you'll pay his fee.

At the time of the operation, you have an obvious growth in your throat. Any doctor who was paying attention would recognize it as something that will cause problems if not treated immediately. As it happens, your doctor ignores it, and years later, it evolves into a serious and disabling condition. You think your doctor should pay for his carelessness.

Can the doctor escape liability for missing the growth because he contracted only to take out the tonsils? As you might suspect, the answer is no.

True, the law says, the doctor may have complied with his contract. But the law of torts is separate from the law of contracts, and the doctor had an obligation to comply with both.

It is like driving through an intersection—you not only have to watch for the green light, you also have to abide by the speed limit.

In the doctor's case, although he respected his contract duties, he ignored his tort obligations by failing to act reasonably. That means he was negligent—with or without a contract—and he owes you compensation for the consequences.

This seemingly simple, just concept has some significant applications throughout the business community.

For instance, accountants hired to prepare routine financial statements and tax returns usually require their clients to sign contracts (the accounting profession calls them "engagement letters") with language something like this: "We undertake and assume no responsibilities to detect any irregularities, administrative problems, bookkeeping deficiencies, or embezzlements."

There have been many cases in which such an accountant, in the course of his work, sees, but fails to recognize, obvious, blatant indications of an embezzlement in progress. The client then sues the accountant—had the accountant done something about what he saw, says the client, the embezzlement would have been nipped in the bud. The accountant points to the contract: no responsibility to detect embezzlements. How, the accountant asks, can he be liable for not detecting what he had no responsibility to detect?

The accountant may not have had a *contractual* responsibility to ferret out embezzlements, but he still had the responsibility to act reasonably under the *tort* law. A court could easily find that having seen evidence of the embezzlement, the accountant was negligent when he failed to recognize it for what it was— just as the doctor was responsible for understanding the significance of what he saw, contract or no contract.

Building contracts almost always say that the builder should build "in accordance with the plans and specifications" prepared by the architect. But suppose the architect makes a mistake, and gives the builder faulty foundation blueprints. Shortly after the building is completed, a portion collapses. The builder built it exactly as the contract said he should. Can he be held responsible?

The tort law says yes—if the builder should have recognized the problem, he could be held liable for negligence, even though he did everything the contract required.

The list of examples could go on, encompassing consultants and engineers and manufacturers and entrepreneurs of every kind and description. Tort law is a wide-ranging field that extends into many different areas in complicated ways. Just remember not to read your contracts too literally; even though you do just what the contract says you're supposed to do, you may still run afoul of tort law. You must treat contracts and torts as separate obligations. The extent of your potential tort liability can sometimes be limited by some careful contract draftsmanship—but not always. It is another area that, unavoidably, requires competent legal assistance and planning.

THE HOME FIELD ADVANTAGE

You decide that it is time to take your New York office staff from electric typewriters to word processing. You investigate the market in detail, and you decide on a California company. The system is expensive—$100,000—but you figure it's worth it. You pay the bill, the company's men install it, and they head back to the West Coast.

A month later, the system is consistently down, your staff regularly and inexplicably "lose" data, and the service personnel don't know how to fix it. You get a sinking feeling as you start to think about what happens next. You are a New York business, and now you have to sue a California company. You wonder about the cost of coast-to-coast litigation. How many times are you going to have to go there to testify? How are you going to find a California lawyer? How many times is your lawyer going to have to come east, and what is that going to cost you?

In fact, it's the Californians who ought to be sweating.

Most states are very protective of the companies within their borders, and they enact laws designed to protect them from foreign marauders. As a result, when an out-of-state company does business with you in your state, you can usually sue it on your home field—even though it is located thousands of miles away.

What happens if you sue in New York and the California company decides not to show up, figuring that a judgment against it in New York doesn't really matter? The Constitution of the United States supersedes any laws that individual states might decide to enact, and it has a provision called the "full faith and credit" clause. Basically, that requires California to give "full faith and credit"—that is, total respect—to a New York verdict. You can take your New York result and transfer it to California, and the California courts will enforce it for you as if the case had been tried and won in Los Angeles.

Like just about any other right the law gives you, however,

you can give it up in a contract—knowingly or unknowingly. Most well-advised companies that do business cross country will try to slip a clause into the deal that keeps them from having to litigate out of their home state. Look at their forms, and more often than not you will see something like this buried in the fine-print boilerplate: "All claims and suits shall be commenced and maintained only in a court located in the jurisdiction of our home office."

TO ERR IS HUMAN . . . BUT IT CAN STILL BE A BREACH OF CONTRACT

It is not at all uncommon for business executives to make mistakes while making contracts.

One of the most common varieties is illustrated by a famous nineteenth-century case, in which a cattle breeder agreed to sell a cow to a banker. The cow had an extremely distinguished ancestry, but the agreed price was only $80 because both parties thought the animal to be sterile. Shortly before the breeder was to deliver the cow, however, the breeder discovered that she was pregnant. Both parties had been mistaken about what they were buying and selling, and the breeder refused to go through with the deal.

When the banker sued, the court was faced with what judges call a "mutual mistake"—a situation in which the two sides have a shared misunderstanding about the subject of the contract. Said the court: "If there is a difference or misapprehension as to the substance of the thing bargained for and intended to be sold, then there is no contract." In other words, if I agree to pay $1 million for your painting, which we *both* believe to be a genuine Rembrandt, I don't have to go through with the deal if it turns out to be a worthless forgery. An exception lets me off the hook, as it did the breeder. The judges found there to be a momentous difference between a sterile and a fertile cow of that lineage, and voided the agreement because of the mutual, fundamental mistake.

This exception works only if the mistake is *mutual*. For instance, suppose you agree to sell me a painting you found in your attic. You have no idea what it's worth. I look at it and conclude that it's a Rembrandt. I offer you $50,000 for it, and you immediately accept. But when I get it home, I have it appraised, and I find that it is a worthless forgery. Can I get my money back?

Courts classify this as a *unilateral*, as opposed to mutual, mistake, and in most cases the law will provide no relief. *You* didn't make a mistake; you didn't know what it was worth. Moreover, you didn't tell me it was something it's not, or mislead me, or conceal any information from me. (Had you done so, a court would find a way to void the contract.) There's no reason to take the benefit of a good deal away from you. Let the buyer beware, says the law. My mistake is your profit.

There's an important lesson to be learned here. Business executives take risks every day. Sometimes they pay off, and sometimes they don't, and in most instances the law lets you pay your money and take your chances. Although the law is rife with equitable exceptions, it won't protect you from yourself. It isn't set up to undo your bad bargains, and you shouldn't assume that a judge will automatically help you out if you get into trouble. You can still buy—or sell—a pig in a poke, with the law's blessing.

THE "I COULDN'T HELP IT" EXCEPTIONS

The law will sometimes, but by no means always, take pity on you when through circumstances beyond your control you get stuck in an intolerable situation.

For example, suppose you accept an offer while ill and on medication, not really understanding what you're doing. Or, as happens more often than you'd think, suppose you sign a contract involuntarily, under a threat of physical violence. Assuming such circumstances can be proved, the law recognizes them as exceptions to the usual rules. Even though you appear to have accepted the offer, the law gives you an "out."

In an ancient but famous case, another excuse was recognized, known as the doctrine of "impossibility." A concert hall was booked for a musical performance, tickets were sold, and then the hall burned to the ground. Were the owners of the hall liable to the concert promoters? After all, they had signed a contract in which they promised to make the hall available, and the promoters now stood to lose a lot of money in ticket refunds.

The court let them off the hook. If, the judge said, it is genuinely impossible, through no fault of his own, for a person to do what the contract says he must do, he won't be liable for breach of contract.

In applying this rule since, however, other judges have drawn a distinction between impossibility and impracticality. Be careful. For instance, just before the oil crisis, suppose you agreed to deliver 100,000 barrels of oil to a customer in two months. When the delivery date came due, you couldn't get the oil without paying a ridiculous price. Your performance isn't impossible; it's impractical, and although in extreme cases most courts will give you a break, you can't always count on it.

A related exception arose in England in 1902. It had been announced that Edward VII's coronation procession would pass along Pall Mall on June 26. As a result, numerous contracts were signed in which flats along the route were leased for that day, at exorbitant prices. The King then fell ill, and the ceremonies were postponed. The one-day tenants refused to pay, and the flat owners sued for the rent.

A doctrine known as "frustration of purpose" was created to relieve the hopeful coronation watchers from their burden, and it has since been widely applied in various commercial settings. For example, courts have decided cases in which a company contracts to buy an item for resale, and the government then makes it illegal. Through no one's fault, the purpose behind the agreement is frustrated, and the buyer is excused from the deal.

The "frustration of purpose" doctrine applies only if the purpose behind the venture is just about totally destroyed by circumstances out of your control. It won't save you just because things didn't pan out the way you had hoped. And it won't help if you had any reason to know about the risk of things' going sour beforehand.

The law may still be "unfair" in many respects, but it is seldom stupid or ill-intentioned. When confronted with a Katie Scothorn or a mistaken cow breeder or a disappointed King watcher, it—meaning the judges who create it—attempts to strike a balance between what's clearly the law and what's clearly "right." We may be a government of laws and not men, but men make the laws, and they do attempt to conform them to society's view of what's right and wrong.

Still, although the law is changeable, it doesn't change very easily. As a result, it doesn't change very fast.

And until it does change, it's still the law, fair or unfair.

But if you find yourself in a situation in which, by any reasonable, moral standard, you are "right," even though the law seems to say you're wrong, don't give up too easily. With the help of an equitable exception, you just may be able to snatch a victory from the jaws of an obvious defeat.

FIVE

HOW TO LOOK GOOD WHEN THE DEAL GOES BAD

As most executives know all too well, when Murphy invented his "law," he knew what he was talking about. Even the best-intentioned agreements between honorable parties can and do turn sour in the most unpredictable ways. And thanks to another kind of law—the business law—the "downside" is frequently far worse than anyone in the deal imagined it could be.

Suppose, for instance, you tell your customer that your 50-cent sprocket is just what he needs for his million-dollar machine. The sprocket turns out to be defective, fails, and ruins the equipment.

What's your liability? Your customer understandably wants a new machine. It wasn't *his* fault that the sprocket failed. But it wouldn't be "fair," you argue, not unpersuasively, to hold you responsible for $1 million. After all, the sprocket cost only 50 cents.

To your outraged amazement, the law is on your customer's side. You breached the contract by supplying a defective sprocket, and the law says you're responsible for a new machine, no matter what it costs. As in so many disputes, there's no verifiable "right" or "wrong," and a convincing case can be made for either position. But the law has to make a choice, and like the rule book for a board game, it arbitrarily dictates who wins and who loses—and how badly. Fair or unfair, known or unknown, common sense or nonsense, the law is the law. Period.

Much of business law amounts to a similar array of preprogrammed rights and wrongs that tell executives when a deal is binding, whether it's been breached, who's entitled to recover damages, how much those damages should be and, generally, who looks good when the deal goes bad. Sometimes the law is on your side. Other times, it's dead set against you. Sometimes the law makes sense. Other times, it seems unreasonable, or even silly.

That's why "Just make sure I'm protected" is probably the most common admonition that lawyers hear from their business clients. Executives count on their lawyers to spot the mysterious and little-known pitfalls in the law's rule book, and to come up with ways around them.

Usually, it's a matter of getting the other party to agree to amend or eliminate certain rules. Attorneys who represent sprocket sellers bargain for contracts that limit the customers' right to sue; attorneys who represent sprocket buyers negotiate against such rule changes. And when they finally reach a compromise, it's often expressed in the convoluted terminology of a forty-page document.

Which is all well and good, but what happens in the "borderline deals," which make up the vast majority of transactions, in which it's the clients and not the lawyers who make the deal?

This, of course, is where the real problems are born. Even if all you do is sell 50-cent sprockets, there are fundamental laws and judicial rulings that can predestine your financial disaster when things get nasty. Obviously, if you don't know about these laws and rulings you won't be able to amend them or eliminate them from the deal. For better or worse, you'll be stuck with the cards the law deals you.

But looking good when the deal goes bad can be a matter of choice, not chance. In effect, whether or not you're an attorney, the law lets you stack the deck in your favor. And it doesn't always require a forty-page agreement. In most cases all it takes is a working relationship with a lawyer, an awareness of some of the law's more important protective rules and techniques, and the ability to ask the right questions.

11 FORESEEING THE FORESEEABLE

Aside from the problems caused by dishonesty and insolvency, most disputes between buyers and sellers of anything—be it products, expertise, services, or whatever—come in three, foreseeable varieties:

1. The buyer claims that what he bought isn't as good as the seller said it would be. This is a variety of breach of contract case called a "breach of warranty."

2. Whatever the seller was supposed to do or provide, the buyer claims that he didn't do it when he said he would. The buyer says that the seller's delay breached the contract.

3. The buyer claims to have suffered damages as the result of the seller's not living up to his end of the bargain, and he says that merely returning his money won't make him whole. The law calls this a claim for "consequential damages"—the term used to describe all the damages suffered as a consequence of a breach of contract.

The law has its way of dealing with these predictable disputes. In most cases, it favors the buyer. Foreseeing these foreseeable problems, sellers' lawyers will attempt to negotiate contracts that change the usual rules in a way that limits the seller's liability for breach of warranty, delay, and consequential damages. Buyers' lawyers, on the other hand, know what the sellers' lawyers are up to, and they try to adjust the contract language so that they don't give up too much.

And as the lawyers realize only too well, whoever prevails in the contract drafting stage usually prevails in the contract lawsuit stage, should it come to that.

Executives involved in "borderline deals" have to handle their negotiations from the same perspective. If you're the seller, you have to be familiar with the standardized, protective techniques that sellers use to protect themselves against breach of warranty, delay, and consequential-damage lawsuits. There is, in effect, a catalogue of court-tested clauses and concepts designed to tilt the scales in the seller's favor in these legally explosive areas.

If you're the buyer, you have to be on guard for the terms and conditions the seller will try to slip into the deal. You must understand what it all means to your financial well-being, and you have to be prepared with some protective techniques of your own.

WARRANTIES: THE CONTRACT GIVETH, AND THE CONTRACT TAKETH AWAY

A warranty is the law's word for that part of a contract which includes promises or statements about the nature or quality of what the seller is selling and the buyer is buying. For example: "This car will get 25 miles to the gallon"; "We guarantee that our product will be free of defects in material or workmanship for 90 days"; "We will complete all repairs in one month." If the warranty is breached, the contract is breached.

A warranty that's clearly stated right in the contract, be it written or oral, is called an "express warranty." A building contract, for example, will usually require the builder to complete his work in a "good and workmanlike manner" or "in accordance with industry standards." A sales contract for a piece of machinery often warrants that it will comply with detailed technical specifications. These are express warranties, and if they're violated, the violator is liable.

Most sellers realize that from their point of view, the fewer express warranties, the better. The less the seller promises, the smaller the target the buyer has to shoot at if there's a problem.

But a seller still has to get his customers to buy what he's selling. At the least, he has to describe his product or service. An advertisement, a manual, a brochure, or an informal sales pitch ("It slices, it dices . . .") that makes statements about what a seller will provide can easily be the source of enforceable express warranties. And where there are warranties, there are claims for breach of warranty.

WHAT TO PUT IN A WARRANTY

Most warranty problems, however, can be prevented through precise, thoughtful draftsmanship. Don't say that your hedge trimmer will give the customer trouble-free usage for years to come, unless you really mean it. Say that in normal usage, with proper maintenance, it can be expected to provide years of quality service, as long as it is operated in accordance with the manual. Now you have an out. You can "hype" your product or service with adjectives and plaudits ("durable and long-lasting"; "manufactured to our highest standards"), but once you start getting specific, you're out of salesmanship and into warranties, and you should never even come close to warranting what you might not be able to deliver.

A common law school example involves a $5 mail-order device that was "unconditionally guaranteed to kill flies when used according to instructions." It sounded too good to be true, and it was. Customers who sent in their money got two blocks of wood. The instructions said: "Place fly on block A. Then place block B on block A, killing fly." Whatever else the manufacturer might be guilty of, careful draftsmanship protected him from breach of warranty lawsuits.

If properly done, an express warranty will take away more than it gives. By stating what his product or service *can* do, a seller, by inference, also describes the countless things it *can't* do. That minimizes claims based on the unrealistic expectations and unreasonable disappointments of his customers.

When a client refuses to pay its ad agency, claiming that the agency's services failed to increase its sales, the ad agency will be in good shape if it made—and didn't make—the right express warranties. "We didn't say anything about how successful the ads would be," the agency could say. "All the contract says is that we would perform certain work for a certain price, and that our ads would get attention." Having made *some* express warranties, the ad agency can effectively argue that if *other* warranties had been included in the deal, they too would have been expressed in the contract document.

Suppose you sue a paint company because the paint you bought in 1984 peeled and faded in 1987. If the company said nothing about how long the paint would last, a judge or jury might decide that the paint should have lasted longer than it did, and you could recover damages. But if the company warranted the paint for only two years, it has a solid defense. You got what you paid for.

Even if the seller's express warranties are as good as they can be, however, a disappointed buyer (or his lawyer) will often have a fallback position: "Maybe it's not in the contract documents, but when I agreed to retain you, you told me that if I spent ten thousand dollars on advertising, I could expect a big sales increase. That's the only reason I spent the money." Or, "I don't care what the fine print says. The salesman told me the paint was the best on the market and would last for ten years."

Whether or not it's true, the seller now has a reliance case on his hands, and a court is going to have to decide it on a "my word against yours" basis. If a judge believes the buyer, the seller will be on the hook—unless the contract has the right kind of warranty disclaimer.

DO YOU NEED A DISCLAIMER?

Over the years, lawyers who represent sellers have figured a way around the "Forget what the contract says, you told me something else" argument. They have their clients routinely stick what's called a "disclaimer" into the deal. A disclaimer, which is a type of merger clause, says that if it's not written down, it's not part of the contract, and the buyer agrees not to sue for it. In standard-form contracts, it will often look something like this:

> There are no other warranties, promises, representations, or affirmations respecting the product or service to be supplied aside from those set forth herein. Any prior or subsequent oral or written warranties, promises, representations, or affirmations are specifically revoked and disclaimed and are agreed not to be a part of any agreement between the parties unless included in a written agreement signed by all parties.

As usual, the disclaimer can be expressed informally, as long as it's clear:

> This letter includes all of the express warranties that exist. We agree that any other warranties made in the past or to be

made in the future won't be valid unless we agree to them in writing.

A disclaimer of express warranties protects a seller from claims based on things supposedly said or promised and not written down. It helps a seller define his duties while minimizing surprises. And conversely, a buyer who sees a warranty disclaimer has to be on guard. If he based his decision to buy on what the seller or his representative told him, he'd better be sure that the contract document fairly states what's been said.

IMPLIED WARRANTIES: LET THE SELLER BEWARE

In the law's early days, the predominant theme was "Caveat emptor"—Let the buyer beware. If the seller didn't say anything about the quality of the goods or services being sold, the buyer could not complain if what he bought didn't measure up to his expectations. If, for instance, a department store bought a thousand light bulbs and they all burned out in two hours, it would, of course, seek a refund. But unless the manufacturer expressly warranted that the light bulbs would last longer than two hours, the department store would be out of luck.

The rule made it so easy for sellers to avoid claims by buyers that eventually buyers had virtually no recourse against sellers, even when the goods or services were below any reasonable, minimum standard of quality. And so the pendulum began to swing the other way. To provide the buyer some level of basic protection, the doctrine of "implied warranties" was born.

An implied warranty is a provision that the law puts into a contract without regard for what the parties might have intended or agreed between themselves. It is a warranty that the law effectively forces on the parties. It's not written anywhere. In all probability, the parties never even talked about it. Nevertheless, it is as enforceable as any contract term.

The law inserts several implied warranties into contracts for the sale of "goods" (as opposed to services, or real estate, for example). The two most important are the "implied warranty of merchantability" and the "implied warranty of fitness for particular purpose." The former says that in all sales contracts, the seller will be deemed to have warranted that the goods he sells are "merchantable"—no worse than average quality, fit for ordinary purposes. In other words, no matter what the contract says, the light bulbs are impliedly warranted to last at least as long as most light bulbs do. The department store can make a claim.

The latter says that if the seller knows the purpose for which the buyer intends to use his product and that the buyer is relying on the seller's judgment, the seller will be deemed to have warranted that the goods are fit for the purpose.

If you tell the man at the hardware store that you need something to fix the crack in your driveway, the law says that, impliedly, he warrants the suitability of the patching cement he sells you. He might as well have written "guaranteed to fix driveway cracks" on the sales receipt.

Courts will also imply warranties into contracts that have nothing to do with the sale of goods, but the laws in this respect differ markedly from state to state. Almost all courts will imply a warranty requiring a provider of services to act reasonably and to conform to generally accepted commercial standards. Even if the contract says nothing on the subject, for instance, a carpenter will be required to do his work in accordance with sound carpentry practice, and a lawyer will be obliged to do what a reasonably competent lawyer would do.

The propensity of courts to protect buyers from sellers through the use of implied warranties appears to be broadening. Many states, for instance, will insert an "implied warranty of habitability" into residential sales and leases. It amounts to a forced representation by the seller or the landlord that the residence is fit for habitation. If it's not—for example, if it has a polluted water system—the implied warranty is breached. Even if the sales contract or the lease says nothing about the water, or anything else, the buyer or the tenant could turn to the courts for help.

CAN YOU DISCLAIM IMPLIED WARRANTIES?

Like express warranties, the implied warranties that arise when goods are bought and sold can usually be disclaimed, although it's a bit more difficult. To make sure that buyers don't unknowingly sacrifice their rights under the implied warranties of merchantability and fitness for a particular purpose, the law requires that the disclaimer be expressed in plain and clear writing. The word "merchantability" must be specifically used. And the type has to be conspicuous, as opposed to the disclaimer's being buried in the fine print of paragraph 43. That's why so many sales documents include something like this, always in capital letters:

> THERE ARE NO OTHER WARRANTIES WHICH EXTEND BEYOND
> THE DESCRIPTION ON THE FACE HEREOF, EXPRESS OR IM-
> PLIED, INCLUDING THE IMPLIED WARRANTY OF MERCHANTA-
> BILITY OR FITNESS FOR A PARTICULAR PURPOSE.

If it's not done right, the disclaimer will be ignored by the court, and the seller will be bound by these implied warranties. At that point, all the seller's efforts to limit his responsibilities to what's clearly stated in the contract will be wasted. "Merchantability" is a particularly vague, amorphous term that can mean virtually anything a judge wants it to mean. It gives a disenchanted buyer an almost limitless platform on which to complain about everything he doesn't like, and it opens the door to a variety of arguments and defenses that most sellers would just as soon avoid.

Outside the sale-of-goods context, a contract provision that clearly and specifically disclaims implied warranties will normally be effective, even if it's not written in conspicuous type, but there are occasional problems. Many states disallow certain types of warranty disclaimers. And if a seller manufactures a dangerous product or performs a service carelessly, the "law of torts" equitable exception often allows a buyer to sue for damages no matter what the contract says (although tort suits, unlike most breach of contract actions, will often be covered by the seller's standard business insurance).

But although not fail-safe, disclaimers remain an extremely important weapon in the battle between buyers and sellers. Although the law's rule book gives the buyer substantial rights, disclaimers let the seller build a fortress that will withstand most of the buyer's onslaughts. If the buyer goes along with the seller's disclaimers, then so be it. In only the exceptional cases can the buyer expect a court to help him when he failed to help himself. And if, on the other hand, the seller fails to win a contract that adequately protects him, the law will allow the rule book to take its course.

Look for the presence or absence of disclaimers, and you will usually be able to tell who will look good if the deal goes bad.

Anticipating Delays

What happens when you agree to deliver your product by January 1, but you can't get there until January 2? What happens if the painter promises to finish the job in fifteen days, but it takes him a bit longer?

In most cases, it depends on the circumstances. Sometimes late performance is a breach of contract, and sometimes it's not. It often depends on how important the deadline was. For example, did the buyer need your product on January 1 because he was committed to resell it to his customer on January 2? If so, the one-day delay is a breach. If not, a court might excuse it. But it might not. Different jurisdictions and judges see things in different ways, and in a lot of courtrooms, January 1 means January 1, period.

To avoid the uncertainty, it helps to address the issue of delay in the contract. If you're the one who wants things to be done on time, without excuses, put the following term in the agreement: "It is agreed that time is of the essence of this contract." In legalese, that means that "Any delay constitutes a breach of contract."

If, however, you wish to keep things more flexible, there are many ways to do it. For example, you might try a "best efforts" clause: "Seller will use his best efforts to deliver by January 1." That doesn't commit you to the delivery date; it commits you only to do your best.

Or you can use an "unforeseen circumstances" provision (often called a "force majeure" clause) which might say something like this: "Fabrication will be completed by January 1, with the exception of unforeseen circumstances beyond our reasonable control, such as, without limitation, Acts of God, strikes, government regulations, delays caused by our suppliers, unanticipated complications in the work, or otherwise."

Many a lawsuit has been won on the basis of a simple sentence like this one: "We will do our best to meet all deadlines. However, they are only estimates, and cannot be guaranteed."

By the way, best efforts and unforeseen circumstances provisions can be used to soften the consequences of minor deviations from contract terms in all kinds of situations. Instead of agreeing to ship 100 sprockets per day, you might rephrase the deal so that you're required only to use your best efforts to meet that criterion. Instead of blanketly warranting that your services will reduce your client's energy consumption by 10 percent, make that your goal, contingent on unforeseen circumstances. It's an excellent way to hedge your bets.

CONSEQUENTIAL DAMAGES: HOW MUCH CAN THEY COLLECT?

The law's rule says that a party who breaches a contract should compensate the other party for all "consequential damages"—every reasonably foreseeable monetary loss that results from the breach. Basically, if the breach of contract caused it, the breaching party is supposed to pay for it.

That sounds just and logical, but it can sometimes get out of hand. Suppose, for instance, that a company president charters a jet to get to an important business meeting. "I've got to leave by one," he tells the owner. "If I don't get to Des Moines on time, my company will lose its most important customer." The jet develops a mechanical problem and cannot take off at the appointed time. He misses the meeting, and the company loses its customer. It sues the jet owner for lost profits amounting to hundreds of thousands of dollars—more than the cost of the jet.

Or consider a case in which a movie studio stages a spectacular, $1-million chariot race, and buys special movie film to capture the event. The film turns out to be defective, and the studio sues the supplier who sold it for the $1 million it will take to redo the scene.

In each example, a relatively routine transaction could lead to an enormous consequential damage award. The only limit the law places on the rule is that the type and amount of the claimed consequential damages must have been reasonably foreseeable to the parties at the time they made the contract. If, for instance, the jet owner was not told about the importance of the trip, the amount of recoverable consequential damages could be limited. Or if, in the example described in the beginning of this section, you didn't have any reason to know what might happen if your sprocket failed, you might have a defense.

But other than that, no matter how small the deal or innocent the breach, there is ever-present the risk of a consequential damage claim that ranges from the annoying to the cataclysmic.

Many businesses could not survive if consistently exposed to such liabilities, which is precisely why lawyers have conceived techniques that effectively restrict the right to recover consequential damages. Perhaps more than anything else, this is what determines who looks good when the deal goes bad. If, as an employee of a product seller, you structured the deal so that your company is not liable for the buyer's momentous losses, you look quite good. But if you were the employee who handled the deal for the buyer, it might be a different story. Through no fault of its own, your company is out of pocket—perhaps out of business—with nowhere to turn. And it's your fault.

THE DAMAGE DISCLAIMER: MAKING THE PUNISHMENT FIT YOUR CRIME

Sellers of goods, services, expertise, and everything else live in constant fear that buyers will sue them for consequential damages. But in most states, a seller can use a disclaimer, similar to a warranty disclaimer, to eliminate a buyer's right to recover consequential damages. For example, you'll often see something like this in the fine print of a company's terms of sale:

> In no event shall seller be liable for consequential damages of any kind, including but not limited to lost profits, increased expenses, damage to property, loss of use of productive facilities, delay, or otherwise. Seller's liability shall be limited to the repair or replacement of defective parts or components supplied by seller, at its option.

Look for the talismanic words "consequential damages"—almost all disclaimers will use this term—and you'll usually find a restriction on the buyer's right to recover for damages caused by the seller.

A seller can also state an effective disclaimer in a letter agreement or memorandum of understanding, using more informal language. If the contract can be fairly interpreted as a restriction on the buyer's right to recover consequential damages from the seller, it will do the job. This provision, for instance, would protect the seller quite nicely:

> *We agree that I will not be liable for any consequential damages. Instead, your right to claim any damage will be limited to a refund of the purchase price.*

Those two simple sentences could be all that stands between the seller, the buyer, and a million-dollar verdict.

THE LIMITS ON LIMITING CONSEQUENTIAL DAMAGES

As much as the law favors freedom of contract, however, it won't let a seller's disclaimer go too far.

In most transactions, the law requires that the seller provide the buyer with *some* remedy if the seller violates the deal. It doesn't have to be a good remedy—it can be, and typically is, limited to the right to seek a repair or replacement, or a return of the purchase price. But the buyer has to have at least a minimal amount of recourse. If the contract attempts to negate *all* the buyer's rights, a court may well invalidate it—leaving the buyer with the law's rule book, complete with the right to recover consequential damages.

Furthermore, the seller has to respect the limited rights the contract gives the buyer. If, for example, the contract says that the seller will repair or replace the defective product, he'd better do it. If he doesn't, or if he makes only token or incompetent efforts, a court might find that as a practical matter, the contract allows the buyer *no* rights, and it will invalidate the consequential-damage disclaimer.

A buyer will often try to set up a seller by developing a record of his unresponsiveness to the buyer's complaints. If the buyer succeeds, a court will no longer restrict his right to sue the seller, no matter what the contract says.

And even the law can develop a conscience. For example,

suppose a consumer buys a lawn mower. The microscopic print in the sales documents says that if the product is defective, he cannot sue for anything other than a repair or replacement. The consumer takes it out of the box and starts it up, and the blade comes loose, causing a severe injury. After running up thousands of dollars in medical bills and lost wages, he sues the manufacturer.

Under the contract, the consumer has no right to recover damages for his injuries. But the law, unwilling to stomach a society in which consumers routinely and often unwittingly give up their right to hold product sellers responsible for their carelessness, developed a rule of "unconscionability." If, says the rule, the contract is so one-sided and repugnant as to be socially offensive, a court can refuse to enforce it. On this basis, when a product or service is sold to a consumer (as opposed to transactions between businesses, which presumably are in a position to know better), courts will almost always invalidate consequential damage disclaimers that purport to limit the right to recover for personal injuries.

There are other situations in which a consequential damage clause could fail to protect a seller, so be careful. Although properly drafted disclaimers are generally respected by the courts, different jurisdictions react in different ways. Some states, for example, have legislation that restricts a seller's right to limit his potential liability. Other states have markedly broadened the unconscionability concept. As a result, a seller cannot safely put all his eggs in the disclaimer basket. Sound business planning calls for appropriate liability insurance coverage to pick up where the contract language leaves off.

And that caution goes double for buyers of goods and services. In many industries, a buyer won't be able to find a supplier who will sell him what he needs without a disclaimer. Try to find a truck or a pump or a copying machine without one. Looking good when the deal goes bad sometimes means having the right kind of business interruption or casualty insurance to protect you from losses caused by those who, although responsible for your problems, stand safely behind the protective shield of a contract.

12 MAKING THE OTHER SIDE THINK TWICE

When a deal goes bad, each side assesses its options. Should it cut its losses and walk away? Should it try for a compromise? Or should it play hardball, push for damages and file a lawsuit if the other side doesn't come across?

More than anything else, the process normally entails weighing what each option will cost against the potential payoff. As long as it doesn't have to risk more than a few thousand dollars in legal fees, a company probably won't mind taking a flyer on a $100,000 lawsuit. But if, by becoming involved in the litigation, it stands to lose substantially more than that, it's going to think twice.

THE "SKUNK FACTOR"

That simple fact of business life can, and should, be an integral part of your business planning. Ideally, you'd like to give your adversaries something to think about each time they so much as consider tangling with you. Whenever possible, you want to be more trouble than you're worth, and you want them to know it, so that whether you're making a claim or defending against one, the other side will more seriously consider the merits of backing off and seeing things your way.

I call that the "skunk factor."

Some insurance companies, for example, operate on the philosophy that bona fide claims made against their insureds should be promptly paid. That, they think, saves them legal fees and operating expenses.

But other insurance companies approach things differently. As a matter of policy, they take everyone to the wall. Like the skunk, they want you to know that even if you win, by the time the fight is over you'll feel as if you'd lost, and you'll regret ever having become involved.

The net effect is to deter the "What the hell, what do we have to lose?" lawsuits that are often filed merely for the purpose of provoking a possible settlement. You don't take a swipe at a skunk just for the hell of it. And even the serious lawsuits settle much more quickly and cheaply—there's no sense messing with a skunk any longer than you have to. It becomes a matter of diminishing returns.

Emulate the skunk. The more "skunk factors" you can build into your business deals, the less people will want to fight with you—and that, of course, leads to the sweet smell of success.

COLLECTING WHAT YOU'RE OWED: MAKE THEM PAY INTEREST

For instance, suppose your customer owes you $1,000. He admits owing it, but says he doesn't have the money. You tell him to borrow it, but why should he? In many states, the interest you can charge him in the absence of an agreement to the contrary—referred to as the "legal rate of interest"—is about 6 percent. And it's usually simple, not compound, interest. He'd rather owe it to you than to a bank.

So you file a lawsuit, and because of court backlogs and the other lawyer's delaying tactics, you get to court in four or five years. You win the trial—and the customer appeals. Another two years goes by before the whole affair concludes in your favor. You finally get your money—plus less interest than you would have earned on a passbook account.

In most states, your customer has an incentive to delay. Owing money to you is like getting a low-interest loan. But things might work out differently if you include a term like this in the contract: "All outstanding balances shall bear compound interest at the rate of 1½ percent per month."

Now your customer can probably borrow the money from the bank more cheaply than he can owe it to you, and the incentives are switched. You're no longer worth fighting with, and your customer will most likely start weighing the benefits of a negotiated payoff.

When you try this tactic, you have to be careful about a couple of things. First, different states have different usury laws —the statutes that regulate the maximum amount of interest you can charge. Violation of usury laws can sometimes result in civil and even criminal penalties. And depending on the nature of the credit you extend to your customers, you may have to comply with certain technical statutes and regulations relating to credit terms and disclosures. Be certain to consult with your counsel.

Second, be sure that the higher interest rate is a part of the contract. Many executives make their deals without providing for interest to be paid on outstanding credit balances. They wait until they send the invoice, where, typically, the interest rate is printed on the form. But by then it's too late. The deal has already been finalized, and a higher-than-legal interest rate wasn't part of the bargain. An educated customer will ignore the terms of the invoice.

REQUIRE THEM TO PAY YOUR ATTORNEY'S FEES

Many businesses take a shot at bringing or defending a lawsuit, basically because there's no good reason not to. If they see a palpable downside, however, it's often a different story.

For instance, to give a customer an incentive to avoid playing fast-and-loose, a seller of goods or services might try to get him to agree to a contract provision like this: "In the event of non-payment or any other act resulting in litigation between the parties, the losing party shall pay all reasonable counsel fees and costs incurred by the prevailing party." That kind of language gives the seller an edge. Because the customer can lose a lot more than what he owes if the seller sues for his money and wins, it puts the seller at the top of the customer's list, way ahead of other creditors.

It works both ways, however, so be careful. If your customer has a good reason for not paying, and you sue him and lose, *you'll* be stuck with *his* counsel fees. It's theoretically possible to make the arrangement one-sided, so that only your customer pays if *he* loses a lawsuit, but it never happens if the other side is paying attention.

If you're the buyer instead of the seller, you might want to turn the tables, especially if you're a bit worried about the seller's ability to do what he says he can do. Ask for this: "In the event of a breach of contract resulting in litigation, the losing party shall pay all reasonable costs and counsel fees incurred by the prevailing party." Your only obligation as the buyer is to pay on time; once you do that, you're off the hook. The seller is the one who then has to perform, and this contract provision can be of great assistance in case he fails to make good on his warranties.

MAKE THEM FIGHT IN YOUR BACKYARD

If you can require your adversaries to litigate where you are as opposed to where they are, you may win the lawsuit before it begins.

If a Utah company has to litigate in Pennsylvania against a Pennsylvania company, its trusted Utah counsel won't be able to handle it. Most lawyers can practice only in their home jurisdiction. The company will have to retain Pennsylvania counsel, whom it doesn't know; it will generally want its Utah lawyer to be involved in a supervisory capacity, which means that its legal fees increase; its executives will have to incur the time and expense it will take to travel to Pennsylvania for pretrial proceedings and, eventually, a trial; and it will be forced to present its case on foreign turf against a native son, which even today can subject it to some prejudices and problems.

All of this gets factored into the Utah company's decision-making process. Do we really want to fight this fight? Maybe we'd better settle.

The law's rules on where a lawsuit should take place—called "jurisdiction and venue"—can normally be altered by a contract provision like this: "The parties agree that all lawsuits or other claims which either of them may bring against the other shall be commenced and maintained only in the federal or state court which sits in the jurisdiction of seller's home office." Often, the law provides that a suit on a contract can be brought only where the contract was "made." That's sometimes tough to figure out, especially when the contract is formed via correspondence or telephone calls between parties in different states. In any event, just to cover all the bases, many contracts also include a clause something like this: "The parties agree that this contract was made at the seller's offices."

The net effect, if you're the seller, is to require them to come to your backyard if there's a problem. That doesn't necessarily eliminate the dispute, but it certainly makes them think twice about pursuing it and makes them more willing to settle it— which is what "skunk factors" are all about.

Be creative, and develop "skunk factors" tailored to your business. If you sell large pieces of equipment, perhaps your contract ought to say that if you're not paid within sixty days, you have the right to repossess the goods at the customer's expense. If you regularly buy components for incorporation into your company's products, you might want to include a contract clause that gives you the right to have any defective components replaced, no matter the cost, at the seller's expense.

It's all a matter of making *your* problems *their* problems, which is a fundamental lawyer's technique for looking good when the deal goes bad.

13 THE BATTLE OF THE FORMS

Many agreements are finalized orally or via a letter agreement, a memorandum of understanding, or a lengthy contract document. Such agreements take shape over time, through negotiation, until the terms and the language are out in the open and mutually agreed. But not all deals evolve along that path.

Picture a situation in which you wish to strike a deal concerning the purchase of certain materials for your business. Using your preprinted form, entitled "Request for Quotation," you ask your suppliers for prices. The form describes what you want in the quotation, and it specifically says that you will not accept quotes that disclaim the seller's responsibility for consequential damages or implied warranties.

A week later, you receive several quotes, all of which say that they are "subject to our standard terms and conditions attached hereto." In the fine print are boilerplate consequential damage and warranty disclaimers.

In accordance with your company procedures, you send the low bidder your purchase order, again using your company's standard form. It says that you are ordering 1,000 units, "in accordance with and pursuant to our terms of purchase on the reverse side hereof." Your terms say that no disclaimers of consequential damages or implied warranties shall be effective, and that the seller should not ship the goods if this is unacceptable.

They respond with their form, entitled "Confirmation of Purchase Order." It says that they received your order, which they will ship in two weeks, pursuant to their standard terms and conditions, which are again attached. They ship on time, along with an invoice that includes another statement of their terms and conditions; you acknowledge receipt with, of course, another copy of yours.

What happens if the products violate the implied warranty of merchantability, causing significant consequential damages? Were implied warranties and consequential damages disclaimed, as provided for in *their* forms? Or do *your* forms govern?

This all-too-common scenario—known in the law as "the battle of the forms"—crisscrosses the nation and plagues business executives in all fields of enterprise. It stems from the fact that buyers and sellers, on advice of their lawyers, routinely employ forms that address the same issues through contradictory approaches.

Most executives know that the forms are designed to protect them in the event of a dispute, but the exchange of fine print has become so commonplace that, typically, the forms are perfunctorily swapped as if the whole process were a meaningless formality. Some executives think that the first form governs; others think it's the last one sent that makes the difference; still others figure that having sent the form, they're protected, no matter what. And courtrooms across the country are clogged with fallout from the confusion.

THE CONTRACT LAW PROBLEM

According to contract law, a contract can be formed only if an offer is met by a definite, unequivocal acceptance that conforms with every aspect of the offer. Unless the offer and acceptance are in total harmony, there's no deal.

In the battle of the forms, however, neither party *ever* accepts an offer. Instead, the two trade contradictory documents. Nevertheless, the parties go through with the purchase and sale, *assuming* they have a contract. Their disagreements are hidden in the exchange of boilerplate, which neither side quite understands. As a result, all the issues surrounding consequential damages, warranties, and the multitude of other mutually exclusive terms addressed in the forms remain up in the air—until there's a problem.

There's a deal, but at the same time there's no deal. Unscrambling who's supposed to do what is about as easy as unscrambling an egg.

THE CONTRACT LAW SOLUTION

As the use of standard forms increased, the law had to figure out a way to decide which form would prevail. As a result, a set of uniform rules has been adopted in almost every state which, theoretically, provides a framework within which the problems can be analyzed.

These rules apply only to transactions involving the sale of goods—in the sense of tangible objects—between businesses. They are meant to impose some sense on this area of commerce, which is dominated by the use of forms. The rules do not apply to consumer transactions, or agreements concerning the sale of services, advice, land, securities, and so on—deals that are not affected nearly so often by the battle of the forms.

Basically, here's what the rules provide:

1. In a major departure from the usual contract law rules, a buyer and a seller *can* form a contract involving the sale of goods between businesses, *even if* the acceptance includes terms different from or additional to those in the offer. As long as there's a basic agreement on the terms of the purchase and sale, the forms exchanged by the buyer and the seller can be vastly different and the deal will still be binding.

2. But on what terms? As in other contracts, the offer will control. The contract will follow the offering party's form. However, it's not always so easy to pick out the offer among the interplay of confirmations, orders, acknowledgments, quotations, and the rest of the forms that characterize dealings between buyers and sellers. The buyer will usually contend that his purchase order was the offer. The seller will usually argue that the purchase order was merely an acceptance of his offer to sell the goods to the buyer.

3. There is a commonsense exception to Rule 1 and Rule 2. If the form that responds to the offer specifically says that it is not to be considered an acceptance unless *all* its terms are agreed to by the party making the offer, then there is no contract. But without that kind of language, an offer that says "no disclaimers" can be met by an acceptance that has pages of disclaimers. The deal will still be binding—and it won't include disclaimers.

4. Although the offering party's terms and conditions govern, the accepting party's terms and conditions can also be a part of the contract as long as they don't "materially alter" the deal. If they are significant enough to be "material" to the transaction, however, they are excluded. And, additionally, the offering party can keep them out of the contract if his form says that no additional terms can be added to the deal, or if he promptly objects to their inclusion. The bottom line: whatever the offering party wants, the offering party gets.

PUTTING THEORY INTO PRACTICE

Although the rules themselves are not particularly complicated, they are very difficult to apply. They are like the scoring rules in boxing or gymnastics—clear and concise, and impossible to use objectively or predictably. It is a lawyer's job to push and pull on the law to see if it can be stretched to a point at which it will accommodate his client's position. It is the job of the law to fight back, maintaining limits and lines between the permissible and the impermissible. Euphemistically, the rules in the battle of the forms have proved to be overly elastic.

For instance, it is obvious that under the rules, the offering party is in the driver's seat. But distinguishing the offering party from the accepting party is largely guesswork. Striving for the upper hand, both sets of forms often include competing clauses something like this: "This form is to be construed as an offer to be accepted by you and is not to be construed as an acceptance." Having been coached by counsel, each party will write letters that refer to its form as "the offer," hoping to build a record to support its side of the story. How do courts untie the knot? Inconsistently and erratically.

Once a court decides who made the offer, it has to determine which of the nonconforming terms in the acceptance "materially alter" the deal. Those terms won't be part of the contract, but the other, "nonmaterial" terms can be. Terms pertaining to disclaimers and warranty limitations will always be material changes. But there's substantial disagreement from case to case over such terms as interest rates, unforeseeable circumstances clauses, attorney's fee provisions, and so on. You won't know which terms are in and which terms are out until you hear about it from the judge and jury.

In compliance with Rule 3, the form sent in response to the offer frequently says that there's no deal unless its terms are included in the contract. If the offering party never responds one way or the other, which is normal, a contract is never created. But the goods end up being shipped and paid for anyway. What happens if there's a subsequent dispute?

Typically, a court will compare the forms. To the extent to which they agree, those terms will be included in the contract; otherwise, the law's rule book takes over—often to the horror of a seller who thought that his airtight boilerplate would protect him from a million-dollar consequential damage judgment.

The rules of the battle of the forms can be helpful. At times, you'll find yourself dealing with an uninformed adversary, and with an understanding of the rules, you'll be able to put yourself in the offering party's chair and take control of the deal. The rules provide the foundation for office procedures that, while not guaranteeing success, can improve the odds in your favor.

But an understanding of the rules in the battle of the forms also serves a different, more valuable purpose: it points out the momentous risks and inevitable uncertainty that a cavalier reliance on forms can promote.

Don't Fight when You Can't Win

The best solution to the battle of the forms is not to fight it, because you can never be sure that you'll win.

When a business executive habitually relies on a form, it's usually because he believes it will automatically take care of whatever problems the deal might present down the road. That, as we've seen, is unrealistic at best. Forms create a false sense of security that keeps the parties from confronting and resolving their disagreements before it's too late.

The solution? Use your forms to highlight, not hide, the differences between you and your adversary.

Initially, you should know *your* forms backward and forward.

That means understanding the language and, more important, understanding which provisions are absolutely crucial and which ones are negotiable. If you sell a flammable product, for example, you know that your consequential damage disclaimer has got to be a part of every deal. But perhaps you can compromise on interest rates, or freight charges, or delay issues, or insurance requirements. If you sell a product that's not likely to cause consequential damages even if there's a problem—office supplies, for example—you can give up your disclaimers, but you might need to take a hard line on the "time is of the essence" or suit location clauses. It's your responsibility to sit down with your lawyer and ask the right questions.

Once the battle of the forms breaks out, nip it in the bud. You can save yourself an infinite amount of legal torment if, instead of blindly responding to their form with your form, you make a substantive response geared toward bridging the gap.

Send a letter that says there's no deal unless their disclaimer is deleted. Or get the other side on the telephone, and decide whose terms and conditions are going to govern which parts of the deal. Compromise in accordance with your priorities, and check with your lawyer along the way so you can make sure you know what the competing clauses mean. If you can't agree, don't make the deal unless you've concluded that the risks are worth taking.

If the negotiation concludes successfully, get it in writing or send a confirming letter: "Confirming our conversation, we agree that paragraphs 1 and 16 of my form will govern our deal, along with the first five paragraphs of your terms and conditions. The rest of our forms aren't applicable, and we agree they won't apply. Please advise if this misstates our understanding."

There is no easy shortcut to looking good when the deal goes bad. But you *can* protect yourself without sacrificing efficiency, profit, and control. It takes preparation, forethought, and sometimes a bit of cunning. But unfailingly, it will be worth the effort. A courtroom is a terrible place to conduct business, especially from the wrong end of a lawsuit.

PART SIX

THINGS YOU'LL
WISH YOUR LAWYER
HAD TOLD YOU

Any lawyer who has practiced for any length of time begins to notice certain familiar refrains that run through his dealings with clients. The following exchange is so common, it could practically be set to music (a dirge, perhaps):

CLIENT: I wish you had told me about this problem earlier.

LAWYER: I wish you had asked me earlier.

CLIENT: How could I ask you about a problem I didn't know I had?

One of the business world's unfortunate Catch-22's is that by the time executives realize they have a legal problem, it may already be too late. There is a broad array of laws that apply to business, and many of them are not the kind you can anticipate through your experience or common sense. They are somewhat arbitrary and random. Either you know about them or you don't. And if you don't know about them, you're not likely to guard against them or ask your lawyer about them.

It's the kind of thing that can really shake you. Discovering that you have unintentionally obligated yourself to a bad deal, or are powerless to enforce a good deal, is bad enough. But when you find out that you've gotten yourself in trouble simply by doing things the way you always do them, you start losing confidence, and for that matter, sleep. Your actions can be businesslike, routine, logical—and patently illegal.

Fortunately, you don't need to memorize a law library in order to deal with this problem. All you need is a familiarity with the most common danger signals—you have to know just enough to know when you need legal help, before it's too late.

When business lawyers discuss things with their clients, they listen for telltale indicators that the client, unaware of these danger signals, is about to walk off a legal cliff. I've collected and catalogued some of these pregnant tip-offs, and they serve as the topical dividers for the next three chapters. If any of them rings a bell—that is, if you catch yourself talking or even thinking along similar lines—stop, pick up the telephone, and give your lawyer the chance to tell you what you'll wish you'd always known.

14 DEALING WITH THE ENEMY

Everyday business can be a dog-eat-dog affair. What some call ruthlessness and treachery is, to others, merely "competition." Business as usual. Survival of the fittest, and all that.

Still, there *are* limits, even when it comes to competition. And when you cross the line, you could be in trouble—even criminal trouble.

Most of the legal problems that arise out of competition are caused by getting either too competitive, or not competitive enough. That, as you might imagine, sets up a situation in which business executives are pulled in two different directions at the same time. The law gives out conflicting signals that can be quite difficult to interpret, even among lawyers and law professors.

Nevertheless, you must comply with the law, especially in this area, even if you don't know and can't figure out what it is.

"I THINK IT'S TIME WE HAD A LITTLE TALK WITH THE COMPETITION"

DEALING WITH THE ANTITRUST LAWS

I once had a client who owned a small, neighborhood business. Everything was fine until one of his competitors, who traditionally operated on the other side of town, decided to grab some of my client's customers by offering ridiculously low prices. My client knew he had to retaliate to protect himself, so he, too, lowered his prices and went after a few of his competitor's customers. The raids continued for several months, until my client's competitor asked for a meeting.

"This is ridiculous," he said. "I know I started it, but I'm losing money on the customers I took from you, and you're probably losing money on the ones you took from me. Let's call a truce and go back to the way it was." They agreed not to raid each other's turf any further.

It was a levelheaded solution that saved both businesses . . . right up to the moment they were indicted for dividing up their competitive territory. My client, a family man with a spotless record, was aghast. He had heard of antitrust law, but wasn't it just intended to keep the oil companies and the auto manufacturers in check? He could not believe it could apply to a small, pragmatic business deal.

The antitrust laws are designed to eliminate anticompetitive flaws in the free enterprise system, called "restraints of trade." Promoting a healthy level of competition, goes the theory, will benefit the economy and the general population.

Antitrust difficulties arise most frequently when competitors start to cooperate instead of compete. In a typical case, businesses that would normally be at each other's throats divide up the customers or territories, or they agree not to undercut each other's prices. Such "restraints of trade" remove the incentive to give the consumer better service at a cheaper price.

The popular image of an antitrust violator is a fat cat tycoon who meets in smoke-filled rooms with other fat cat tycoons for the avowed purpose of cheating society; but the issues are usually not that clear-cut. In truth, many antitrust violations are committed unwittingly. The antitrust laws run directly against the grain of many executives' basic instincts, imposing momentous civil and criminal penalties for what appear to be innocent and routine solutions to typical business predicaments. One man's restraint of trade is another man's sound business practice, and that's what makes this area of law so dangerous.

Most executives, for instance, know that "price-fixing" is illegal. They understand "price-fixing" to be an agreement among competitors to set and maintain prices at artificially high levels. But consider these actual antitrust cases:

• A group of companies sold the same product in the same market. Historically, prices fluctuate wildly. Sometimes the market is flooded with the product, and prices plummet. Other times, supply is scarce, and prices skyrocket. So the companies met in the effort to stop the chaos. They agreed to release quantities of the product more evenly throughout the year in the hope of stabilizing the market.

Although they did not agree to charge the same prices, their deal affected prices and restricted competition. All the participants were convicted of price-fixing.

• A group of gas station owners, in a cost-cutting move, agreed not to advertise prices or give away free glasses or trading stamps, although they could still charge whatever they wanted.

The court found that the agreement tended to regulate prices and reduce competition among them. They were all convicted of antitrust violations.

• A trade association of container manufacturers supplied its membership with data on the prices being charged and quoted by the other members of the association.

There was no agreement to fix prices, but the court found that the exchange of this type of information among competitors tended to limit price competition. Antitrust penalties were imposed.

If you're thinking about making a deal with the competition, you need to be alert to the possibility of trouble. Not every understanding among competitors is an antitrust violation, but you'll never be able to tell the ones that are legal from the ones that are criminal unless you get your lawyer involved from the very start.

"I'VE GOT SOME GREAT IDEAS FOR DISTRIBUTION AND PRICING"

OTHER ANTITRUST TIP-OFFS

There are many other areas in which the antitrust laws have an impact that is difficult to anticipate. Routine decision-making in areas involving marketing, pricing, and distribution, for example, does not normally involve a high degree of legal risk. But antitrust law can change that very quickly. Watch out for these danger signals:

• Many manufacturers require the stores that sell their products to charge a certain minimum price, and they take retaliatory action against those which fail to comply. The law dislikes this kind of arrangement. It reduces competition among retailers who sell the manufacturer's product. Sometimes such a practice is legal, and sometimes it isn't; a business that takes part in this kind of arrangement—be it a manufacturer, distributor, or retailer—had better consult counsel.

• The same is true of exclusive territory arrangements, by which, for example, a manufacturer guarantees a distributor or retailer the exclusive right to sell a product in a particular area. Sometimes it's legal, but other times it's not. Don't do it without legal advice.

• The antitrust laws often try to stop the big fish from eating the little fish. For instance, imagine a market in which there are several small companies and one very large company vying for customers. In the effort to drive the small companies out of business, the large company might offer its products at below cost. Because of its size, it can absorb the loss, but eventually the smaller companies would have to fold, leaving the large company free to raise prices as high as it wants.

This and similar "predatory practices," as the antitrust law calls them, are illegal. If the larger company were able to sell at a lower price because of its efficiency or technical superiority, it would normally be permitted to do so. But the law draws the line at purposefully losing money or committing other acts beyond the limits of "healthy" competition, especially where the overriding purpose is not only the acquisition of business, but the destruction of competition.

• Some computer companies used to make their customers sign a contract requiring them to use only the computer company's paper, punch cards, and other supplies. Fast-food franchisors used to require that their franchisees use only the hamburger meat the franchisors sold to them. Movie distributors would sell certain films to theaters only if they agreed to buy other films they did not really want.

Deals such as these are called "tying arrangements"—the seller will sell only if the buyer also agrees to buy something else. They limit competition—for instance, other manufacturers of computer supplies lose the ability to compete for customers who bought a particular make of computer. Tying arrangements are generally illegal. Don't try this variety of marketing without legal advice.

• When a manufacturer or distributor of a product sells it to one retailer at one price and another retailer at another price, antitrust issues arise. Those two retailers cannot compete on an equal footing; the one who buys for less has an unfair marketplace advantage over the one who buys for more. Sometimes the price differential can be logically explained—one retailer may pay cash and the other may want credit, or one may buy in greater volume than the other. But in many cases, this practice, called "discriminatory pricing," is illegal. Involve your lawyer in this kind of pricing decision.

Whatever you decide concerning distribution, pricing, and in general, getting a "leg up" on the competition, check out your ideas with your lawyer first. They might be highly effective and profitable. But they also might be illegal.

"THERE'S NOTHING WRONG WITH A LITTLE HEALTHY COMPETITION"

INTERFERENCE WITH CONTRACTS

Well, maybe, but be careful. Antitrust law says you have to compete, but there are limits on what you can do to your competitors.

Salesmen often visit an account to find out what the customer is buying from the competition and how much he's paying for it. Then the salesman tries to make the customer a better deal. That's the way it's supposed to work.

But suppose the customer tells the salesman something like this: "I wish you'd been here a few weeks ago. You have the better price, but I've already signed an agreement to buy from your competitor, so I guess I'm stuck."

That's a danger signal. Many salesmen, eager to get the business, try to talk the customer out of his prior deal. "Just tell them you got a better price. They won't do anything—do you realize how much business they'd lose if they sued a customer?"

That's a tort, called "interference with contract." It was, for instance, the basis of Pennzoil's $11-billion verdict against Texaco. As a general rule, you cannot induce a party to a contract to breach it. If you do, the other party to the contract has the right to sue you for damages, and there's nothing more humiliating or painful than having to pay damages to your competitor.

The law tries to strike a balance between the sanctity of contracts and the promotion of competition. You can still make your sales pitch, even if the customer is under contract to someone else. If he decides to take his chances and breach the deal without your direct inducement, you're not responsible. (You might tell the customer that you know he can't make a deal with you now, but having heard what you have to say, maybe he'll consider calling you when his present contract expires.)

But there's a fine line between telling a customer how your deal is better than the contract he already has, and advising him to violate his agreement. And even if you do it right, good luck proving it when your competitor sues you. If you're in the sort of business in which you run into this problem frequently, you ought to have your lawyer analyze your individual circumstances with a view toward developing a specific list of "dos and don'ts."

15 DEALING WITH EMPLOYEES

Perhaps no area of business law in recent history has come under closer scrutiny, and been changed more fundamentally, than the law that affects employer–employee relations. It's an area that demands informed and deliberate action—the stakes are high, and it's very, very easy to slip up.

Many executives, having come up through the ranks when the law had a much different orientation, presume that the old way is still the best way. But the rules have been changed, and the days of "I run this company and I'll do what I think is right" capitalism are long gone.

"I Hired You and I Can Fire You"

FIRING EMPLOYEES

Most executives understand that unless an employee has an employment agreement that says otherwise (for example, a union contract, or an agreement that says the employee can be fired only for "just cause"), the employer can dismiss him at any time, for any reason. The law calls such a person an "at will" employee—he serves at the will of the employer.

At least, that's the way it used to be. But things are not so clear anymore.

Very recently, some courts started carving exceptions into the "at will" employment rule. These cases first arose from situations in which an employee was fired for having reported his employer's safety violations or criminal offenses. The firings were invalidated as being "contrary to public policy." At present, most states recognize a restriction on an employer's right to fire a "whistle-blower" employee, and some have even passed legislation to make it absolutely illegal.

Once the door was opened, it became a floodgate. Courts started finding other reasons to restrict what an employer could do to an "at will" employee. There is no consistency from state to state, and employers still win most of the time. But consider the following cases in which fired employees without employment contracts recovered damages from their former employers:

• An employee claims she was discharged because she failed to accept a date with a superior.
• An employer fires an employee shortly before the employee would have become entitled to a large sales commission, resulting in a substantial saving to the employer.
• An employee is dismissed allegedly because he made a worker's compensation claim, or because he exercised some other right to a benefit, such as disability insurance.
• An employee is fired for refusing to take a lie-detector test.

And to further complicate matters, there are numerous federal statutes that restrict what an employer can do to an employee. Here are just a few:

• The National Labor Relations Act prohibits firing employees for union activity.
• The Fair Labor Standards Act prohibits firing employees for making claims for minimum wage and overtime payments.
• Title VII of the Civil Rights Act of 1964 prohibits firing employees on the basis of race, religion, sex, or national origin. This often leads to cases based upon a sophisticated statistical analysis of an employer's work force in order to document the motivation behind the employer's hiring and firing practices.
• The Age Discrimination in Employment Act prohibits discharges based on age.
• The Employee Retirement Income Security Act prohibits discharges motivated by a desire to keep employees from obtaining vested pension rights.

Firing an "at will" employee can lead to an obligation to reinstate the employee and reimburse him for all back pay lost as a result of the firing. All a court has to find is that the employer's actions were improperly motivated. It is becoming more and more common for employees to sue their former employers, either because they truly believe they were fired for unjustifiable reasons or, recognizing how risky this kind of case is becoming to employers, in the hope of generating an out-of-court settlement.

In addition to the need for restraint, one lesson employers ought to derive from all this is the need to document the bona fide reasons that support a decision to discharge. If, for example, an employee has not been performing his work properly, his file ought to include evidence of written warnings and work evaluations given before his termination. When the employee later claims that the employer's actions were discriminatory, or intended to punish him for whistle-blowing, the employer will have a response and a means to prove it.

And finally, have your counsel go over your employer–employee procedures—courts are finding all sorts of previously unseen legal ramifications in employee handbooks, bulletin-board notices, and even unwritten company policies. There are ways around a lot of the confusion, but it's going to take legal know-how and creativity.

"WE'LL GIVE THEM A FEW SHARES OF STOCK. THAT'LL KEEP THEM HAPPY"

THE RIGHTS OF MINORITY STOCKHOLDERS

Employee stock purchase plans are a very popular and profitable employee benefit in many large corporations. These programs are structured to take advantage of certain tax laws, and if the stock rises, the employees receive an asset of increasing value. It's a good way to keep employees happy.

Owners of small or medium-sized corporations also have to reward or risk losing their important employees. Taking a cue from their larger brethren, they will often afford such employees the right to buy a limited amount of stock in the corporation, or they will give the stock as a "bonus." From the employees' point of view, it gives them a feeling of ownership, of being part of the organization in a real sense. From the point of view of the principal owners, it's a lot cheaper than cash or a salary increase.

But unless the stock plan is structured by professionals—as it is in large corporate employee benefit programs—giving a few shares of stock to a trusted bookkeeper can cause havoc. Corporate stockholders have certain legal rights. If the corporation is owned by an individual, a family, or a group of original founders, the complications are minimized. But once an outsider acquires the rights of a stockholder, look out.

For instance, minority stockholders have the right to insist that the corporation conduct business formally, according to the corporation's bylaws. Forget the informal decision-making you're used to. They have the right to inspect the corporation's books and records—they can see who's making what, what expenses are being reimbursed to the officers, whether business is being diverted to other enterprises owned by the primary stockholders, and so on. Forget the extra "perks" that are customary in a closely held company—unless all the "i's" are dotted and "t's" are crossed, a minority stockholder can require the officers and directors to reimburse the corporation for any extra benefits or diversions of assets.

If there's extra money in the business, a minority stockholder has the right to insist that dividends be paid before salaries are increased. In some circumstances, a minority stockholder can keep the corporation from firing him, even if he doesn't have an employment contract. Minority stockholders have the right to vote for directors—the people who, by law, run the corporation —and depending on the company's overall stock structure, they may have the right to elect a director. They have the right to request a court to appoint a "receiver" or "custodian" to look over the shoulder of the primary stockholders, making sure they don't take anything to which they're not specifically entitled. It can be a nightmare.

But, you say, your trusted bookkeeper would never do such a thing? Maybe not. But what happens if he dies and leaves the stock to his uncle, who is not nearly so cooperative? What happens if he gets sued, and a creditor takes the stock from him in satisfaction of a judgment? What happens if, desperate for cash, he sells the stock to your competitor at a hefty price, giving your worst enemy minority stockholder rights in your business?

And perhaps worst of all, suppose you want to sell your business. A prospective purchaser who knows about minority stockholder rights will not want to buy your corporation unless he can acquire 100 percent of the stock. That's when a minority shareholder starts acting like someone who owns a candy store in the middle of the block that GM wants to buy for its office-building complex. He'll know how important his 1 percent has become—and he'll negotiate accordingly.

So before you decide to transfer an "inconsequential" few shares of your business as an employment benefit, consult your lawyer. Perhaps a nice profit-sharing plan or an extra week's vacation would serve your purpose more appropriately.

"THANKS FOR WORKING LATE. THERE'LL BE A LITTLE SOMETHING EXTRA IN YOUR PAYCHECK THIS WEEK"

PAYING OVERTIME—THE LEGAL WAY

One of my clients runs a business in which all the employees regularly work more than forty hours a week. He was keeping separate time cards on each and paying time-and-a-half, as the law mandates. Finally, the bookkeeping hassles were more trouble than they were worth—some employees worked 51.3 hours one week and 49.2 hours the next week and 55.6 hours the following week. Multiplied by fifty employees, calculating each paycheck each week became a major production.

So he sat down with the employees and struck a deal. "Suppose I pay each of you the same flat amount each week, no matter how many hours you work. We'll pick a number that's fair—your regular wage, plus your average overtime, plus a little more, just to make sure. I'll save bookkeeping problems. You'll be assured of an overtime income, and if you think it's not working out, let me know and we'll change it."

The employees thought it was a great idea, and the system operated for years without complaints. But one day, my client received a visit from the U.S. Department of Labor, which audited his payroll records. It was the beginning of an expensive lesson.

Federal law requires that employees be paid time-and-a-half for overtime. My client had no objection to that, and he explained the deal he had made with his employees. In fact, the flat sum he paid ended up being more than time-and-a-half.

Not good enough, said the Department of Labor. "We don't care if you pay them ten times the amount they've got coming to them. You've got to keep records showing what you pay for forty hours, and showing the extra payments for the overtime. You can't estimate."

"What about the employees?" my client asked. "Don't they have the right to decide how they want to be paid?"

"Wrong again," said the Department of Labor. It would take a written, signed agreement with each employee, and sometimes even that wouldn't be good enough.

The upshot was that my client had to pay substantial damages to the Federal Government, ostensibly for distribution to the "underpaid" employees. Some of them, as a matter of conscience, refused the money. Other employees had long since left and could not be found. None of that mattered to the Department of Labor, which kept the money anyway.

These standards apply to most but not all businesses, and there are some exemptions in certain industries. But to this day, my client cannot believe it happened to him. He keeps asking me a question I don't know how to answer: "Don't they have to tell you in advance that you can't do something that makes sense?"

"ANYONE AROUND HERE WHO WANTS A UNION HAD BETTER START LOOKING FOR ANOTHER JOB"

DEALING WITH A UNIONIZATION EFFORT

What do you do when you find out that union representatives are attempting to unionize your employees? Many executives are shocked, scared, and angry, and the actions they take in the first few days (or, often, the first few minutes) before consulting their lawyer can seal their fate for years to come.

The law gives employees the absolute right to engage in "concerted activity"—they can join together to seek improvements in their wages and working conditions through "collective bargaining." Most often, employees exercise this right by electing a union to be their "bargaining representative." The union negotiates for the employees as a group, and the employees agree to do what the union tells them to do—for example, to keep working, or to go on strike. In exchange, the employees hope to get the bargaining leverage and expertise that unionization is intended to provide.

In attempting to unionize a business, a union will first recruit a small group of interested employees. Operating on the inside, they can effectively "talk up" the union, distribute literature, arrange meetings, and attempt to develop support. As other employees are won over to the union side, the union will ask them to sign "authorization cards" evidencing their desire to be represented by the union.

Sometimes, an employer finds out about the union campaign at an early stage, bars the union from the premises, and makes it clear that those employees who favor unionization had best look for other employment. Other times, the employer doesn't find out until the union has persuaded a majority of the employees to sign authorization cards. At that point, a union representative will pay the employer a visit. "Here's proof that a majority of your employees want us to represent them," he'll say, displaying the cards. Panicked, many employers immediately commence efforts to discover and terminate the union sympathizers in the work force.

These are natural reactions to what employers often perceive as attacks on their autonomy and profitability. But these sorts of responses blatantly violate federal labor laws—and they're the quickest and surest way to guarantee a union victory. Here's what you need to know to stay out of trouble.

• In most cases, the union will have to win a government-supervised election among the employees before it can become their collective bargaining representative. Remember this if the union attempts to pressure you into signing an agreement appointing it the employee representative before an election is held. Do not meet with the union representatives, even for a minute or two, without your lawyer. You would be surprised at the legal consequences that can arise from seemingly harmless

union—management discussions about the possibility of unionization.
• Up to the day of the vote, the employer and the union have
the right to campaign for employee support. The law recognizes, however, that because of the economic power it can wield
over its employees, an employer can unfairly influence the vote.

Therefore, the employer's conduct during the campaign is
watched very closely. If the employer commits "unfair labor
practices," the National Labor Relations Board, which super-
vises the election process, has the power to declare the union to
be the representative of the employees even if the union loses
the election. An employer must walk a well-advised line between
an aggressive, hard-fought campaign and overly coercive or intimidating "persuasion."

Here are the kinds of campaign tactics that are most often
labeled "unfair labor practices":

• Intimations by the employer that he will close or move the
business if the union wins.
• Promising extra benefits or raises if the union loses.
• Threatening to reduce wages or benefits if the union wins.
• Firing or demoting union sympathizers, or rewarding anti-
union employees.
• Spying on employees, or launching investigations in order to
determine which employees favor the union.
• Initiating new employee benefits during the campaign, espe-
cially while hinting at take-backs if the union wins.

In addition:

• The law gives the union a fair amount of access to the employer's premises so that it has an equal chance to speak with employees. An employer's initial reaction to news of a unionization
effort typically bars all union people from the property, forbids
the distribution of union literature, and so on. That sort of
blanket restriction can cause problems. Check with your lawyer
first.
• The union representative usually tries to show the employer
the authorization cards, but at all costs, the employer should

not look at them. It's a trap. Once the employer sees who signed the cards, he knows who's for the union and who's against the union. If the union loses the election, it will try to prove that the employer influenced the election by favoring the anti-unionists and discriminating against the pro-unionists. But to prove it, the union has to show that the employer knew one from the other. That's why they want the employer to look at the authorization cards. If he doesn't, he'll have a much better chance of avoiding unfair labor practice charges.

How to fight unionization—or, for that matter, whether to fight unionization—is well beyond the scope of this book. But an executive has to realize that when the union comes knocking, it brings a significant amount of legal firepower with it. You have to fight your urge to counterattack with guns blazing. The battle has to be waged within certain limitations, pursuant to legal advice, or the law will see to it that you lose the war.

16 COVERING YOUR ASSETS

Business is, at its core, a struggle to make what's theirs into what's yours, while keeping what's yours from becoming what's theirs.

You want their customers; they want your customers. You want your customer's money, and your customer doesn't want to give it to you. You want to keep your ideas and methods to yourself, and your competitors would like nothing better than to steal them from you—just as you'd like to steal theirs from them if you could get away with it.

It's the law that gives you the weapons you need to wage this war successfully. Many of these weapons are vastly underutilized; the effectiveness of others is consistently overestimated.

To protect your assets effectively, you have to understand the strengths and limitations of *whom* you're fighting with. But you must also understand the strengths and limitations of *what* you're fighting with.

"I've Got This Great Idea I'd Like to Show You"

PROTECTING YOUR IDEAS
The stock-in-trade of many businesses includes ideas, designs, solutions to problems, or other products of expertise, creativity, or sheer intelligence. Unlike that of a company which sells bricks or trucks, the "inventory" of such businesses is difficult to protect. For example, if an engineering consultant designs and sells a computer program to a client, can he prevent the client from selling the program to others? If a company develops a new manufacturing technique, can it keep its competitor from stealing the idea?

Many if not most times, it can't; but I've seen a great num-

ber of businesses, especially consulting firms, derive a false
sense of security from the copyright laws. They affix a copyright
notice to their reports, manuals, or procedures, believing that it
prevents anyone from using their solutions or strategies without
their permission. It's not that simple.

A "copyright" gives the copyright holder certain rights to the
tangible things he creates—books, poems, articles, reports,
logos, plans, sound recordings, photographs, sketches, and so
on. And in most instances, a copyright is quite easy to obtain.
All you have to do is affix a copyright notice to the work—
normally the symbol ©, followed by the date that the work was
first distributed to the public, followed by the name of the copyright holder. An example of a copyright notice appears at the
beginning of this book. Adding the phrase "all rights reserved"
gives some added protection. Although it's not always mandatory, the copyright should then be registered at the copyright
office in Washington—a simple matter accomplished by filling
out a form and paying a small fee. Registration gives you other
rights, such as the right to sue anyone who copies or sells what
you've copyrighted without your consent.

But copyright protection goes only so far.

For instance, suppose you create and copyright a recipe for
Eggs Benedict. What rights do you have? Is no one else allowed
to cook Eggs Benedict according to your recipe without your
permission? Or suppose you copyright an article on how to ride
a bike. Is no one permitted to ride a bike according to your
description without your okay?

That's not the way it works. The governing statute, known as
the Copyright Act of 1976, says that a copyright does not protect
"any idea, procedure, process, system, method of operation,
concept, principle or discovery." That means that a copyright
protects only the *tangible* part of your creation—what appears
on the paper in the form of the words you choose to express
your thoughts. It doesn't protect the *ideas* behind your words.

Therefore, you don't own the Eggs Benedict "process," in the
sense of having the right to prevent others from preparing your
dish according to your recipe. Although your write-up of the
recipe is protected, anyone else could use the recipe, or write it
up a bit differently than you did and put it in a cookbook. Your
article on bike riding describes a "procedure" or a "system."

COVERING YOUR ASSETS   179

Your copyright doesn't mean that you own a bike-riding method.
It means that you own a *description* of a bike-riding method.

As metaphysical as that distinction may seem, it has tremendous business significance. A company that comes up with a
unique technique wants to keep others from using it or selling
it. But all a copyright protects is the company's written explanation of the technique, not the technique itself. The same goes
for an engineer's computer program (although the law is chang-
ing quickly in this area), an advertising agency's marketing
ideas, a toy company's product concepts, and so on.

Still, there are alternatives—if you get legal help at an early
stage in your idea's development. For example, you may be able
to obtain a patent on some of your methods and processes,
although that's a very difficult, technical, and lengthy process.

Many consultants use contracts that effectively prohibit their
clients from distributing the consultant's work product to others. They include clauses like "Customer agrees that the ideas,
concepts, processes, and work product supplied pursuant to this
agreement shall remain the property of the consultant and shall
not be disclosed or sold to any third party." That, too, requires
a large measure of legal know-how.

Employment agreements can also be structured to prevent
your employees from disclosing your trade secrets, and there
are various trade secret laws which might also apply to your
situation.

But all these techniques require competent legal assistance.
There is simply no easy, quick way to protect your ideas. Don't
assume you can do it yourself. And don't put yourself in a position in which, after the horse has left the barn, you wish you
had asked your lawyer for help.

"EMPLOYMENT CONTRACTS? I DON'T NEED THE COMPLICATIONS"

RESTRICTIVE COVENANTS, AND OTHER SURVIVAL TACTICS

Most companies shy away from signing their employees to
written employment agreements. But a properly drafted employment agreement can prevent a wealth of problems.

An employee departure can devastate a business. In a typical scenario, a company hires a young salesman, trains him, watches him progress—only to have him accept a job with a competitor. The salesman is in a position to destroy his former employer. He can disclose customer lists, markups, pricing policies, business plans, and everything else that a business can't afford to leak to the competition.

Or, quite often, a key employee in a consulting firm, insurance agency, investment counseling firm, dentist's office, advertising agency, or similar business will leave and take a large chunk of the business with him. The principals in the company probably lost money on the employee until he learned the ropes —only to have their pocket picked just when they could start recouping their investment.

But if your employee is subject to an employment agreement, much of this can be avoided, or at least minimized. In most jurisdictions, the agreement can include a "restrictive covenant." This is a provision that legally prevents your employee from competing with you, taking your business, or working for the competition. As long as it's "reasonable" in terms of how long it lasts and what geographic area it covers, a court will enforce it. For instance:

> *Employee agrees as a condition of employment that, in the event of termination for any reason, he will not engage in a similar or competitive business for a period of two years, nor will he contact or solicit any customer with whom Employer conducted business during his employment. This restrictive covenant shall be for a term of two years from termination, and shall encompass an area within a 50-mile radius of Employer's place of business.*

And you can add provisions that protect your business' "trade secrets" from disclosure—who your customers are, how you do business, and so on.

> *Employee agrees that Employer's customer lists, processes, manufacturing techniques, sales materials, and pricing information constitutes the sole and exclusive property of*

> *Employer, and that same are "trade secrets" under the law. Employee promises that under no circumstances shall he disclose same, during or after the term hereof, and upon violation of this provision Employee agrees that Employer shall be entitled to an injunction, compensatory and punitive damages, and reimbursement for its counsel fees.*

These kinds of clauses are hypertechnical, and to be certain of the maximum protection, you'll need a lawyer to draft them. But it's worth the effort. A business has to protect its assets—not just its cash, but its goodwill, its methods, its strategies, and all the rest. An employment agreement with the right provisions is an excellent way to do it.

"I'VE GOT A WILL AND LIFE INSURANCE. AT LEAST I KNOW MY FAMILY'S PROTECTED"

WHY YOUR BUSINESS, AND YOUR FAMILY, NEED A BUY–SELL AGREEMENT

Over the last ten years, I'm sure my law firm has represented at least a dozen clients with the same fundamental business problem. They explain it like this:

"Twenty years ago, me and my partner started a business. On the advice of our accountant, we made it a corporation and we each took fifty percent of the stock. Over the years, the business prospered, but last month, my partner died.

"His will left everything he had to his four kids—and the lawyer for his estate tells me that included the stock in the business. The kids are willing to sell the stock, but I don't have enough cash to give them what it's worth, and if I took the money out of the company I don't think it would ever recover. I used to be in business with my partner; now I'm in business with his kids. And I don't know what I'll do if they decide to sell it to someone else."

At best, a stock purchase involving some kind of deferred payout is arranged, but that drastically compromises cash flow and profitability. Just as often, no agreement can be reached, leading to lawsuits and an out-of-business corporation.

A device known as a "buy–sell" agreement prevents this kind of problem. It comes in limitless varieties, but usually each partner will sign a contract which requires his estate to sell his stock either to the other partner or to the corporation upon his death. The business then takes out life insurance on both partners. When one of the partners dies, the proceeds are used to pay the deceased partner's estate for his stock.

Everybody (except, of course, the deceased partner) wins: his heirs get a fair price and immediate cash for stock they probably didn't want anyway, and the remaining partner keeps the business without having to come up with the money to pay for it. And during their lives, each partner has the peace of mind that comes from knowing that if he dies first, his estate is in order, and if he doesn't, the business can continue. As an alternative to life insurance, the partners can build up a cash reserve, or they can make other arrangements. Lawyers and accountants work hand in hand to design the best business and estate planning approach.

Buy–sell agreements can be used to avoid all sorts of other problems as well. For example, in the minority stockholder situation referred to previously, the employees who receive the stock could be required to sign a buy–sell agreement that gives the company the right to buy their stock back (at a low price) upon death or termination from the company. It can also provide that they're not permitted to sell it to a third party without first giving the company the right to buy the stock, again at an artificially low figure. That helps the company keep its stock away from outsiders.

Business partners often enter similar buy–sell agreements designed to keep the stock away from strangers. For example, it's quite typical for the stockholders in a closely held company to sign an agreement that prevents any of them from selling stock to a third party without first offering it to the other stockholders. That gives them the perpetual right to keep the business in the hands of the people they know and trust. Without a buy–sell agreement, there's no way to control where the stock—and the business—ends up.

"WE'RE PROTECTED. THEY SIGNED A NOTE THAT SAYS THEY HAVE TO PAY US IN THIRTY DAYS"

PROMISSORY NOTES AND JUDGMENT NOTES

Suppose your customer admits that he owes you money, but he says he doesn't have it. He tells you that he expects to be able to pay you in a few months, and he asks you to be patient. How can you protect yourself?

You could write up an agreement whereby the customer admits responsibility for the debt and agrees to pay by a certain date. That saves you from having to prove your entitlement to the money, just in case he changes his mind later. This sort of agreement is often called a "promissory note," which is just another term for a writing in which one party agrees to pay money to another.

But what happens if he doesn't honor the agreement? You're left with a breach of contract lawsuit, and you can't do anything to collect your money until it works its way through the court system, which could take years and thousands of dollars in legal fees. In the meantime, a lot of other creditors could also be pursuing your customer, and there might not be any assets left by the time your case gets to trial.

In many jurisdictions, you can take advantage of a much better alternative, called a "judgment note."

A "judgment" is what you get if you sue someone and win. A judgment puts the power of the court behind your efforts to collect what you're owed. If you have a judgment, the court will make the debtor disclose all his assets, and it will sell whatever he has and give you the proceeds. You can freeze his bank accounts. You can take his inventory. You can grab his accounts receivable or any other money he might be owed. Short of throwing him into debtor's prison, a judgment gives you a broad range of tools that you can use to get what's coming to you.

A "judgment note" gives you the judgment without the necessity of filing and winning a lawsuit. It's like a promissory note, except it gives you the right to enter a judgment for what you're owed, as if there had already been a trial. If the debtor doesn't pay, you can immediately commence enforcement proceedings

—saving the time and expense of litigation. And many judgment notes even let you collect your legal fees from the other side.

Typically, a debtor who is dealing with you in good faith will agree to sign a judgment note if you'll agree to delay collection efforts for a stipulated period, or for as long as he makes monthly payments. Your lawyer can tell you if judgment notes are permitted in your state and if the technique will work in the particular facts of your case.

"WHY SHOULD I WORRY? IT WASN'T MY FAULT"

HOLD HARMLESS AND INDEMNIFICATION CLAUSES
How could you protect the assets of your company in the following situations?

• Your company owns a small office building. It contracts with a management company to maintain the property, arrange for snow removal, and the like. The management company fails to clear the ice off a sidewalk, and one of your tenants slips and falls, sustaining a serious injury. The tenant sues your company for failing to keep the sidewalk safe.
• Your company manufactures electric motors. One of your suppliers tells you that, as a specialist, it can make and install the controls for the motors better and more cheaply than you can. You subcontract that part of the manufacturing to your supplier. The controls fail, and twenty of your customers file suit.
• Your company is retained to write a sales brochure. You hire a writer to produce the copy as an independent contractor. The week after the brochure is distributed, your customer gets sued for copyright infringement by a competitor. It turns out that the writer you hired plagiarized what he wrote, and the customer understandably demands a refund plus damages from you.

In each case, you have clear rights against the person or business who caused the damages. But to assert those rights, you will have to pay a lawyer to defend against the claim you face, while at the same time pursuing your own claim for reimbursement against the guilty party. That is an expensive, two-front proposition. And as was discussed in Chapter 1, even though the whole mess was someone else's fault, you won't be able to sue for your legal fees. It could easily cost you more than it's worth.

The solution is a legal device known as a "hold harmless and indemnification" clause. It looks something like this:

> *We hereby agree to defend, indemnify, and hold you harmless from and against any and all claims or suits that may be brought against you arising out of or related to the work to be done by us for you as set forth herein.*

The exact wording may vary a bit from jurisdiction to jurisdiction, but provisions of this type mean that in the event of trouble, they agree to pay your legal costs, and they also agree to pay any damages that you might incur in the event someone makes a claim against you. In short, you get a free ride. A hold harmless and indemnification clause is like a private insurance policy. Even if you get into trouble, somebody else defends you and pays the tab if you lose.

You should consider negotiating for a hold harmless and indemnification clause in any situation in which you could be sued for what someone else has done. Anytime you hire a supplier or subcontractor to provide materials or work for which you are ultimately responsible, this sort of provision could be a lifesaver.

The problem with hold harmless and indemnification clauses, however, is the solvency of whoever's doing the holding harmless and indemnifying. It's only as good as the party that stands behind it. If it's General Motors that's agreed to protect you, fine. But if it's Harry's Pizza and Janitorial Services Inc., you may have problems. The hold harmless and indemnification clause doesn't affect the claim of whoever's suing you. An injured party doesn't lose its right to seek and collect damages against you, just because the company that was supposed to bail you out doesn't have the money to back up its promise.

In some instances, you can solve this problem by coupling the other party's hold harmless and indemnification obligation with the responsibility to obtain a bond or an applicable insurance policy that protects you, just in case they can't. That puts some substance behind their promise. A clause like this will do it in most cases:

> *We shall provide a bond or suitable insurance policy naming you as an insured or otherwise protecting you from liability, in the amount of $100,000, in such a form as you may reasonably require.*

There are some complexities having to do with bonding and insurance law that your lawyer will have to cover. And the precise wording of the hold harmless and indemnification provision will also require some fine-tuning, depending on your jurisdiction and the sorts of risks that usually affect the type of business you do.

But if you're interested in protecting your assets against lawsuits, there's nothing like a contract clause that requires them to pay everything and you to pay nothing. You can't do much better than that.

17

TRICKS OF THE TRADE:
The Problem Solvers

Lawyers are trained to appreciate the value of a compromise. They know, perhaps better than anyone else, how frustrating and expensive it can be when a "do-able" deal falls apart at the seams, or when an argument needlessly turns into a lawsuit.

What follows are some Solomonesque, hard-to-argue-with techniques that lawyers use to break free from the most common deal-making logjams. I've found them to be great "gap closers," and they're especially applicable to the "borderline deals" that business executives tend to negotiate by themselves, without legal counsel.

THE "MEET IT OR BEAT IT" FIRST OPTION

Not so long ago, when a team in the National Basketball Association signed a player out of college, that team owned the rights to the player for all time. When the player's contract expired, his options were to sign a new contract with his team, or not play. He had to hope his team would treat him fairly, because he wasn't allowed to sign with another team that might be willing to pay him more money.

The rationale behind the system had to do with the risk behind the team's initial investment. No one could tell for sure what college players would make it in the pros, and at best, paying a 21-year-old athlete a six-figure salary was a gamble. But under the old NBA system, the chance was worth taking. If the player became a star, the team had the right to hold on to him. It was guaranteed the benefit of its investment.

Recent court decisions invalidated the system, allowing players to offer their services to the highest bidder. That upset the applecart. Now the team that ran the risk, paying the player a bundle when he was still an unknown quantity, could lose him to another team as soon as his contract expired. "That's not fair," said the owners. "We invest the money, take all the chances, and some other team gets the payoff." The league was in trouble.

But the NBA and the players' union solved the problem with a compromise technique often referred to as a "meet it or beat it" first option; now, at the end of a player's contract term, he is free to solicit offers from whomever he pleases. But before he can accept another team's offer, his original team gets the chance to "meet or beat" the best offer he receives. If it does, the player has to stay. If it doesn't, the player can go.

The player is happy. He gets his market price. The team is happy. It gets the opportunity to hold on to him without paying any more than anyone else was willing to pay.

I've seen this technique work in numerous other businesses. Many deals focus on one party's willingness to do something now, as long as he gets something later. A publisher will agree to publish a book now, as long as it gets an option to publish the author's next book. An insurance broker will agree to write a policy for a low premium now, as long as it gets the right to hold on to the business when the policy expires. A builder will agree to complete a developer's project for a specified price now, as long as it gets to do the next project as well.

Negotiations often break down at that point. The author doesn't mind if the publisher does his next book, but before he agrees to it, he wants to know how much he's going to be paid. The publisher doesn't want to commit to a high price, because it can't tell how successful the first book is going to be. The author doesn't want to commit to a low price, just in case his first book is a smashing success.

The insurance broker can't quote a premium now for a policy to take effect two years from now. Who knows what the market will be like then? The client, however, doesn't want to commit to the insurance broker. Perhaps he'll be able to get a much lower price from a different broker when it's time to renew the coverage.

The builder can't quote a price for a project that's not supposed to start for a year. It depends on the details, material costs, and so on. And the developer must go with the lowest bidder. Maybe that will be this builder, but maybe it will be somebody else.

A "meet it or beat it" first option stops the arguments over what the future might bring. It solves the problem by postponing it, allowing the market, not the parties, to set the terms of the deal. The publisher will have the right to publish the author's second book, but only if it matches the best offer some other publisher gives the author. The insurance broker will keep the client's business, but only if it agrees to charge no more than the best deal some other broker is willing to give. The builder will have the option to handle the developer's next project, but only if it's willing to meet the low bid.

There are numerous variations to the "meet it or beat it" first option. For instance, you can require the option holder to beat the market's best offer by at least 10 percent. That gives the other bidders more of an incentive to get involved in the auction —their offer has to be beaten, and not just tied, before they're out of the running.

But no matter how you do it, one side of the deal (the basketball player, the author, the insurance client, the developer) is guaranteed the best deal the market has to offer. The other side of the deal (the team, the publisher, the broker, the builder) isn't locked in and has to make the deal only if it wants to. It can be a very effective compromise.

THE "MOST FAVORED NATION" AGREEMENT

A close relative of the "meet it or beat it" first option is the "most favored nation" agreement.

Amalgamated Steel buys large quantities of coal, using various suppliers. Suppose one of the suppliers proposes that Amalgamated Steel sign a contract agreeing to purchase a million tons a week for one year at its current price. It guarantees to have sufficient quantities available so that Amalgamated Steel is never caught short, and it offers favorable payment terms.

"Fine," Amalgamated Steel says, "but how do we know the current price will be fair six months or a year from now? Suppose the market price drops? How do we know you'll treat us fairly?"

The parties could commence complex negotiations defining the price to be charged, but in many cases a "most favored nation" provision could solve the problem. It would guarantee that for the duration of the contract, the supplier would never charge Amalgamated Steel more than it charges any other customer—Amalgamated Steel would be "most favored." That, by itself, could give Amalgamated Steel the assurance it needs.

Other variations could be added, such as capping the price at a stated maximum, or lowering the price if the supplier's competitors are charging significantly less to Amalgamated's competitors.

But again, the market, and not the parties, would set the price, and both sides come out feeling that they've been treated fairly. One side protects its precedent. It's like saying, "We can't go along with that, but we will agree that if we ever agree to it in the future, we'll give it to you as well." The other side knows that it won't be at a later disadvantage—it will always have the best deal.

And it works wherever there are buyers and sellers: a building owner agrees that if it ever offers space to another tenant at a lower rate than you're paying, it will lower your rent; a food company promises a farmer that it will never pay more for someone else's corn; a television station agrees to raise your salary if it pays another newscaster more than you.

It's a good way to snatch a deal from a disagreement, and it turns convoluted contracts into simple transactions.

The Agreeable Point of Future Reference

When money markets got volatile a few years ago, mortgage lenders were petrified to lend money at 11 percent for thirty years when in a year or two, the going rate might be 15 percent. Mortgage money was tough to come by, until someone came up with the idea of making the mortgage rate adjustable. It was linked to an agreeable point of future reference—various Treasury or consumer price indices—so it could shift with the tide, neither benefiting nor burdening the borrower or the lender.

The same idea can work whenever you can't agree on a price, a discount, an interest rate, an escalation rate—anything numerical. Tie whatever's holding up the deal to the prime rate, or the Dow Jones average, or the commodities futures index, or the consumer price index, or an industry average, or any other statistical compilation that makes sense. It's another way to compromise painlessly.

The "You Divide and I'll Choose" Ploy

I once represented a woman who was involved in a messy divorce suit. There was a great deal of valuable art, furnishings, and antiques involved, and after bitter negotiations with her husband, we managed to settle all the issues except for the division of the property in the house.

Just before the trial began, the judge who was to hear the case called everyone into his chambers.

"I have an idea that might resolve this case," he said. "When I was a boy, my brother and I used to fight over everything: who got the bigger piece of pie, who got to play with what toy—we were fighting constantly. One day, my grandfather came to visit during the midst of one of our toy fights. To stop all the bickering, he had me divide all the toys into two piles, but my brother got to choose which pile he wanted to play with."

It worked brilliantly. My client did the dividing. Not knowing which half she would end up with, she had to make them equal, which satisfied her husband. By the time she finished, she didn't care which half he chose.

I've used this device in several business disputes since. For instance, I was once involved in a suit between two companies, each of which claimed to have the right to purchase the assets of a defunct company. They were willing to "split the difference," but they still couldn't decide who would get what. It solved the problem instantly.

Another time, I represented a participant in a joint venture that was acquiring numerous small tracts of residential land. The parties were realistic business executives who knew that nothing lasts forever, and they wanted their joint venture agreement to provide for what happened if they ever parted company. The last thing they wanted was some judge deciding which of them would be entitled to what property. The "You divide and I'll choose" idea worked like a charm.

And there's an interesting variation on the theme. If two partners want to split up their business, for instance, one could make an offer like this to the other: "I think that half the business is worth one million dollars. Either you can buy my interest for that price, or I'll buy your interest for that price. You choose." It's very tough to question the honesty or fair-mindedness of that kind of proposal.

It works just as well if you provide for the procedure in advance of any dispute, by contract:

> Should either party wish to buy out the other, that party shall make a written offer, stating the proposed price. When the offer is received, the party who receives it shall have the option to either accept the offer, or buy out the interest of the offering party at the same price.

That's the kind of clause that tends to keep partners together or, at worst, ensure reasonable buy-out proposals.

The "Best Efforts" Clause

Suppose a company hires a consultant to improve its efficiency. The consultant charges $1,000 a day, with a minimum contract of one week. The company is willing to pay the price, but wants to know what it's getting for its money. If it pays the fee, will its efficiency be improved?

"No guarantees," says the consultant. "Until I put in the time to see what needs to be done, I can't tell. And I might make some suggestions that you won't put into effect. It's not necessarily my fault if my services don't improve your bottom line."

The company wants to hire the consultant, but finds it hard to justify a sizable payment for an undefined result. The consultant wants to work for the company, but can't guarantee what he might not be able to produce.

There's really no good way to solve this problem, but if both sides are willing to take the chance that the deal will most likely work itself out anyway, they can agree to disagree for the time being. A good way to do that is through a "best efforts" clause, providing something like this:

> *Although no specific results can be guaranteed, Consultant represents that he is capable and qualified in this field, and he agrees to use his best efforts so that Company receives the maximum benefit for the least expense.*

Neither side is totally protected, but they haven't given up any rights, and each has an argument it can use against the other in the event of a dispute. If the consultant charges a lot and does very little, the company can claim that the consultant didn't try as hard as he could to give the company its money's worth. The company still doesn't have any guarantees. But it can make the consultant show how a qualified individual could have charged so much for so little. That makes the deal much more palatable. It gives the company confidence that it will not be "taken."

From the consultant's point of view, he doesn't promise specific results, only time well spent. That gives him a defense against an unreasonable client who expects miracles and feels he didn't get his money's worth.

As noted in Chapter 11, "best efforts" clauses can be used to narrow, if not solve, a multitude of problems. An advertising agency might not be able to guarantee an increase in its client's sales, but it can agree to use its best efforts. A company might not be able to guarantee a two-week delivery, but it can undertake to use its best efforts. When you can't say "absolutely, positively," try a "best efforts" clause. It gives both sides a reasonable measure of protection, but it also includes a "fudge factor," just in case.

THE LAST RESORT: ARBITRATION

When all else fails, the ultimate problem solver is an agreement to have someone else solve the problem for you.

In a lease negotiation, for example, the landlord and the tenant might agree to escalate the rent after two years, but they might not be able to agree on the amount. Two partners starting a business might agree that in the event of a later dispute, the business should be sold, but they can't decide how, whether to get it appraised, or what to do if one wants to buy out the other.

To break the deadlock, the parties could agree now to submit the dispute to arbitration later, just in case they can't work it out between themselves.

Arbitrations can be handled in a variety of ways. There are commercial arbitration companies (such as the American Arbitration Association) which will supply everything from the ground rules to the arbitrator. The parties could select their own mutually acceptable arbitrator. Or they could each pick an arbitrator (presumably, someone who could be expected to see things its way), and those two would pick a third arbitrator who, in effect, would make the decision.

Arbitration is much quicker and much cheaper than litigation. It is especially well suited to the resolution of disputes in which the decision-maker ought to have a specialized expertise not found in most judges. For that reason, many technical, construction, labor–management, and regulated-industry disputes are arbitrated privately more frequently than they are litigated in courtrooms. The disadvantage is the loss of appeal rights—there's no second bite at the apple, and very few of the procedural safeguards that characterize (and delay) most lawsuits. And the decision is only as good as the arbitrator. On that score, you have to be willing to take your chances.

Where the issue is not one of life and death, or where the parties want to avoid the publicity, delay, and expense of a trial, arbitration can be a good alternative. At the contract negotiation stage, it's a good way of moving the deal forward. You agree to disagree later on, leaving the decision to a neutral third party. And arbitration can also be useful when a deal goes bad and lawsuits are threatened. Depending on the particulars, it may provide a better alternative than a judge and jury. Get your lawyer's advice when the time comes.

SEVEN

THE REAL WORLD
OF LITIGATION

Some business executives can't wait to get their "day in court." "It's not the money," they claim, "it's the principle." Or, sometimes, "I'll show those sons of bitches."

To others, the mere threat of lawyer's fees, cross-examination, and legal doubletalk sends them running for cover. They'll do almost anything to avoid a lawsuit.

But when those same executives consider hiring more employees or buying new equipment, for example, they dispassionately study alternatives, hire consultants, and run spread sheets on their computers. They look for objective, verifiable business justifications for their actions. The only thing that matters is the bottom line.

That dichotomy has always frustrated me. Litigation decisions are as important as any decisions an executive is likely to make. Yet litigation decisions so often are made out of anger or anxiety more than analysis. Deliberate, cautious executives yield to the temptation to "teach those guys a lesson," whether or not it makes practical sense. Or, as often happens, fear and loathing replace bravado, and they overreact in the other direction—backing off from a fight they can win, rather than get involved in the legal system. The businesslike, "cost–benefit" analysis that predominates everywhere else seems to fade when the subject is lawyers and lawsuits.

Neither the fervor nor the fear of litigation is totally justified. Lawsuits exact a heavy toll, not only in time and money, but emotionally as well. Still, a just debt ought to be collected, and a breached contract can't always be ignored.

But the decision to settle out of court, stand your ground, or walk away has to be a *business* decision. And business decisions—even those influenced by gut judgment and intuition—have to be made on the basis of fact, not emotion.

The purpose of Chapter 18 is to take you, step by step, through the litigation process, for in making the decision to sue and in deciding what to do if you get sued, the process itself is one of the cold, hard realities that must be considered.

Once you understand the medium in which lawsuits are handled, you'll understand the message: avoid them if you can. The purpose of Chapter 19 is to give you some advice and some alternatives—what to do so you won't have to reread Chapter 18.

18 "SEE YOU IN COURT!"

A lawsuit is the process by which we, as a civilized society, resolve our disputes. The same basic concepts and procedures apply whether the lawsuit involves a claim for $30 or $30 million. Fundamentally, those concepts and procedures are nothing short of brilliant, being the product of centuries of imagination and refinement by some of history's greatest minds. Everything about it—from the use of a jury, to the rules of evidence, to the mandatory oath to tell the truth—is meant to guarantee, as far as possible, a just, fair verdict.

But somewhere along the way, something went awry.

How It's Supposed to Work: An Overview

It helps to begin with an overview of how things are supposed to work. Think of the scales of justice. It's a useful metaphor.

A lawsuit begins when the "plaintiff" decides to spend the fifty bucks or so it costs to file a "complaint" with the court. Through itemized "allegations," the complaint states the plaintiff's claim against the "defendant." Eventually, the defendant files an "answer" to the complaint, stating his view of whether the allegations are true or false, and perhaps making some allegations of his own. These documents, called the "pleadings," tell the parties what they're fighting about. They define the conflict.

At this initial, accusatory stage in the lawsuit, the scales are evenly balanced. Neither side has an advantage. Having started the lawsuit, however, the plaintiff has the "burden of proof"— the obligation to tip the scales in his favor.

Accordingly, and assuming that the parties have been unable to negotiate an out-of-court settlement, the plaintiff begins the trial, presenting testimony from his witnesses. As his lawyer finishes questioning each witness—the process referred to as "direct examination"—the opposing lawyer gets to ask questions—the process referred to as "cross-examination."

By the time the plaintiff "rests his case," he must have presented enough solid evidence so that the scales move his way, however slightly.

If he doesn't, the judge can stop the trial and enter a verdict against the plaintiff right then and there, even before the defendant "opens his case"—that is, before he calls any of his witnesses. In some jurisdictions, that's called a "nonsuit"; in others, it's referred to as a "directed verdict."

For example, suppose cars driven by the plaintiff and the defendant collide at an intersection. The plaintiff starts the lawsuit by filing a complaint in which he alleges that the defendant ran a red light. At the trial, the plaintiff attempts to meet his burden of proof through the direct examination of a witness who was walking on the sidewalk at the time of the accident. The witness testifies that the defendant in fact drove into the intersection when the light was red.

Then the lawyer for the defendant cross-examines the witness.

"What was the weather like?"

"It was raining."

"Were you looking down, to keep your face out of the rain, at the time of the collision?"

"Yes, I guess I was, now that you mention it."

"And isn't it true that when you first heard the collision, you looked at the cars, not the traffic light?"

"That's true. The noise is what caught my attention and I guess I looked into the intersection first."

"And isn't it true that you looked at the intersection for at least a couple of seconds?"

"I think so."

"So a couple of seconds went by before you looked at the traffic light?"

"I guess."

"You don't *know* whether the light was red when the defendant entered the intersection, do you? For all you know, the defendant may have had a green light, or at worst a yellow light, at that point. Right?"

"I guess that's so. I don't know what color it was before the collision."

The plaintiff's case has just evaporated. A skillful cross-examination has a way of doing that. If that's all the plaintiff has, he's in trouble. At best, the scales are still even, which means that the defendant wins.

In most cases, however, the plaintiff will be able to at least nudge the scales in his favor by the end of his case. If the plaintiff himself testifies that he had the green light, for example, and if his story holds up after cross-examination, that will be enough.

At that point, the burden of proof shifts to the defendant. Using his own witnesses, each of whom will be cross-examined by the plaintiff's lawyer, he must counterbalance the plaintiff's version of what happened. Maybe the defendant will have a witness who says that it was the plaintiff who ran the red light. Perhaps he'll admit what happened, but he'll present an excuse, called a "defense"—his brakes failed, or he had to swerve into the intersection to avoid a child.

Finally, at the end of the trial, each lawyer presents an argument, and the court then "weighs" the plaintiff's evidence against the defendant's evidence. It takes into consideration the credibility of the witnesses, the clarity of their testimony, the amount of evidence, and anything else that might be relevant to the decision-making process.

If, at that stage, the scales are still even, or tipped toward the defendant, the plaintiff hasn't met his burden of proof, and he loses. But if they tip toward the plaintiff, even by just a hair, he wins. In a criminal case, the defendant's guilt has to be established "beyond a reasonable doubt." But in a civil case, it's much different. The defendant's liability to the plaintiff has to be established only by what the law calls "a preponderance of the evidence"—51 percent to 49 percent will do it.

So what's the big deal? You each present your evidence, and the court makes a decision. Why does it take years and thousands of dollars to handle a lawsuit?

WHY LITIGATION COSTS SO MUCH AND TAKES SO LONG: THE ADVERSARY SYSTEM

Much of the explanation—some would say blame—rests with the very foundation of our legal process.

We operate through what the law calls an "adversary system." Every lawyer is sworn to be an adversary to the other side and an advocate on behalf of his client. Once the lawsuit is filed, it's not a lawyer's job to mediate a compromise. It's not for him to decide who's right and who's wrong. It's a lawyer's sworn duty to go for an all-out, take-no-prisoners wipeout for his client.

And if there is any potential avenue of attack or defense that could lead in that direction, then he's got to pursue it. Within certain ethical boundaries, he's got to do everything he can to win.

At the same time, however, the system is designed to help the plaintiff get everything he's entitled to, without the defendant's paying any more than he owes. To serve that goal, the plaintiff is given a vast amount of ammunition to use against the defendant. But the defendant gets every imaginable form of defense. The theory is that with such all-powerful tools at their disposal, each relentless adversary will effectively refute the unsupported positions of the other, leaving only the irrefutable truth behind.

Take two adversaries. Require that they fight each other to the best of their abilities. Equip them with diverse, complex weapons and defenses. Of necessity, the result will be a long-term, expensive struggle—and that, in a nutshell, is why litigation is the way it is. For as long as the lawyers for plaintiffs and defendants have the right to file motions, write briefs, take depositions, and pose interrogatories—some of the various tactics discussed in the remainder of this chapter—they will use them in the effort to win their cases. It's their legal obligation. In a kind of litigation arms race, each side must presume that the other is going all out to win, and each side has to respond in kind.

NOT-SO-EQUAL JUSTICE UNDER LAW

Still, if that's what it takes to produce just, fair results, so be it. But it's not that simple. In practice, the adversary system, though an engaging idea, is marred by a monumental flaw: it works only when each of the participants can afford the fight that the system inevitably produces. As between litigants of similar size and strength, the system takes its toll, but seems to do its job. But when it's David versus Goliath, it's a different story. Nothing could be more repugnant to our concept of justice than the notion that "might makes right." Yet that's often the way the adversary system works.

To carry his burden of proof, a plaintiff has to uncover the facts and document them to the court's satisfaction. Especially against a writhing, fighting defendant, that takes a great deal of legal time and, therefore, money. To avoid being steamrollered, a defendant has to do everything he can to resist a plaintiff's unremitting efforts to stick him with the responsibility for something he feels he didn't do. That, too, is time-consuming and expensive. In fact, every legal parry and thrust costs money, and speaking practically, in the adversary system a litigant can go only as far as his money will take him, no matter how "right" he may be.

Knowing that, the attorneys for a wealthy plaintiff will frequently use all of the law's well-intentioned devices not for their intended purpose, but rather to coerce a poorer defendant's acquiescence to an otherwise unjustified out of court settlement. Similarly, in the guise of good lawyering, a wealthy defendant will impose one expensive procedural obstacle after another in the path of a poorer plaintiff, until the amount the plaintiff receives becomes more a function of his staying power than of the merits of his position.

This sort of tactic is impermissible—some have termed it "legalized blackmail"—and there are rules that allow courts to punish lawyers and litigants for taking unsupportable positions designed to run up the other side's costs. Nevertheless, it's very difficult for a court to determine when a lawyer, as part of the adversary system, decided to try a tactic in good faith on behalf of his client, and when he did it for the sole purpose of waging a war of attrition against a weaker opponent.

The War of Attrition Begins: Discovery

The best example of the potential for abuse inherent in the system is that stage of a lawsuit called "discovery."

The adversary system presupposes that fairness and justice are best served if neither side has the ability to keep secrets from the other. The battle should be fought in the open, with everyone's cards on the table.

Therefore, once the pleadings are filed, the law equips plaintiffs and defendants with the ability to find out just about whatever they want to know about the other side's allegations. Everything is "discoverable," and in the discovery stage, each of the litigants gets the investigative power of a Watergate prosecutor. For example:

• *Interrogatories*. Each side can send lists of written questions that the other side has to answer in writing, under oath.

• *Document requests*. Each side can generically describe the documents he'd like to see (for instance, "all documents that you relied on in making your allegations"; "all documents you used in preparing your answers to interrogatories"), and the other side has to find them and produce them.

• *Depositions*. Each side can require anyone who might have relevant information—be it the other side, or an independent third party—to appear and be questioned under oath, in the presence of a court reporter who transcribes every word for future reference.

• *Subpoenas*. A subpoena is the equivalent of a court order that requires a person to disclose information or documents. Each party has the right to subpoena records, confidential memos, correspondence, diaries, telephone bills—virtually anything. If a party has difficulty persuading a witness to appear for a deposition, he can serve him with a subpoena. If he doesn't show, the witness can be sent to jail.

Discovery can, and does, serve an indispensable function in the administration of justice. An employee's complaint against a company, for instance, might allege that he was unconditionally guaranteed a job for at least five years, and that he was wrongfully fired for reporting the company's safety violations. The company might answer by alleging that the promise of continued employment for five years was not unconditional, and that the employee was fired for a lack of qualifications and poor work performance.

The employee doesn't need to hire a team of private investigators in order to prove his case. He can subpoena his employer's internal memoranda, which might show why he was really fired. He can require the company to answer interrogatories seeking the names of witnesses who attended meetings where his employment status was discussed, and he can then take their depositions to find out what was said. Discovery can be a powerful, truth-seeking equalizer.

Discovery is also one of the reasons that so many lawsuits settle out of court. If the lawyers do their job, no "surprise witnesses" can materialize from the back of the courtroom at a crucial stage in the trial. By the time they've completed discovery, both the employee and the company know basically who will testify on behalf of the other, and they know basically what each witness will say. They may disagree about how a jury will react or what a judge might do, but this kind of fundamental knowledge about the other side's case gives the lawyers a feel for the probabilities—who's more likely to win; what are the probable high and low verdicts. There's a basis for negotiation and compromise which, given the time and expense involved in a trial, is what usually happens.

But discovery can also be used as an intimidating, expensive club.

The company, for example, can easily use discovery to bankrupt or embarrass the employee into dropping the suit. Its interrogatories could number in the hundreds, and the employee will have to pay for his lawyer's time in answering all of them. The employee's deposition could take days, as could each of ten other depositions the company might decide to take—more legal fees and court reporter costs. The company could pursue its discovery rights against the employee's current employer, endangering his job. It could take the depositions of his family and friends, humiliating him. And the company could contest every effort at discovery undertaken by the employee's attorney, causing him to file motions and appear in court and thus run up his fees—all for the purpose of wearing the employee down.

The employee's only recourse, aside from giving up or settling for a token sum, is to fight fire with fire, if he has the resources.

There are probably documents in the company's files it would just as soon not disclose—internal memos respecting the safety violations that the employee says he was fired for reporting, for example. The employee's counsel could take the depositions of the president of the company and the chairman of the board, and drag them out for days, making the lower-level executives who were responsible for his termination look bad. He could file motions with the court asking that the company be punished for its abuse of the discovery processes.

The net effect is the inexorable corruption of a worthwhile investigatory procedure into a weapon it was never intended to be. More than anything else, discovery is why lawsuits take so long and cost so much.

THE WAR OF ATTRITION CONTINUES: JOINDERS, CROSSCLAIMS, AND COUNTERCLAIMS

When a defendant gets sued, he gets the right to blame the whole affair on somebody else. That, too, leads to legal fees, delays, and expenses.

For instance, suppose you sue the company that sold you your new telephone system. It simply doesn't work, and you want your money back. Very simple.

The telephone company, however, blames it on the installer and brings him into the lawsuit, claiming the problems are his responsibility. He, in turn, brings in the electrical engineer who laid out the wiring, blaming the defects on his careless plans and drawings. The engineer says it's the fault of the switching equipment the installer used, so he brings in the company that manufactured it.

Each gets the opportunity to say "him, not me." The process is known as "the joinder of a third party defendant" (or, in some courts, "the joinder of an additional defendant").

Once the third party defendants are in the case, they and the defendant can make claims against one another, referred to as "crossclaims." Perhaps the installer will crossclaim against the engineer for extra costs he says he had to incur because of the faulty plans. Maybe the company that manufactured the switching equipment will crossclaim against the installer for an unpaid bill.

And finally, the defendant, and any of the third party defendants, can make claims against the plaintiff, referred to as "counterclaims." The installer might counterclaim against you for hiring an engineer who didn't know what he was doing, thereby increasing the installer's costs. The company that manufactured the equipment might counterclaim against you, saying that if the installer won't pay his bill, you ought to pay it. And so on.

Courts have the power to limit the joinders, crossclaims, and counterclaims, but they usually don't. In most cases, they'll let everything that arises from the same general transaction be litigated at one time. A geometric increase in mass confusion is the frequent result. When discovery begins, for instance, each party gets to serve interrogatories, request documents, and take depositions, focusing on the particular aspect of the dispute that concerns them most.

Your "simple" lawsuit for the return of your money can get lost in a directionless melee among persons and companies about whom you couldn't care less.

STILL MORE ATTRITION: MOTIONS AND BRIEFS

The term "motion" usually refers to a document that a lawyer files with a court, requesting the court to make a ruling on a question being raised by the lawyer. (In some jurisdictions, there are "motions" and "petitions." As a practical matter they are the same thing, although there are slight differences in form.) A "brief" (if ever there was a misnomer, this is it) is a written legal argument submitted in support of the motion.

Motions can be filed with respect to the simplest or the most complex matters; they can deal with niggling details of form, or they can lead to a victory for the plaintiff or defendant before the trial begins; and as with discovery, they can be used to foment delay and expense, for purely tactical reasons. Some examples of typical motions:

• *Motions relating to the pleadings.* Often, a defendant will contend that a plaintiff's complaint is not clear or specific enough. Or a plaintiff will claim that a defendant's answer includes legally impermissible statements which ought to be stricken. Or the third party defendants will get into the act, citing technical defects in joinders. All these issues are presented through motions.

• *Discovery motions.* A witness, on the advice of counsel, might refuse to answer a deposition question, claiming it to be improper. The defendant might answer the plaintiff's interrogatories vaguely or ambiguously. A plaintiff might fail to produce the documents requested by a defendant. Whenever a party wants the court's assistance in the discovery process, he files a motion.

• *Demurrers.* A demurrer is the law's way of saying "So what?" (In federal courts, it's called a "Rule 12b6 Motion.") It's a motion filed by a defendant contending that even if everything the plaintiff alleges in the complaint is true, the plaintiff is still not entitled to a verdict under the law, and the lawsuit ought to be dismissed as a result. For example, the plaintiff's allegations might describe a transaction which, according to the defendant, does not amount to a contract. If the court agrees, it will "sustain the demurrer" and dismiss the complaint.

• *Motions for judgment on the pleadings.* After the defendant files his answer, the plaintiff might contend that the defendant admitted enough of the complaint so that the plaintiff ought to be entitled to a judgment in his favor on the basis of the pleadings alone. That argument can be raised through a motion.

• *Motions for summary judgment.* During the course of discovery, the facts might develop totally in favor of one party or the other. The plaintiff, for example, might make some crucial admissions during his deposition, or he might produce some evidence that clearly refutes his position. In that event, the defendant would argue that he is entitled to "summary judgment"—that is, a pretrial judgment in his favor upon the filing of a motion.

• *Posttrial motions.* After the trial is over, the losing side almost always feels that the judge made certain mistakes in the way the proceeding was handled. How the judge ruled on the lawyers' objections might be challenged, or it might be argued that the judge failed to give the jury a proper explanation of the law. Before an appeal to a higher court is pursued, these matters are raised in posttrial motions, in essence asking the court to change its mind and perhaps conduct a whole new trial.

When the motion is important and the stakes high, the brief that accompanies it will often take fifty, one hundred, or even more hours to prepare. Legal research—that is, finding and analyzing legal precedents that might be analogous to the issue in question—can keep teams of lawyers busy for hours on end. Before the brief is finalized, it will go through numerous drafts. Even routine motions require briefs that might easily take twenty or thirty hours of a lawyer's time.

After one side files a motion and brief, the other side is given an opportunity to file an answer to the motion, along with a reply brief. Depending on the complexity and importance of the motion, that could take a month or two. Frequently, the party who filed the motion then gets the opportunity to write and file another brief replying to the reply brief.

And finally, when all parties have had their say, the court has to rule on the motion. It might schedule "oral argument," in which the lawyers appear in court to present their positions, debate, and answer the court's questions. Thereafter, a conscientious court could take weeks to complete its analysis; if the court is backlogged, the weeks often turn into months.

In the meantime, the case remains at a standstill.

FINALLY, YOUR DAY IN COURT: THE TRIAL

In most jurisdictions, it takes years—sometimes five or more years—for a case to get to trial. The sheer volume of lawsuits, combined with the vast amount of time and trouble it takes to process each one, has completely overwhelmed the limited number of judges and courtrooms in many areas of the country.

There's a legal maxim that "Justice delayed is justice denied." Truer words were never spoken. While awaiting your "day in court," you might run out of money, your witnesses might die or forget what they saw and heard—or for that matter, *you* might die or forget what you saw and heard.

But if a party can hold on until the trial begins, anything can happen, and both sides know it. Although discovery narrows the possibilities, trials are still essentially unpredictable. That's why so many cases settle "on the courthouse steps." Face to face with the uncertainties of litigation, and having failed to pressure a better settlement up to that point, plaintiffs often opt for "half a loaf" rather than risk getting none, and defendants often choose to pay money they don't think they owe as "insurance" against a verdict that might be much higher.

Sometimes, however, the parties simply can't reach an agreement, and a trial becomes their only alternative. They ask the court to tell them which party is "right," who's telling "the truth," and what's "fair."

Win or lose, both sides inevitably learn how elusive, vague, and relative the concepts of "right," "truth," and "fair" can be, especially in a courtroom.

SELECTING A JURY

Not every case is heard by a jury. In many jurisdictions, for instance, where small claims and injunction lawsuits are concerned, a judge decides the case without a jury. And even when the law permits a jury trial, the parties can agree to waive it if they want. Juries will normally favor the "little guy"—most jurors are, themselves, "little guys"—so an employee suing his employer, or a small businessman suing an oil company, would want a jury trial. But if a Fortune 500 company sues a bank, neither side expects a lot of sympathy from a jury, and they often prefer to take their chances in front of a judge.

If a jury is to hear the case, the jurors have to be selected. This is accomplished through a process called the "voir dire" (pronounced "vwar deer"), in which the lawyers pose questions to prospective jurors in the effort to find those most likely to favor their client's position. The lawyers aren't allowed to ask direct, "How would you decide this kind of case?" questions, but they try to probe for information on background, prejudices, and inclinations, and they make their judgments on that basis.

At the start of the voir dire, courthouse personnel assemble a group of jurors, usually called a "jury panel," from which the lawyers select the jurors they want. In a typical case involving one plaintiff, one defendant, and one third party defendant, there will be twenty-four prospective jurors on the jury panel. At the close of the questioning, each of the three lawyers will get four "peremptory challenges"—the right to "excuse" (dismiss) four persons from the jury panel for no reason other than gut feel or personal preference. They may, in addition, request the judge to excuse any number of jurors for "cause"—such as bias, acquaintance with the parties, physical or mental disability, and so on. When the voir dire is completed, a jury of twelve has been seated, and the case begins.

Trial lawyers develop their own preconceived biases and stereotypes about what "kinds" of people favor what sorts of cases, and they select jurors on that basis. Some feel that particular ethnic backgrounds are more apt to favor certain kinds of cases. Some feel that age, sex, or socioeconomic status is crucial. Some feel that occupations are the key. If a lawyer intends to prove his case by reference to numbers, graphs, and details, for example, he'll try to staff the jury with people who hold jobs that indicate a preference for that sort of approach—engineers, accountants, bank tellers, and so on. There are even companies that specialize in developing "jury profiles." Teams of psychologists interview hundreds of people, developing the characteristics of the "ideal juror" for a particular case.

THE TESTIMONY

Once the jury is selected, the trial itself starts with "opening statements" by the lawyers. Both sides get the opportunity to explain what they intend to prove during the trial. The opening statement lets the judge and jury know what the puzzle will look like when all the witnesses who constitute the pieces have testified.

The plaintiff then opens his case through the direct examination of his witnesses. The plaintiff's lawyer has met with and prepared each witness in advance, so that each knows what he's going to ask, and he knows how each is going to answer. His goal is to get the story out, through the witnesses, as clearly, smoothly, and convincingly as he can. He can use documents, charts, photographs, or anything else that might make the plaintiff's position more credible or convincing.

The plaintiff's lawyer will also have prepared each witness for the opposition's cross-examination, which follows the direct examination. He'll try to anticipate what the other lawyer is going to ask, and he'll discuss potential answers with the witnesses— not for the purpose of putting words in their mouths, but to make sure they're not caught by surprise or tricked into saying something they don't really mean.

The defendant's lawyer, recognizing that the witnesses will be expecting certain kinds of questions, will devise cross-examination strategies designed to catch them with their defenses down. The idea is to approach the witnesses from a direction they're not expecting, increasing the odds that they'll contradict themselves, or perhaps panic and forget their preparation. And if the defendant's lawyer can't get a damning admission or retraction, he'll at least try to make the plaintiff's witnesses look shifty and unreliable.

A good cross-examination can mortally wound the other side's case, but it can also be a terrifically risky and difficult enterprise for the cross-examiner. Jurors identify with the witness much more than with the lawyer. The witness is one of their own, as insecure as they are among the black robes and strange rituals of the courtroom; the lawyer, on the other hand, appears to be right at home. As a result, a lawyer has to be very careful about how he handles a witness in front of a jury—he can't "turn up the heat" until he's sure that the jurors won't take offense at his tactics. But he also must question forcefully if he's going to make any headway. It's a tough balancing act.

Moreover, when a lawyer cross-examines a witness, he frequently has no idea how the witness might answer. Unlike the case in direct examination, he hasn't had the opportunity to "script" the questions and answers with the witness, who as often as not considers the lawyer a mortal enemy. Whenever a lawyer appears shocked or rattled by the witness' answers, he loses credibility in the eyes of the jury. Cross-examination requires the ability to ad-lib while still appearing to be in control, no matter how badly it's going.

A trial is a constant "cat and mouse" struggle, and a cagey lawyer will often set traps for an unwary opponent. For instance, if the issue focuses on what was said at a meeting, the plaintiff's lawyer might call a witness who took reams of notes. But the plaintiff's lawyer won't ask him about the notes. He'll just ask about the witness' recollections, banking on the fact that the defendant's lawyer will take the bait.

When the defendant's lawyer begins the cross-examination, he's likely to ask, with great flourish, something like this: "And will you tell the jury, Mr. Witness, how you came to possess such a detailed recollection of a meeting that took place so long ago, without the benefit of any notes?"

The plaintiff's attorney will have the witness prepared. "I took pages of notes. Would you like to see them? They back up everything I say. I studied them before I testified." The defendant's attorney now looks rather silly, and the witness appears especially credible.

At the close of the plaintiff's case (assuming the plaintiff has met his burden of proof), the defendant begins his case. The roles are now reversed, but other than that, the trial proceeds in the same fashion—the defendant's lawyer puts on the testimony of his witnesses, and the plaintiff's lawyer gets his chance at cross-examination.

If the plaintiff presented a good case, the jury is probably leaning in his favor by the time the defendant starts his presentation. But if the defendant has a well-prepared case, consisting of credible witnesses who contradict those called by the plaintiff and who stand up relatively well to cross-examination, the jury starts to suffer from what psychologists call "cognitive dissonance"—they don't know whom to believe.

THE SUMMATIONS

Thus, when the testimony is finished the lawyers get to deliver "summations" or "closing arguments" to the jury. In their most effective and persuasive rhetoric, they attempt to alleviate the confusion and persuade the jury to see things their way—creating more confusion in the process.

The lawyers will, for instance, present reasons the jury ought to believe one witness as opposed to another. They'll focus on which version of the facts "makes common sense." They'll high-light subtle contradictions in the testimony. They'll point to one witness' bias as opposed to another's lack of a personal interest in the outcome—one witness might be the plaintiff's uncle, and another might be a passerby who doesn't care who wins the case.

And of course, a good lawyer will attempt to arouse the jury's empathy and concern for his client's plight—the innocent, damaged plaintiff, or the unjustly accused and put-upon defendant, as the case may be.

THE CHARGE

If the case has been tried before a judge without a jury, it ends at this point. Usually, the judge defers a decision and "takes the case under advisement." He'll study the testimony and the law, and he'll require the lawyers to submit briefs and other legal documents expressing their positions.

But if there is a jury, the judge must now give them his "charge"—a description of their duties, and an explanation of the law as the judge conceives it.

Consider a case in which a plaintiff sues a defendant for breach of contract. The plaintiff says that the contract was formed during a particular conversation. The defendant recollects the conversation much differently, and denies the existence of any contract. Various witnesses testify, and they contradict each other.

When the jury begins to deliberate on its decision, it first has to determine the facts of the case. It is the jury's job to resolve contradictions and assess credibility. It decides what was really said during the conversation between the plaintiff and the defendant. It decides who's telling the truth.

But the jury has a second task as well. It not only has to determine what happened, it also has to determine its legal significance. That's what lawyers call "applying the law to the facts." The jury has to decide whether the words spoken during the conversation amount to a contract, as claimed by the plaintiff, or harmless banter, as claimed by the defendant.

The charge is designed to equip the jurors for the task. It would sound something like this:

As I have explained to you, members of the jury, it is up to you to assess the credibility of the witnesses and to determine the facts of the case. But once you accomplish that task, you must apply the law, as I explain it to you, to those facts.

I charge you that a contract is formed when one party makes an offer which is then accepted by another party. An offer is an expressed willingness to make a binding agreement on certain terms. An acceptance is an unqualified and unconditional assent to the offer. A contract does not have to be in writing, and it does not require the involvement of lawyers or any special legal terminology.

Therefore, if you find that there was an offer and acceptance in the conversation that took place between the plaintiff and the defendant, as I have explained those terms to you, then you should find that there was a contract, and the plaintiff will prevail. But if you find that the conversation did not include both an offer and an acceptance, then there was no contract and the defendant will prevail.

The jurors have to accept the law as the judge defines it for them. They can't decide what the law ought to be, and they can't hypothesize about what they think the law is. They have to take it as the judge gives it to them, and they have to make their decision on that basis alone.

THE VERDICT

The jury then deliberates in total privacy. If the jurors choose, they can spend hours analyzing the lawyers' brilliant arguments and the witnesses' sincere testimony. Or they can flip a coin—it's up to them. Be they young, old, dropouts, professors, drug addicts, ministers, business executives, poets, or any other imaginable combination of backgrounds, prejudices, and sophistication, they can do what they want, for their own reasons. The fate of the parties is exclusively in their hands.

WHY IT DOESN'T ALWAYS WORK: THE SOFT SPOTS

If you live through the attrition, last through the delay, and make it out of the courtroom, you may well get the just, fair verdict that the system envisions. But then again, you might not.

There are soft spots at almost every stage of a trial—points at which the whole trial can be turned against one side or the other for no good reason, no matter where "right," "truth," or "fairness" may lie.

THE JURORS

People are by nature unpredictable, despite the efforts of trial lawyers to classify their biases and predilections according to their ethnicity and occupations. There is no reliable way to foretell how an individual juror will react to a particular case. Jury selection is always a crapshoot.

Which would be fine, as long as the process always produced an objective, unprejudiced jury. But that's not always what happens.

Jurors react positively or negatively for all sorts of rational and irrational, conscious and subconscious reasons. One of the jurors may have a friend who was unjustly ruined by a lawsuit, and he may have a latent prejudice against plaintiffs in general. One of the parties may remind one of the jurors of his obnoxious Uncle Herman; without even knowing why, that juror won't believe a word that party says. Another juror may have been cheated by a company in the same business as one of the litigants, and he may be convinced that everyone in that field is no good. Another may have been so impressed with the competence of one of the attorneys as to figure that his client can't possibly be in the wrong, no matter how the facts develop.

THE DELIBERATIONS

When a jury starts deliberating, some jurors become leaders and some remain followers. Some state their views articulately and persuasively, and others stay in the background. The verdict is often the result of which jurors, with what prejudices, assume positions of control. Most trial lawyers feel that the jury system works quite well, most of the time. But it's not at all unusual to see a courtroom of experienced litigators scratching their heads in amazement. "How could they possibly have decided the case *that* way?" is a frequent refrain. There's no explaining it, there's no predicting it, and there's no preventing it.

Even with a completely impartial jury, things can easily go awry. In most jurisdictions jurors are not permitted to take notes. It's felt that the collective recollections of the group will be more reliable than what a few happen to write down, and maybe that's so. But what about a lengthy case, involving fifty witnesses? How are the jurors to recall all the testimony? Even in a one-day trial, the judge's charge could take an hour. How are they to remember, let alone master, all the points of law he read to them?

In a technical case involving the testimony of sophisticated experts, a jury of laymen is unfairly asked to make judgments on whether the Harvard nuclear physicist made more sense than the Yale chemical engineer. The jurors are left to decide on the basis of general impressions—who sounded more credible, who spoke more persuasively—which has very little to do with right and wrong.

And even in simple cases, involving a plaintiff who says "black" and a defendant who says "white," there is no reliable way for a jury to determine who's telling the truth. Almost in desperation, the jurors will seize on anything they can during their deliberations. That's why notes, confirming letters, and documents are so important. They give a jury a reason to pick one witness over another.

THE WITNESSES

Often a lawyer can make a party or a witness look bad in the eyes of the jury, and that can easily turn the tide. For instance, a plaintiff's deposition in a fairly complex business litigation could take a day or two to complete. The transcript of the deposition will consume hundreds of pages. A well-prepared trial lawyer will study it for hours and index it so that he can find any passage he wants at a moment's notice.

When the plaintiff testifies, the lawyer will be looking for any inconsistencies between the deposition testimony—which may have been taken a year or two before trial—and the trial testimony. As understandable as such inconsistencies may be, a jury can be given a very different impression of their importance.

I once tried a case involving a suit by a consultant against one of my clients. The consultant claimed that my client had orally agreed to pay him an extra fee if the work was completed by a certain date. My client denied it. During his deposition, the consultant said that the conversation took place in my client's office, in early 1981. At trial, he said it was a telephone conversation, in the fall of 1981.

It really wasn't a very significant difference; the question was whether the promise was made, not where or when. But my client won the case, and I think it had a lot to do with the cross-examination of the consultant, which went like this:

> "Do you remember having your deposition taken?"
> "Yes."
> "Were you sworn to tell the truth at that time?"
> "Yes."
> "And did you tell the truth?"
> "I did."
> "Were you sworn to tell the truth today, in this trial?"
> "Yes."
> "And did you tell this jury the truth?"
> "I did."
> "Let me direct your attention to page twenty-three of your deposition, when you were asked where the promise was made. Read the jury the answer you gave, under oath, at that time."
> "I said it was in your client's office."
> "Did you hedge, or say you weren't sure?"
> "No."
> "And what did you say, under oath, today?"
> "I said it was on the telephone."
> "Do you understand the meaning of an oath to tell the truth?"
> "Yes."
> "Yet you admit having told two different stories on two different occasions, even though you were sworn to tell the truth both times, don't you?"
> "I made a mistake. I'm sorry. It was at your client's office, like I said at the deposition."
> "Did you make any other so-called mistakes today?"
> "I don't think so."
> "How about page eighty-two of your deposition, where

*you say the meeting was in early 1981. Yet today, you say it
was a different time. Another mistake, under oath?"*

"I guess it is."

*"Now, tell the jury whether the version you gave while
under oath at your deposition is correct, or whether the one
you gave while under oath today is correct."*

"I'm not sure."

*"You're not sure of exactly what happened, period. Isn't
that the real, sworn truth?"*

The judge said the last question was improper, but the jury
got the point. The cross-examination really amounted to making a mountain out of a molehill, but it gave the jury a reason,
however artificial, to choose our version of the facts over theirs.

APPEALS AND COLLECTIONS

Congratulations! You won. Now what?

If you were the plaintiff, you try to collect your money, which
often is no mean feat. If the defendant won't pay up, you have
to chase him. But the law puts a slew of weapons at your disposal for that purpose: you can use depositions and interrogatories to search for assets; you can grab bank accounts; you can
force the sale of land, buildings, equipment, and so on.

If you were the defendant, you can rest on your laurels.

All of which is great, except . . .

For plaintiffs, the collection process can be another time-
consuming, hideously expensive affair. And if there's no pot of
gold at the end of the rainbow, it will all be for naught. You
can't take what the defendant doesn't have.

And whether you're a plaintiff or a defendant, the losing side
can and usually does appeal. That delays everything for months
or even years, and depending on what the appeals court does,
you might end up going through the whole trial again.

THE LAWYER

Some lawyers are much, much better than others—which is,
of course, another way of saying that some lawyers aren't very
good. There. I've said it.

The problem is, as with everything else in the law, you may
not know you have a problem until it's too late. Your lawyer

might be great on the golf course, or even excellent in the conference room—but a courtroom is a whole different ball game. Trying a case is something very much apart from the other things that lawyers generally do, and no matter how skilled your lawyer may be in those other things, he may be out of his element when it comes time for voir dires and cross-examinations.

And even if he's an experienced, competent litigator, the other lawyer is an unknown variable. He may be so good—or so bad—that the case turns in one direction or the other solely because of it.

THE JUDGE

And finally, judges are just lawyers who got promoted. They have all the same strengths, weaknesses, foibles, and biases as the rest of us. Some of them do a better job of covering for their weaknesses and sublimating their biases than others; they have good days and bad days; they get bored; they like some lawyers better than others; they make mistakes; in short, they're human. But by their rulings, their demeanor, the things they say about witnesses, how they treat one lawyer as opposed to another in front of the jury, they can turn the tide for you or against you.

The point is not that litigation never works. By and large, judges are forthright and competent, and the collective wisdom and insight of a jury can be startling. Not every case gets delayed into oblivion. Not every trial goes haywire. Especially when compared with the alternatives, our system of litigation holds its own quite nicely.

Rather, the point is that like any system of dispute resolution, sometimes it works, and sometimes it doesn't. It's inherently unpredictable. It doesn't even purport to dole out perfect justice, or anything close to it, every time. And it costs a fortune.

Most important, it offers no guarantees. Being right doesn't give you anything except the opportunity to prove it, and telling the truth doesn't give you anything except a clear conscience.

So what do you do? You'd like to avoid lawsuits, but at the same time, you have to stand up for your rights and interests. How do you do it?

That's the focus of the next, and last, chapter.

19 AN OUNCE OF PREVENTION . . .
Nine Ways to Avoid Litigation

In the real world of litigation, every lawsuit is a high-stakes gamble. You pay your money—and lots of it—and you take your chances—and lots of them. It's an expensive, cumbersome, and risky way to solve a business problem, to be avoided whenever and however you can.

I'm not suggesting that you always give up, rather than sue or be sued. Lawsuits and lawyers are sometimes an unavoidable cost of doing business. People can be unreasonable or dishonest, and you have to protect your rights. You can't stop someone from suing you for no good reason. There are unforeseeable and unresolvable disagreements and problems that can be settled only in a courtroom.

But I am suggesting that fighting the good fight and winning the lawsuit is only the second-best thing that can happen to you. Getting what's coming to you *without* a lawsuit—that's what you should be aiming for, and that's where a working knowledge of the law can really help.

There are certain obvious ways to avoid litigation that a business executive doesn't need to hear about from a lawyer: don't do business with people you don't trust; make sure you're dealing with creditworthy companies; don't promise what you can't deliver—and so on. This is one area in which common sense really does matter.

Still, lawyers who deal in lawsuits are in something of a unique position to observe, in concentrated doses, the broken promises and shattered expectations that make up the majority of business litigation. I've tried to assemble that collective experience in this chapter, much of which reviews prior chapters. Not every admonition will apply to every business. And there's no way to assure yourself of a lawsuit-free business life.

But here are the nine best, time-tested ways I know to avoid the expense, the delay, and the hassle of litigation.

ONE: IF YOU CAN'T PROVE IT, IT DOESN'T EXIST

You know the guy on the other side of the table said what he said during the negotiations, no matter what he says now; you know you didn't promise anything remotely similar to what they say you promised; you know that despite what they claim, they didn't do what they were supposed to do.

You know you're right; but how are you going to prove it? If the case goes to court, they'll testify one way, and you'll testify another way. Maybe you'll win. But maybe you'll lose.

That uncertainty is what encourages lawsuits. Each side has an equal chance to win the case, so why not give it a shot?

But it need not work that way if, after the two of you draw the battle lines, you're able to produce a clear confirming letter, written contract, or business record that substantiates your position. The other side will still gripe and moan—he may still believe that he's right—but in the back of his mind, he'll start to question whether he can win the case. With each bill his lawyer sends him, he'll wonder whether he's throwing good money after bad; he'll curse "the system"; and he'll start looking for a way to salvage something, even if it's only pride, out of the whole affair.

As far as the law is concerned, if you can't prove it, it doesn't exist. Every minute of every business day, you should force yourself to think: How am I going to prove this later on, just in case? People are not as apt to fight if they're not so sure they can win. Being able to prove you're right when you know you're right will keep you from having to sue, and it will keep you from being sued, in a great many cases.

TWO: WHAT YOU SAY IS WHAT YOU GET

By now, you know that the law takes everything literally. What you say, and not what you mean to say, is what's important. And that leads to litigation.

There are three parts to the strategy of avoiding this trap.

First, say what you mean. To do that, you first must decide what you want to say—offer, rejection, continued bargaining without committing yourself . . . You must then choose your words so that your thoughts are clear and complete.

Second, know the legal meaning of what you say. If you don't know what an offer is, or you don't know the difference between an acceptance and a counteroffer, you could get into trouble, no matter how careful you are. You've got to speak the law's language.

And third, document it. Once again, even if you say just the right thing, they might remember it differently than you said it, and then you've got the "If you can't prove it, it doesn't exist" problem.

THREE: DEVELOP A HEALTHY PESSIMISM

You can't worry yourself out of every good deal. In business, a lot of risks are worth taking. But a healthy, realistic pessimism would prevent a lot of litigation.

Suppose the salesman tells you that the machinery is trouble-free, and it's warranted for a year. "We'll do whatever it takes to make things right," he says.

The unrealistic optimist thinks, "Great. I have nothing to worry about."

The healthy pessimist, however, looks at the sales documents a little more closely. He sees a merger clause, which effectively negates anything the salesman might say. And he sees a consequential damage disclaimer—if anything does go wrong, the seller's liability is minimized.

"Then I guess you won't mind putting your promise in writing and withdrawing that disclaimer," he says.

If the answer is no, the healthy pessimist has a choice to make. Maybe he'll decide to buy it anyway, but he's more likely to check the experience of other users, his own insurance coverage, and the warranty terms the competition offers. He won't assume that a salesman's promise and "a warranty" will solve all his problems, no matter what.

You can't always assume that things will work out; and you can't effectively protect yourself unless you act before the problem surfaces. If you try to get the protection you need and fail, at least you'll know what you're facing—you can decide intelligently whether to take the risks, and you can search for other ways to protect yourself.

For example:

• If you're the buyer, be careful of disclaimers and merger clauses. If you're the seller, make sure they're part of the deal.
• Ask the "what" and "why" questions when you're putting together an agreement. Don't assume that you'll be able to work out the details as they come up. Fill in the blanks in the deal, and if you get promises about delivery times, completion dates, service terms, or anything else, document them.
• Build in as many "skunk factors" as you can. And be careful if they try to "skunk" you—for example, look for clauses which require that all litigation be in their backyard if something does go wrong.
• Remember how important techniques like restrictive covenants, buy–sell agreements, and judgment notes can be when things go wrong.
• Read the fine print, and find out what it means if you're not sure. Don't be afraid to negotiate for changes. Often, the other side thinks the fine print doesn't really mean anything, and they'll be willing to go along.

FOUR: GET TO KNOW THE DANGER SIGNALS

As a matter of routine, my law firm develops a profile of the danger signals that apply to each of our clients, according to the client's business, history, and method of operation. We then sit down with the client and tell him what to look for—a sort of "you know you'd better call your lawyer when . . ." presentation. We've found it to be a great way to nip problems in the bud.

For instance, we represent a company that serves as sales representative for a variety of high-tech product manufacturers. Here are some of the danger signals we tell its key personnel to look for:

• In the fine print on the sales documents, some customers insert a clause that says something like this: "Payment shall be

made to seller from buyer at such time as buyer receives payment from its principal."

That's trouble. Sometimes our client will sell a product to a
company, and that company will resell it to another company
as a part of a larger system. This clause means that if my client's
customer doesn't get paid by its customer, then it doesn't have
to pay my client, even if my client did everything it was supposed to do. When my client sees this kind of language, I get a
telephone call.

• Our client could not stay in business if it ran the risk of being
liable for consequential damages every time it sold a product.
To protect against that problem, we've built the appropriate
disclaimers into its sales agreements and confirmations, and
we've educated the appropriate personnel on how to win the
"battle of the forms."

Once in a while, however, a customer writes a letter or sends
a form indicating that it, too, knows how to deal with forms—it
will refer to my client's form as the "acceptance" and its own
form as the "offer," for example. Our client now knows how to
spot that, and when it happens someone alerts us to the problem. We can then call the signals, behind the scenes.

• Like any sales organization, sometimes our client has problems getting paid. Many of these can be handled routinely,
through its own credit department. But other problems require
prompt legal action. We've coached our client's personnel on
how to recognize these kinds of problems, which generally involve matters pertaining to payment bonds, mechanic's liens,
bankruptcy, and other hypertechnical areas.

Not every danger signal applies to every business. Some companies negotiate each deal separately, and have to be especially
sensitive to "offer–acceptance" danger signals. Others use
forms, and need to focus on "battle of the forms" issues. Some
companies deal in long-term relationships, and they need to
watch for different things at different stages. Others operate on
an "in and out" basis—sign the deal, deliver the product, and
leave. They've got a whole different set of concerns. Some have
to worry about protecting ideas, concepts, customer lists, and
the like. Others couldn't care less.

But in every business, one of the keys to avoiding litigation is the early detection of problems that might lead to litigation. Sit down with a lawyer or other adviser, and get to know the danger signals that specifically apply to your business.

FIVE: ALWAYS LEAVE YOURSELF AN "OUT"

Nobody's perfect. Sometimes you're going to foul up. Sometimes it will be as a result of problems you couldn't foresee or control, and other times it might even be your fault. You've got to anticipate this fact of life, and leave yourself as many "outs" as you can.

If you're in the business of providing products or services by a particular deadline, you know that sometimes you're going to be late. Make sure the agreement doesn't have a "time is of the essence" clause. Say you'll use your "best efforts" and you're not responsible for problems out of your control, like shipping delays, unforeseen circumstances, and so on.

Some companies are in the business of making their customers more efficient, happier, or richer—they might sell advice, machinery, telephones, books, accounting services, or even legal expertise. But you can't please all the people all the time. Maybe a clause like this would be appropriate: "Our services are designed to increase output, but because individual situations differ, we cannot guarantee any specific level of improvement." Or, "Our products are warranted to be free of defects in material or workmanship, but we cannot guarantee specific results unless agreed to in writing."

Think about the kinds of things that have gone wrong in the past, and provide an "out" for the future. Have customers complained when you try to charge them extra for your services, even if unanticipated problems come up during the work? Provide an "out": "Company reserves the right to charge additional reasonable fees for time expended as a result of circumstances not known to Company as of the date of this contract."

Have your customers told you that they're not going to pay because the salesman told them something that turned out to be untrue? Provide an "out" in the form of a merger clause:

"This agreement replaces and supersedes any promises or representations made heretofore, and constitutes the complete agreement between the parties."

Every lawyer has clients who, often justifiably, are dissatisfied with something they bought, often for a great deal of money. "I thought it would do an awful lot more than it did. I think I'm entitled to some of my money back," they say.

When the adversary has given himself the right kind of "out," however, the lawyer has to tell the client that litigation may not be worth the time and trouble. "Next time, call me before you sign anything" will be about the best he can do. An "out" stops the lawsuit before it gets started.

SIX: DEVELOP PREVENTIVE FORMS AND PROCEDURES

Rigid, mechanistic forms and procedures, if properly and consistently used and updated, can help you and your employees say and do the right thing without always having to think it through, look it up, or call counsel. You don't always have to know the intricacies and rationales of the law. Many times, all you need to know is what you're supposed to do. Why you're supposed to do it doesn't matter.

For example, the following kinds of forms and procedures can be of great help:

• Many businesses have preprinted forms for buying, selling, and contracting, but the employees who deal with the forms aren't quite sure what to do with them. Employee manuals can solve that problem. They tell the employees when to send what form, what to say in cover letters, how to respond when they receive forms, what not to say on the telephone, and when to notify superiors.
• In this age of word processing, it's not at all unusual for a business to keep various lawyer-drafted form paragraphs on a computer, from which they can assemble letter agreements, proposals, and confirming letters which cover the typical issues that come up.
• There are manuals and forms that tell employees when and how to "paper the file."

• Many executives use "deal checklists" prepared by their law-yers—lists of points that need to be covered in different kinds of negotiations that take place in different kinds of businesses.
• Many businesses have detailed manuals that tell salesmen what they can and can't say, in order to avoid interference with contract suits, trade libel litigation, and so on.
• Many businesses provide their management employees with standard-form hiring and firing procedures and agreements.

All these forms and procedures are preventive in nature. They're designed to head off legal problems right from the start, especially in areas where common sense wouldn't be much help, and might even be counterproductive. And by institution-alizing a way to handle situations that arise repeatedly, they keep a business from continually having to reinvent the wheel. There isn't a company I can think of that wouldn't benefit from this approach.

SEVEN: GET YOUR LAWYER INVOLVED BEFORE YOU HAVE A PROBLEM

For your lawyer to do you as much good as possible, his role must extend beyond the obvious tasks of writing your contracts, designing your forms, and advising you on problems. Avoiding litigation also means minimizing the hidden problems that catch you by surprise—the ones you never knew you had, until it's too late—and that's where your lawyer's help will make the dif-ference.

For this purpose, there's nothing better than lunch (absent the usual three martinis). Time and again I've had "So how are things going?" lunches with clients, only to find out that they weren't going nearly so well as my client thought.

Not too long ago, for example, a client told me he was leaving his current company to take a high-level job with a brand-new company. He had checked everything out, he said—there were stock options, the company had money in the bank and a line of credit, and the principals were reputable people.

I asked him what the company was all about, and he told me

that it was in the business of marketing a revolutionary industrial technology. It sounded great—until I asked him who owned the legal rights to the process. Was it patented? Was there a patent pending? Were there licensing agreements or pending disputes about it?

Those were lawyer-type, "You worry too much" questions, he told me, but I was eventually able to determine that he didn't know. Either he had never thought to ask, or he assumed that details of those kinds had already been taken care of. I persuaded him to hold off for the time being.

As it turned out, I checked a little further and found out that the rights to the technology weren't at all clear. Before too long, my client's prospective employer got sued by another company which claimed that it was the owner of the process. The case is still in litigation, and will be for years to come. The future of the company is, at best, in doubt.

During similar informal lunch meetings, I've found out all kinds of things I would never have known about otherwise, and I was able to do something before situations really got out of hand. I've had clients proudly tell me how they're firing all the employees who are union sympathizers (a clear violation of federal law); how they and a competitor have agreed to let each other alone (a potential antitrust violation); and how they're going to build a small addition onto their building (a violation of local zoning laws).

It's the kind of thing that makes both the lawyer and the client choke on their sandwiches, but it's worth it.

EIGHT: DON'T GET BOXED IN BY YOUR EMOTIONS

I have a building contractor client who once put a roof on a building for one of his customers. When the work was finished he sent his bill, and with no justification at all, the customer refused to pay. We wrote the usual threat letters, to no avail, and we advised our client that eventually the judicial process would get him his just due, although it would take time.

Our client was incensed and didn't want to wait. So he took the roof back: he literally drove a crane to the building, which was complete and occupied, and removed the roof. Since the customer had never paid for it, he figured it was still rightfully his.

Although a somewhat extreme example, that's what I mean by getting boxed in by your emotions. Our client went from being very right to being very wrong.

People—even hard-boiled business executives—are still people, and they have emotions. It's tough not to be angry when you go out on a limb for a customer who then refuses to pay you, for absolutely no reason. It's tough to bury the burning desire to get even.

In the more typical case, a business executive will make a threat, usually in the emotional heat of the moment, and then feel the necessity to back it up. "I'm walking off this job tomorrow if we don't have this straightened out." Or, "I'm not making another payment unless you do what we've asked." You may not have the legal right to walk off or withhold payment just yet —even if you're "right"—and if you do, you take yourself from a position of strength to a position of weakness.

That's one of the causes of needless litigation. If you had just sat back and fed them enough rope, they would probably have hanged themselves. But now they have a leg to stand on, a potential defense, a chance to win. So they may as well fight you in court.

Emotions do play a role in business: you have to be comfortable with your decisions, and how things "feel" can be important. But fundamentally, the decision-making process comes down to weighing what you have to gain versus what you have to lose. When the advantages are outweighed by the disadvantages, the fact that it felt good is no excuse.

There's a saying in the law: "A lawyer who represents himself has a fool for a client." When you're emotionally involved in a situation—either as lawyer or as business executive—it's tough to make the objective, measured judgments that determine success or failure. When a boxer senses victory, sometimes in his fervor he forgets himself and swings wildly and aimlessly—and he leaves himself open for a knockout punch. It happens a lot in business too.

A high level of emotional involvement isn't a crime, but it is

a danger signal. Back off, and let someone else handle things
for a while.

NINE: EDUCATE YOUR EMPLOYEES

What every executive better know about the law must trickle
down through your company. It's not enough for the sales managers to know about offers and acceptances. The salesmen have
to know some basic contract law also—after all, it's they, and
not the managers, who do most of the offering and accepting.
Similarly, it's not enough for the purchasing manager to know
about the "battle of the forms." The purchasing agents have to
know what's going on too. They're the ones who most frequently deal in the routine boilerplate.

A lot of companies forget that. The executives who deal with
the lawyers are the ones who get educated, but the "hands-on"
employees don't get the kind of understanding that could help
them recognize a trouble spot or think their way around a potential problem in the field, where it counts. They don't learn
the danger signals; they don't develop a feel for what they ought
to document; they remain legally unrealistic optimists and not
healthy pessimists.

I'm not saying that every employee at every level needs this
kind of training. Certainly, many employees need only forms
and clearly defined procedures, if that. But in many companies,
employees below the top echelon—sometimes way below the
top echelon—work with the law every day, whether they know
it or not, and that's where much of the business litigation comes
from.

Some companies attack this problem with in-house seminars;
others with explanatory written materials; others with informal
information sessions.

But the point to remember is that the law is more than just
background information. It's there to be used—sometimes as a
sword, and sometimes as a shield. For that to happen, the right
kind of legal know-how has to get beyond the generals, into the
hands of the foot soldiers.

GLOSSARY

ABUSE OF PROCESS   A right to sue for damages arising from the use of legal process for an improper purpose, as in using a subpoena strictly for harassment.

ACCEPTANCE   An unqualified and unconditional assent to an offer, thereby forming a contract.

ACCORD AND SATISFACTION   A contract in which the parties agree to settle a claim arising from a prior agreement by substituting a new agreement in its place.

ACCOUNTING   A type of remedy that can be awarded by a court, requiring a party to prepare and submit a detailed statement of debits, credits, payments, transfers, and so on, arising from the transaction that is the subject of the lawsuit.

ACT OF GOD   An event caused exclusively by nature or other occurrence, in no way attributable to any person's actions.

AD DAMNUM CLAUSE   A clause placed at the end of a complaint in which the plaintiff states what is being claimed.

ADHESION CONTRACT   A contract characterized by the unequal bargaining strength of the parties; typically, a standard-form contract whereby one party, usually a consumer, is told to "take it or leave it."

AD HOC   Created for a special purpose, as in an "ad hoc committee."

ADMINISTRATOR   A person appointed by a court to manage the assets and liabilities of a deceased person who has not left a will. If female, referred to as an "administratrix." See also "executor."

ADMIRALTY   Having to do with maritime torts, crimes, contracts, and other issues.

ADMISSIBLE   Referring to evidence (testimony, documents, photographs, models, and so on) that conforms to the rules of evidence and is therefore received by a court and considered in reaching a verdict.

ADMISSION INTO EVIDENCE   A court's acceptance of evidence so that it may be considered in reaching a verdict.

AFFIANT   A person who signs an affidavit.

AFFIDAVIT   A written statement signed under oath before a person empowered by law to administer oaths, such as a notary public.

AFFILIATE   A corporation effectively controlled by another corporation.

AFORESAID   Mentioned previously, as in a document that refers to the "aforesaid clause."

AGENT   A person who is authorized by another, called a "principal," to act for him. The principal has the power to control the agent's actions, and can be bound by and liable for what the agent does, pursuant to a complex body of law known as "agency law."

ALIENABLE   Transferable.

ALIENATE   To transfer property; to convey.

ALIQUOT   A fractional interest.

ALLEGATION   An assertion or claim. Often used to refer to the statements that a plaintiff makes in a complaint, setting forth what he intends to prove.

ALLEGED   Asserted; claimed.

ANSWER   A document filed with the court by the defendant in response to the plaintiff's complaint.

ANTICIPATORY BREACH   A statement or act of a party to a contract which indicates that he will not or cannot perform his contractual responsibilities.

ANTITRUST   A body of law designed to protect interstate commerce from acts deemed to be injurious, such as price fixing, divisions of territories and customers, discriminatory pricing, monopolization, group boycotts, and the like.

APPARENT AGENCY   A doctrine of agency law which holds one person liable for the acts of another, as if they were principal and agent, even though they are not.

APPEAL   Exercising resort to a higher court.

APPELLANT   The party who makes the appeal.

APPELLATE   Pertaining to an appeal, such as an "appellate court" or an "appellate brief."

APPELLEE   The party against whom the appellant files the appeal.

APPURTENANCE   As used in deeds and leases, a structure attached to or considered to be a part of the real estate, such as a barn, a greenhouse, an outbuilding, and so on.

ARBITRATION   A process of dispute resolution not involving a court in which the parties agree in advance to be bound by the decision of a third party.

ARGUENDO   For the sake of argument; hypothetically.

ARTICLES OF INCORPORATION   A document filed with a state in order to form a corporation; sometimes called a "certificate of incorporation."

ASSIGNMENT   A type of contract that transfers property or rights. The person who does the transferring is referred to as the "assignor"; the other party is the "assignee."

ASSIGNMENT FOR THE BENEFIT OF CREDITORS   A debtor's transfer of his property and rights to another for the purpose of having the other gather his assets and pay his liabilities.

ASSUMPSIT   Historically, based upon a contract, as opposed to a tort, as in "an action in assumpsit."

ATTACHMENT   The act of seizing property by court order to satisfy the claim of a creditor.

ATTEST   To certify. Often, a contract or other legal document to be signed by the president of a corporation will also include a signature line for the corporation's secretary, next to the word "attest." The secretary's signature constitutes his certification of the president's signature.

ATTORNEY–CLIENT PRIVILEGE   The right of an attorney or client not to disclose communications made by the client to the attorney.

AUDIT   Verification of a business' financial records for the purpose of documenting the accuracy of the information contained therein, usually by a certified public accountant. An "audit" is to be distinguished from an "unaudited" engagement, or a "compilation and review," neither of which attempts to verify the information in a business' financial records.

AUTHENTICATION   The process by which a document is proved to be what it is contended to be. Before it is admissible, for example, a written contract must first be "authenticated" by the testimony of a witness who can verify what it is, who signed it, and so on.

BAD FAITH   Actions based upon fraud, dishonesty, ill will; not by an honest mistake or carelessness.

BAILMENT   A legal relationship in which one party, called the "bailor," delivers his goods to another party, called the "bailee." The bailee has the obligation to use or handle the goods only as directed by the bailor, and to then return them to the bailor.

BENEFICIARY   The person entitled to benefit. For example, the beneficiary of a will or trust is the person who is to receive property as stated in the will or trust.

BEQUEST   A gift of property made in a will.

BEST EVIDENCE   A term used to distinguish primary, as opposed to secondary, evidence. The distinction is important in determining which evidence is admissible in court. For instance, oral testimony respecting the contents of a document is usually inadmissible, since the document itself is the "best evidence" of what it says.

BILL OF LADING   A document, typically used by a common carrier, describing and evidencing receipt of goods.

BLUE SKY LAW   A state statute that regulates the purchase and sale of securities in the effort to protect persons from investing on the basis of misrepresentations or other illegal practices.

BOARD OF DIRECTORS   The body, elected by the stockholders, that has the legal responsibility to operate a corporation.

BOILERPLATE   Standard language that appears without significant variation in contracts, legal documents, and the like.

BONA FIDE   With good faith; honestly; genuine.

BONA FIDE PURCHASER   A person who purchases property, for fair value, without being aware of any other person's claim to the property.

BOND   A term usually used in the sense of a surety bond; an obligation undertaken by the bonding company to pay a person on behalf of the bonded party, in the event that the bonded party defaults in some obligation. For instance, a bonding company may agree to pay a contractor what he is owed on a building project in the event that the owner of the project does not.

BREACH   The violation of a legal duty, as in "breach of contract" or "breach of warranty."

BRIEF   A document prepared by a lawyer and submitted to a court in support of a legal position being advanced by the lawyer, containing arguments and legal citations.

BULK SALE   A sale by a business of the major part of its merchandise, inventory, or other assets not made in the ordinary course of its business.

BURDEN OF PROOF   During a trial, the obligation to prove a position being taken. For example, in a lawsuit based upon a breach of contract, the plaintiff has the burden of proving the existence of a contract, the breach of the contract, and the damages suffered. If he does not satisfy his burden of proof, the defendant wins; if he does, the defendant must then go forward to rebut what the plaintiff has proved. Whichever side has the burden of proof must first introduce evidence to satisfy it before the other side has any obligation to proceed.

BUY–SELL AGREEMENT   An agreement in which stockholders in a corporation agree to restrict their right to dispose of their stock without first affording the other stockholders the option to buy the stock at a price to be determined in accordance with the agreement, and otherwise providing for the orderly conduct of business among stockholders.

BYLAWS   The rules adopted by a corporation pertaining to the fashion in which the corporation is to govern itself.

CAPTION   The heading of a complaint, motion, or other legal document, identifying the parties, the court, and the document.

CASE LAW   The collected decisions of courts, expressed in legal opinions written by judges.

CAUSE OF ACTION   The facts that constitute the right to sue for relief, as in "a cause of action for breach of contract."

CERTIFIED COPY   A copy of a document signed by its custodian (for example, the clerk of the court) to verify that it is an accurate copy of the original.

CHANCERY   A division of a court that resolves disputes on the basis of fairness and equity, instead of by applying the common law and relying strictly on legal precedent. Such courts have the power to act in limited, specific situations.

CHANGE OF VENUE   Transferring a lawsuit from one court in one location to another court in another location.

CHAPTER 11   A section of the Bankruptcy Reform Act that permits a business to reorganize, under court protection from creditors, pursuant to a court-approved plan.

CHAPTER 13   A section of the Bankruptcy Reform Act that permits individuals to repay debts over an extended period.

CHARGE   The trial judge's instructions to the jury, including an explanation of the law, delivered immediately before the jury begins to deliberate.

CHATTEL MORTGAGE   A security interest in personal property given to secure the repayment of a debt or the satisfaction of some other obligation.

CIRCUMSTANTIAL EVIDENCE   A method of proving facts not from firsthand observation, but from knowledge of other facts from which certain deductions can be made. To use a classic example, the fact that there is snow on the ground in the morning is circumstantial evidence of the fact that it snowed during the night.

CLASS ACTION   A lawsuit in which a large group of persons may sue, or be sued, through a representative. The advantage is that it is not necessary for each member of the group to be named as a party in the lawsuit.

CLOSED SHOP   A place of business where union membership is a condition of employment.

CLOSELY HELD CORPORATION   Or "close corporation." A corporation owned and controlled by only a few shareholders, usually operated more informally than larger or publicly held corporations.

CODE OF PROFESSIONAL RESPONSIBILITY   The code of ethics and rules of conduct by which attorneys are governed.

CODICIL   A supplement or amendment to a will.

COGNOVIT NOTE   A note that permits a confession of judgment.

COLLATERAL   Property pledged to secure a debt or other obligation.

COLORABLE   Appearing to be truthful or genuine, but false or counterfeit in reality.

COMMON LAW   The body of law that is formulated from case law, as opposed to statutes enacted by legislatures.

COMPANY   A general term for a business, which could be, for example, a partnership, corporation, proprietorship, or other entity.

COMPARATIVE NEGLIGENCE   Negligence on the part of the plaintiff which contributes to the plaintiff's damages. In jurisdictions that recognize the doctrine of comparative negligence, the plaintiff's recovery is diminished by the proportion of negligence attributable to him. See also "contributory negligence."

COMPENSATORY DAMAGES   Damages awarded in the amount of the actual losses suffered, as distinct from punitive damages.

COMPILATION AND REVIEW   An accounting method in which an accountant compiles data from the financial records of a business, without verification for accuracy, and then presents the data in a financial statement or some other form. To be distinguished, for example, from an audit.

COMPLAINT   The document that a plaintiff files at the commencement of a lawsuit, stating generally the nature of the claim through a series of allegations.

CONDEMNATION   The act of taking private property for public use, through the power of eminent domain, for which just compensation must be paid.

CONFESSION OF JUDGMENT   An authorization by a debtor, in an agreement with the creditor, for a judgment to be entered against the debtor without any hearing or trial.

CONFIRMING LETTER   A letter that recites the existence of a fact, promise, statement, or other matter, for the purpose of providing the sender with a means to prove the fact, promise, statement, or other matter in the event of a dispute.

CONFLICT OF LAW   An inconsistency between the laws of two different jurisdictions, each of which might apply to a particular transaction.

CONSEQUENTIAL DAMAGES   All the damages caused by a wrongful act, whether immediate, long-term, monetary (for instance, lost profits), non-monetary (for instance, pain and suffering), or of any other nature.

CONSIDERATION   Items of value (for instance, money, rights, agreements to do or not do certain things in the future) exchanged between parties to a contract as the mutual inducement to consummate the transaction.

CONTEMPT   A willful failure to obey a court order, or an act done to embarrass or obstruct a court.

CONTINGENT FEE   A fee agreement between a lawyer and a client providing that the lawyer shall be paid a percentage of the recovery he obtains for the client, plus costs expended on the client's behalf. The lawyer earns no fee unless he obtains a recovery for the client. Typically used in personal injury cases.

CONTRACT   A legally binding agreement.

CONTRIBUTION   A duty owed among joint tortfeasors to contribute equally to the satisfaction of the plaintiff's claim against them.

CONTRIBUTORY NEGLIGENCE   A legal doctrine accepted in some jurisdictions which provides that if the plaintiff's own negligence contributed, even in just a small way, to the plaintiff's damages, the plaintiff will not be able to recover against a negligent defendant. See also "comparative negligence."

CONVERSION   A tort involving one person's unauthorized taking of another's property.

CONVEYANCE   Transfer of title to property.

COPYRIGHT   Statutory protection that can be obtained by the author of a literary work, including writings, music, art, motion pictures, and other materials, preventing others from copying or selling the literary work.

CORPORATE OPPORTUNITY   The opportunity of a corporation to acquire profit or other benefits. Those who owe a duty of loyalty to the corporation, such as its officers and directors, are not permitted to take personal advantage of corporate opportunities.

CORPORATE RESOLUTION   An act of a corporation, approved by vote of the stockholders or directors, usually memorialized in writing.

CORPORATE VEIL   The legal doctrine that protects the stockholders of a corporation from the debts and liabilities of the corporation. Under certain circumstances, however, the stockholders can be liable, pursuant to a doctrine known as "piercing the corporate veil."

CORPORATION   A business entity, viewed in the law as a person, created and governed by the authority of state law. A corporation is owned by stockholders and run by directors and officers, but it has a separate, independent existence, with its own rights and liabilities.

COUNT   A section of a complaint, stating a separate cause of action.

COUNTERCLAIM   A claim made by a defendant or third party defendant against the plaintiff.

COUNTEROFFER   An offer made in response to another offer.

COURT OF APPEALS   In the federal system, the court to which appeals are taken from the federal district courts, where the trials are held. There are various courts of appeals, each of which presides over a different geographic "circuit." The appeals courts in several states are also referred to as "courts of appeal."

COVENANT   A contract, or a particular promise in a contract, usually in arrangements relating to real estate.

COVER   The right of a buyer, after breach by a seller, to purchase substitute goods in order to protect himself from further damages, charging the seller for the cost difference and other expenses incurred.

CROSSCLAIM   A claim made by one of the defendants or third party defendants against another defendant or third party defendant.

CROSS-EXAMINATION   The questioning of a witness by a party opposed to the one who called and conducted the direct examination of the witness. On cross-examination, unlike direct examination, leading questions are permitted.

CUMULATIVE VOTING   A system of tabulating the votes of stockholders in a corporation designed to promote minority representation.

DEAL MEMO   Colloquial term for a written agreement used in some businesses.

DECEDENT   A deceased person.

DECLARATORY JUDGMENT   A type of lawsuit in which a party seeks a definition of his legal rights, not an award of damages.

DECREE   A court order or judgment.

DE FACTO   Literally, in fact, or actually. Used to denote a state of affairs which, although improper, must as a practical matter be recognized. See "de jure."

DEFAMATION   A tort involving the making of false, unprivileged statements that damage the reputation of a person. Libel and slander are types of defamation.

DEFAULT JUDGMENT   A judgment entered by default against a party, usually as a result of his failure to respond to a complaint. In that event, the plaintiff is awarded a default judgment for the relief sought by the complaint.

DEFENDANT   The party sued by a plaintiff, against whom relief is sought.

DE JURE   Legitimately or lawfully.

DEMISE   To convey land for a term of years, or to lease.

DEMURRER   A response to a complaint in which the defendant admits the allegations of the complaint and argues that they fail to state facts which would justify an award in the plaintiff's favor.

DEPONENT   A person whose deposition is taken.

DEPOSITION   A discovery device in which a party or witness is questioned under oath, before trial. The testimony is then transcribed into written form for future reference.

DERIVATIVE SUIT   A lawsuit against a third party which a corporation has itself failed to pursue, brought by a stockholder in the corporation on the corporation's behalf.

DEVISE   A gift of real property in a will.

DIRECTED VERDICT   The trial judge's entry of judgment against the party with the burden of proof for failure to satisfy the burden, without allowing the jury to rule on the case.

DIRECT EXAMINATION   The questioning of a witness by the party who called the witness to testify. Leading questions are not permitted on direct examination.

DIRECTOR   A person elected by the stockholders of a corporation to serve on the corporation's board of directors and manage the business of the corporation.

DISCLAIMER   The refusal or repudiation of a duty, a claim, a right or a power. Most often used to denote a party's contractual attempt to eliminate or limit his responsibility for certain liabilities, such as the responsibility for consequential damages.

DISCOVERY   That stage in a lawsuit, after the pleadings are filed and before trial, in which each party is given the right, through various means, to discover facts known to the other parties, and to otherwise investigate and uncover the factual issues raised by the lawsuit.

DISSOLUTION   With respect to a business entity, such as a partnership or corporation, the act of terminating the business entity and resolving its affairs.

DISTRICT COURT   A trial court in the federal court system.

DIVERSITY OF CITIZENSHIP   A basis for obtaining jurisdiction in the federal court system. Historically designed to avoid local prejudice, it permits litigation in the federal, as opposed to the state, court system in certain instances in which the dispute is between citizens of different states, or where noncitizens are involved.

DOCKET   The formal, abstracted record of proceedings before a court, as in a list of the various cases pending before a court.

DUE PROCESS   The constitutional right to be treated fairly by government. Due process is a broad, complex topic dealing with the rights of citizens to be free of arbitrary or unreasonable governmental interference with life, property, liberty, or other rights. In a more general sense, the term is used to refer to fundamental standards of fairness and justice.

DUTY TO BARGAIN IN GOOD FAITH   The obligation of labor and management to deal with each other forthrightly, honestly, and reasonably during collective bargaining.

EASEMENT   A right to use the land, or part of the land, of another for a particular limited purpose, such as for access to a road.

EEOC   Equal Employment Opportunity Commission. A federal agency created by the Civil Rights Act of 1964 for the purpose of enforcing laws against discrimination in hiring and firing on the basis of race, religion, age, sex, or national origin.

EJECTMENT   A cause of action seeking a court order to remove a person who is unlawfully occupying real property.

EMINENT DOMAIN   The right of a government to take private property, upon payment of just compensation, for public use. The property is taken through "condemnation."

ENCUMBER   To place a lien, mortgage, security interest, easement, or similar claim against property—generally referred to as an "encumbrance."

EQUAL PROTECTION   A constitutional guarantee generally providing that no person be denied the same protection of the laws as is provided to other persons.

EQUITY   Courts of Equity, also referred to as Courts of Chancery, resolve disputes on the basis of fairness and equity, instead of by applying the common law and relying strictly on legal precedent. These courts have the power to act in limited, specific situations.

ERISA   Employee Retirement Income Security Act. A federal law governing pension and retirement plans.

ESCROW   Property (for instance, money, a deed, stock, or other asset) held by a third party (often called the "escrow agent"), to be released according to the terms of the "escrow agreement" upon the happening of defined events (such as by a certain date, or if certain payments are made, or if certain authorizations are received, or in other specified circumstances).

ESTOPPEL   A doctrine of law that prohibits a party from taking a position or making a claim to the detriment of another party when the first party's actions, statements, or promises induced the second party's reliance. For instance, the estoppel doctrine can be used to "estop" a party from denying the existence of a contract, if his actions led another party to rely on the belief that a contract existed.

EVIDENCE   Testimony or exhibits introduced in a trial for the purpose of satisfying a burden of proof or persuading a judge or jury.

EXECUTION   The legal process of enforcing a judgment, as by selling the defendant's property at a sheriff's sale. The term also refers to the signing of a document, as in "executing a contract."

EXECUTOR   A person appointed in a will to carry out the wishes and manage the assets and liabilities of a deceased person. If female, referred to as "executrix." See also "administrator."

EXHIBIT   A document, chart, model, or other tangible object introduced into evidence at a trial.

EX PARTE   Describing a legal proceeding conducted in the presence of one party only, without notice to or participation by the other party. For instance, proceedings are conducted ex parte when there is an emergency to which the court must immediately respond.

EXPERT WITNESS   A person proved to the satisfaction of a judge to be qualified by experience or training to express an opinion at a trial. Normally, witnesses at a trial are permitted only to express facts of which they have firsthand knowledge. Experts, if qualified, can express their opinions respecting matters within their area of expertise.

FAILURE OF CONSIDERATION   The failure of a party to a contract to give the other what he bargained for.

FAIR LABOR STANDARDS ACT   Federal legislation setting the minimum wage, declaring a forty-hour week, prohibiting child labor, and making other protective provisions for workers.

FEDERAL COURT   The court system set up by the Federal Government, consisting of district courts, where trials are held; courts of appeals, to which appeals from trial courts are taken; other, specialized courts, such as the tax court; and the United States Supreme Court.

FEDERAL QUESTION   One of the bases of jurisdiction in the Federal Courts. Applies to a lawsuit involving a question of federal importance, such as the interpretation of a federal statute. See also "diversity of citizenship."

FEDERAL RULES OF CIVIL PROCEDURE   The rules that govern the conduct of lawsuits in the Federal Courts. Each state also has its own rules of civil procedure.

FEE SIMPLE   A category of real estate ownership which is unconditional and absolute. When a person has a fee simple ownership interest, he possesses all rights to the land for all time, without limitations.

FIDUCIARY   A person who has the duty to act for the benefit of another, keeping the other's interests primary in all respects; one who owes another a high duty of trust and confidence. A "fiduciary duty" requires full disclosure, total honesty, and the avoidance of any conflicts of interest.

F.O.B.   Free on board, meaning that the price includes delivery to the location named.

FORCE MAJEURE   A clause in a contract designed to protect the parties from events outside their control which prevent contract performance, as in an Act of God.

FORECLOSURE   A proceeding to sell mortgaged property in order to satisfy the mortgage debt.

FOREIGN CORPORATION   A corporation formed in a state other than the state or states in which it conducts business. In most states, a foreign corporation must first register with the state before it can lawfully conduct business.

FORUM NON CONVENIENS   A doctrine that permits a court to transfer a case to another jurisdiction in which it would be more appropriately handled.

FRAUD   An intentional misrepresentation or concealment of the truth, made for the purpose of deceiving another person and causing him to suffer harm, which in fact results in such deception and harm.

FRAUDULENT CONVEYANCE   The unlawful transfer of property for the purpose of hiding it from creditors.

FRUSTRATION OF PURPOSE   A doctrine that will excuse a party's failure to perform as required by a contract if the whole basis and purpose behind the contract has been negated by circumstances occurring after the contract was formed.

GARNISHMENT   A proceeding in which the property of a debtor in the possession of a third party is attached for the benefit of a creditor. A garnishment can apply to money held by a bank, accounts receivable owing to the debtor, and similar assets. The creditor who institutes the garnishment is called the "garnishor"; the person who has the debtor's property, against whom the garnishment is instituted, is called the "garnishee."

GENERAL CONTRACTOR   In the construction industry, one who contracts to complete an entire project, rather than just a segment of a project. A general contractor usually hires subcontractors, who have responsibility to complete specific aspects of the work, pursuant to a contract with the general contractor.

GENERAL DAMAGES   Nonspecific damages such as pain and suffering, loss of goodwill, damage to reputation, and the like.

GIFT   A voluntary transfer of property made without consideration.

GOOD FAITH   Honesty, without intention to mislead; the intention to treat another fairly and honestly.

GUARANTEE   A contract providing that certain things shall be done as promised by a person referred to as the "guarantor."

HARMLESS ERROR   A doctrine that permits an appeals court to affirm the actions of a trial court, even if the trial court made an error, because of the minor or nonprejudicial nature of the mistake.

HEARING   A proceeding, similar to a trial, convened to give a person the right to be heard and confront witnesses, previous to a court or other governmental body's issuing an order which might affect the person's property, liberty, or other rights. A hearing is normally required pursuant to the constitutional guarantee of due process.

HEARSAY   A witness' repetition of what he heard others say outside of court, introduced to prove that what was overheard is true. According to the rules of evidence, hearsay can be inadmissible in court, because, among other reasons, the other party has no effective way to cross-examine the person who made the statement. However, there are many exceptions to the hearsay rule, and testimony relating to such out-of-court statements is often admissible.

HEIR   A person who receives another's interest in property at the time of the other's death.

HEREDITAMENTS   Things capable of being inherited.

HERETOFORE   Previously; referring to things in the past.

HOLD HARMLESS   A provision whereby one party agrees to keep the other free from damages or liabilities that might arise from a transaction.

HOLOGRAPH   A will or a deed written by the person making the will or deed, in his own handwriting, without witnesses. Different states have different laws respecting the validity of such documents.

HORNBOOK   A book that summarizes the law; the phrase "hornbook law" refers to basic, fundamental precepts of law.

HOT CARGO   Goods produced by a company with which a union has a dispute. A "hot cargo" clause in an agreement between a union and a company will permit union members to refuse to handle hot cargo.

HYPOTHECATE   To pledge property as security for a debt.

IMMATERIAL   Referring to evidence that does not bear upon or tend to prove any of the issues in question, and is therefore inadmissible.

IMMUNITY   Freedom from liability; for example, in many states, the government is immune from suit for its torts except in certain limited situations.

IMPASSE   In labor law, the point at which labor and management are stalemated despite their efforts to bargain in good faith.

IMPEACHMENT   The act of damaging the credibility of a witness by showing his lack of believability: for example, by introducing evidence of his prior criminal convictions, or by introducing prior statements which contradict his present testimony.

IMPLIED WARRANTY   A warranty that is created and made a part of a contract not by agreement of the parties, but by the operation of law. For instance, the implied warranty of merchantability and the implied warranty of fitness for a particular purpose are inserted by law into all contracts involving the sale of goods. Implied warranties may, in most cases, be avoided by disclaimers, but the disclaimers themselves must meet certain legal criteria.

IMPOSSIBILITY   A doctrine that excuses a party from the obligation to perform as required by a contract when the performance becomes impossible by virtue of unforeseen circumstances outside the party's control.

INADMISSIBLE   Evidence that does not conform with the rules of evidence and is therefore not permitted during a trial.

INALIENABLE   Not capable of being transferred.

INCHOATE   Incomplete, unfinished. An "inchoate interest," for instance, is a property interest which has not yet come into being.

INCORPORATOR   The persons who form a corporation.

INDEMNIFICATION   An obligation to reimburse a person for all expenses and damages sustained—as, for example, a part of a hold harmless agreement, or by operation of law.

INDENTURE   A type of written agreement, often referring to a deed.

INFRINGEMENT   A violation of rights held by another, as in a "copyright infringement" or "patent infringement."

INJUNCTION   A court order that commands a party to do something or to stop doing something. Injunctions are often referred to as "restraining orders" or "cease and desist orders." An emergency injunction is often referred to as a "temporary restraining order" or a "preliminary injunction." In order to obtain an injunction, a party must prove that he will suffer irreparable harm unless the injunction is issued.

INSOLVENCY   The inability to pay one's debts.

INSTALLMENT CONTRACT   A contract which is to be performed periodically, in stages, as where goods are shipped monthly, or payment is made weekly.

INSURABLE INTEREST   The legal right of a person to insure against the loss of certain property or the death of an individual. Before he can have an insurable interest, a person must show that he will suffer a real loss if the property is destroyed or if the person dies.

INTEGRATION   A contract that includes the final, entire agreement between the parties. An "integration clause" states that the contract is an integration.

INTENTIONAL TORT   A tort committed on purpose, as opposed to negligently. Assault, battery, conversion, defamation, and fraud, for example, are intentional torts.

INTERLOCUTORY   An order or other proceeding during the pendency of a lawsuit which decides some aspect of the dispute, but does not dispose of the entire litigation.

INTERPLEADER   A type of lawsuit in which a person who holds property claimed by others can name them as defendants, requiring them to litigate the dispute and eliminating his potential liability to either.

INTERROGATORY   A written question which one party to a lawsuit may require another party to answer under oath, during the discovery stage of the litigation.

INTERSTATE COMMERCE   Transactions which involve more than one state. Interstate commerce is frequently a prerequisite to the application of federal statutes. For instance, unless a company engages in interstate commerce, it will not be subject to federal antitrust or labor laws. However, the company itself need not do business in different states in order to be found to have engaged in interstate commerce. Ordering supplies, for instance, from out of state may be enough; only minimal interstate contact is required.

INTESTATE   The state of dying before making a will.

INTRODUCE INTO EVIDENCE   To present evidence at a trial, requesting the court to deem it admissible.

IRRELEVANT   Referring to evidence that does not bear upon or tend to prove any of the issues in question, and is therefore inadmissible.

JOINDER   The procedure whereby third party defendants are added to a lawsuit.

JOINT AND SEVERAL LIABILITY   A type of liability in which more than one person is liable for the whole debt or for all the damages suffered, so that the plaintiff can sue all or any one of them, at his option.

JOINT TENANCY   An interest in property in which each joint tenant jointly owns the whole property with the other (as opposed to each owning a divided half of the property). Depending on state law, a joint tenancy can also include a right of survivorship so that, upon the death of one joint tenant, the other becomes the sole owner of the property. Compare "tenancy in common" and "tenancy by the entireties."

JOINT TORTFEASOR   A person who is jointly and severally liable for a tort, along with at least one other person.

JOINT VENTURE   A business entity—not a corporation, but analogous to a partnership—between persons or other business entities, for the purpose of jointly pursuing a particular enterprise.

JUDGMENT   A court's final decision, by either a judge or a jury, respecting a lawsuit. A party who obtains a judgment is thereafter entitled to enforce it through the application of laws and procedures designed for that purpose.

JUDGMENT NOTE   An agreement providing one party the right to confess judgment against the other party upon the other party's failure to pay a specified sum of money when due, or upon the happening of some other defined event. Judgment notes are illegal in some states. See "confession of judgment."

JUDGMENT SEARCH   A search of public records to determine whether judgments have been previously entered against a person or a business.

JURISDICTION   Referring to a particular geographic area over which a court can exercise its power. Pennsylvania, for instance, is a jurisdiction in which Pennsylvania courts sit and can act. The term also refers to the right of a court to assume power over particular litigants and disputes. For instance, a court does not "have jurisdiction" over a person until that person is properly served and notified of the existence of a lawsuit against him.

LAW CLERK   An attorney, usually just out of law school, who performs legal research and other tasks for a judge to assist in the judge's handling of lawsuits, motions, and similar matters.

LEADING QUESTION   A question that suggests the answer desired by the questioner or which attempts to put words in the mouth of a witness, such as "Isn't it true that . . . ?"

LEGACY   A gift of personal property in a will.

LETTER AGREEMENT   A contract put into the form of a letter, signed by both parties.

LETTER OF CREDIT   An agreement, typically entered by a bank on behalf of a customer, assuring third persons that the bank will repay them if they extend credit to the customer.

LETTER OF INTENT   A letter typically used to express a general understanding and the intent of the parties to enter a formal written contract respecting it.

LEVY   A seizure of property pursuant to court order for the purpose of satisfying a judgment.

LIABILITY   The obligation of one person to another under the law.

LIBEL   Defamation expressed in a writing, picture, or other tangible form.

LICENSE   Legal permission, usually in a formal, written agreement, to use, within limitations, the property or rights of another.

LIEN   An encumbrance on property, usually made a matter of public record, evidencing the right to make a claim against the property, such as a mortgage.

LIFE ESTATE   The right of a person to possess property during his lifetime, but not thereafter. Property in which a person possesses a life estate does not pass to his heirs after his death.

LIMITED PARTNERSHIP   A type of business entity, not a corporation, regulated by state statute, made up of one or more limited partners and one or more general partners. The limited partners are not liable for the obligations of the partnership beyond their capital contribution. The business of the limited partnership is managed by the general partners, who can be liable for the partnership debts and obligations.

LIQUIDATED DAMAGES   Referring to a contract clause which provides the amount of damages that a party who breaches a contract shall be required to pay, without reference to the actual damages suffered by the non-breaching party. A clause providing for liquidated damages is valid only under certain limited conditions.

LIS PENDENS   A notice, filed in public records, notifying persons interested in certain real property of the pendency of litigation or claims involving the property.

LITIGANT   A person involved in litigation.

MALFEASANCE   A wrongful act for which there is no legal excuse.

MALICE   An intentional act done for the purpose of causing harm to another.

MALICIOUS PROSECUTION   A tort involving the institution and prosecution of a lawsuit without any reasonable basis. The person against whom the lawsuit was initiated may sue for damages if he can prove that the plaintiff had no basis for the suit, and if the lawsuit terminates in his favor.

MALPRACTICE   Negligence by a professional, usually defined as the failure to employ that level of skill and care typically employed by those similarly situated.

MASTER–SERVANT RELATIONSHIP   A type of agency relationship, typically involving employers and employees. The master can be liable for the torts or other actions of the servant, committed within the scope of the employment relationship.

MATERIAL   Referring to evidence that has a logical connection to the issues in question.

MECHANIC'S LIEN   The right of a person who supplies labor or materials on a construction project to place a lien on the property to secure his claim for payment.

MEMORANDUM OF UNDERSTANDING   A term used to describe a written agreement, or a writing which summarizes the terms of an oral agreement, which may or may not be signed by both parties.

MERGER CLAUSE   A contract clause which declares the agreement to be the full and complete agreement between the parties, superseding and cancelling all other oral and written agreements.

MINISTERIAL   Referring to a task that requires only conformity with instructions, and no judgment or discretion.

MISFEASANCE   Improperly performing an act which if done correctly is proper.

MISREPRESENTATION   A false statement, made either negligently or intentionally, which would have the effect of misleading another.

MITIGATION OF DAMAGES   A legal doctrine that requires a nonbreaching party to take reasonable steps to minimize the damages caused to him by a breaching party.

MORTGAGE   An interest in land given to secure the repayment of a debt, affording the holder of the mortgage the right to sell the land in satisfaction of the debt in the event of a default.

MORTGAGEE   The person who holds a mortgage on property, such as a bank.

MORTGAGOR   The person who owns the property on which there is a mortgage.

MOTION   A request made to a court for the purpose of obtaining an order or other ruling on a pending case.

NEGLIGENCE   A tort involving the failure of a person to do what a reasonably prudent person would do under similar circumstances.

NEGOTIABLE INSTRUMENT   A document, such as a promise by a person to pay money, which is legally capable of being transferred, or "negotiated." To be negotiable, the document must meet certain specific legal criteria.

NLRB   National Labor Relations Board. A federal agency empowered with the authority to enforce federal labor laws.

NOMINEE   A person designated by another to act in his place.

NOTE   A written promise to pay a specific sum of money.

NOTWITHSTANDING   Nevertheless; despite.

NOVATION   A contract in which a new party is substituted, by agreement of all concerned, for one of the original parties to a contract.

OBLIGEE   A person who is owed an obligation. Also refers to a person for whose protection a bond is given.

OBLIGOR   A person who owes an obligation to another. Also refers to a person obligated under a bond.

OFFER   An unequivocal, expressed willingness to make a contract on certain terms.

OFFEREE   A person to whom an offer is made.

OFFEROR   A person who makes an offer.

OFFICER   A person elected by the board of directors of a corporation to operate the business in a specific capacity, such as president, vice-president, secretary, or treasurer.

OPEN SHOP   A business in which union membership is not a prerequisite for employment.

OPTION   An agreement that requires an offeror to keep an offer open for acceptance by the offeree for a stated period of time; the right to purchase something at a later time for a stated price.

OSHA   Occupational Safety and Health Act. A federal law regulating workplace conditions.

PARALEGAL   A person with legal training, not a lawyer, who assists a lawyer in certain tasks.

PARENT CORPORATION   A corporation that owns another, or most of another, corporation, which is referred to as a "subsidiary."

PARTITION   Referring to a cause of action in which a joint owner of property requests that a court divide the property among those who have an interest in it.

PARTNERSHIP   A business entity formed by contract, called a partnership agreement, among two or more partners who agree to devote their time and skill to the enterprise and to share profits and losses in a predetermined way.

PATENT   Statutory protection which gives an inventor the exclusive rights to his invention, and which prevents others from using the invention without his permission, provided that it meets specific patentability criteria.

PEREMPTORY CHALLENGE   An attorney's right to challenge a juror and remove him from a trial without the necessity of giving a reason for the challenge. Each attorney is permitted a specified number of such challenges to be used as he sees fit.

PERJURY   The making of any false statement under oath.

PERSONAL PROPERTY   Property that is movable, as opposed to real property. Often referred to as "personalty."

PETITION   A formal, written request to a court seeking the court's ruling on a certain matter. Similar to a motion.

PIERCING THE CORPORATE VEIL   A legal doctrine which permits a creditor or other person making a claim against a corporation to hold the stockholders liable for the debts of the corporation, contrary to the usual rule. Piercing the corporate veil is permitted when the corporation has been operated as a sham, for the purpose of deceiving creditors or for other unlawful purposes.

PLAINTIFF   A person who commences a lawsuit.

PLEADINGS   The formal allegations of the parties to a lawsuit, set forth in the plaintiff's complaint and the defendant's answer.

PRECEDENT   A prior decision of a court which, because of its similarity to a later case, influences a court's decision in the later case. Our legal system is structured so that courts take their guidance from precedent; later cases are to be decided as were similar, prior cases.

PRELIMINARY INJUNCTION   An injunction, usually entered on an emergency basis, designed to preserve the status quo until a full hearing can be conducted.

PRIME CONTRACTOR   See general contractor.

PRIVILEGE   A specific right, exemption, or benefit. An excuse which permits a person to do or not do something that would otherwise be required. For example, the "attorney–client privilege" permits an attorney and a client to refuse to disclose communications between them, although under ordinary circumstances they could be asked about any of their conversations that might be relevant to the lawsuit.

PRODUCTS LIABILITY   A body of tort law that defines the rights of those damaged or injured by products against those responsible for designing, manufacturing, or selling the products.

PROMISSORY NOTE   A written promise to pay money to another.

PROMOTER   The persons who take the preliminary steps necessary to form a corporation.

PROPRIETORSHIP   An unincorporated business owned and controlled by one person.

PUNITIVE DAMAGES   Damages that may be awarded against a party under certain limited circumstances involving malicious, reckless, or outrageous conduct. Punitive damages are designed to punish the offender, not to compensate the other party for actual losses.

PURCHASE ORDER   A document which authorizes a seller to deliver goods to a buyer.

QUANTUM MERUIT A legal doctrine which requires persons who knowingly receive the benefit of another's labor or materials to pay a fair price for them.

QUASI-CONTRACT An obligation created by law, in the absence of a contract, to prevent the unjust enrichment of one party at the expense of another.

QUID PRO QUO A legal expression referring to the exchange made between parties to a contract; this for that.

QUIET TITLE ACTION A cause of action to determine the validity of competing claims to land and to resolve defects in title.

RECEIVER A person appointed by a court to be the caretaker of certain property, a business, or other object of value.

RECORD The official account and repository of the evidence which has been admitted by the court and which may therefore properly be considered in reaching a decision.

REDEEM To buy back or repurchase. When a corporation redeems stock, it buys it back from the stockholders. When property that has been used as collateral is redeemed, the debt is repaid and the property is bought back, free of any security interest.

REFORMATION The act of amending a written contract so that it accurately reflects the true agreement of the parties. Lawsuits seeking a court-ordered reformation may be commenced when a contract document mistakenly fails to set forth the parties' agreement.

RELEASE The relinquishing of a claim or a right, usually by a written document, as a part of a settlement or compromise agreement.

RELEVANT Designating evidence which tends to prove the issue in question. In determining whether evidence is admissible, a court will, among other things, determine if it is relevant. If it is not, it is inadmissible.

RELIANCE A doctrine of law which can, in certain circumstances, impose liability on a person, even in the absence of a contract, if he acts in such a way as to induce others to depend on the truth of his statements or actions.

REMAND An appellate court's sending back of a lawsuit to the trial court for further action in accordance with the appellate court's instructions.

REMEDY The means by which a party to a lawsuit is given what he is entitled to receive under the law. The right to be awarded damages or the right to receive an injunction is a remedy.

REMOVAL The defendant's act of transferring to a federal court a lawsuit that was commenced by the plaintiff in a state court. When a lawsuit could have been commenced in the federal court in the first instance, the defendant can remove it to federal court against the plaintiff's will.

REPLEVIN A lawsuit that seeks a court order mandating the return of personal property from the defendant to the plaintiff.

RES A term that usually denotes the subject matter of a trust.

RESCISSION A legal doctrine by which a contract is undone, as if it had never existed. A party can sue for rescission if the contract was procured by fraud, for example.

RES JUDICATA A legal doctrine holding that a court's final judgment in a case forever bars the parties from litigating the same claim, or similar claims arising from the same general circumstances.

RESPONDEAT SUPERIOR A doctrine of agency law which holds the "master"
    responsible for the acts of the "servant." For instance, an employer can
    be liable for the torts of his employee, and an employer can be bound by
    the contracts to which his employee agrees.
RESPONDENT The party against whom a petition is filed, by a "petitioner."
RESTATEMENTS A series of legal books, published by the American Law In-
    stitute, written for the purpose of codifying the law into precise, written
    statements, and to set forth what the law ought to be in controversial
    areas. There are various Restatements, such as the Restatement of Torts,
    the Restatement of Contracts, the Restatement of Agency, and others.
    Frequently, courts adopt all or part of various Restatements as the law of
    the jurisdiction.
RESTITUTION A legal doctrine which requires a wrongdoer to restore an in-
    nocent party to the status quo before the wrong was committed. In a
    breach of contract situation, for instance, a party ordered by a court to
    make restitution must put the plaintiff in as good a position as that in
    which he would have been had there been no breach.
RESTRAINT OF TRADE An act that limits free market competition in violation
    of certain antitrust laws, such as, for example, price fixing.
RESTRICTIVE COVENANT A contract clause typically included in employment,
    partnership, joint venture, and similar contracts which restricts a party
    from engaging in similar or competitive work within a specified geo-
    graphic area, for a specified period, after the contract relationship has
    terminated.
RISK OF LOSS In sales contracts, the responsibility for the safety and preser-
    vation of the goods. If, for example, the seller has the risk of loss during
    shipment, he must replace the goods or otherwise compensate the buyer
    if they are damaged in transit.
RULES OF EVIDENCE Court rules that define which evidence is admissible.
RULE TO SHOW CAUSE A court order requiring a party to respond to a claim
    made by another party, usually at a hearing.

SCOPE OF EMPLOYMENT For purposes of the doctrine of respondeat superior,
    acts of the employee which are within the ambit of his employment
    responsibilities so that the employer is liable for them.
SECONDARY BOYCOTT In labor law, a union's interference with a neutral
    company, with which the union has no dispute, for the purpose of bring-
    ing pressure to bear on another company with which the neutral com-
    pany does business.
SECURED CREDITOR A creditor with a security interest.
SECURITY AGREEMENT An agreement that provides a security interest.
SECURITY INTEREST A legal interest in property, acquired by contract, which
    secures the payment of a debt or other obligation by giving the creditor
    the right to sell the property to satisfy the debt, and which establishes
    certain priorities to the property among creditors.
SEQUESTER To separate witnesses from one another so that one cannot hear
    and be influenced by the testimony of the other; to isolate jurors from
    contact with the public.
SERVICE OF PROCESS To provide notice of a lawsuit to a defendant, so that
    he can defend himself, by delivering to him copies of the complaint and

other documents by which the lawsuit was commenced, as provided by the law of the jurisdiction.

SETOFF   A type of counterclaim in which the defendant claims that the amount he owes to the plaintiff ought to be reduced or cancelled because of sums owed to him by the plaintiff.

SHARE OF STOCK   A right to a certain interest in a corporation, which varies depending on the type of stock, the bylaws of the corporation, and applicable law. A share of stock may, for example, afford the holder the right to a proportionate share of the assets of the corporation in the event of dissolution, the right to receive a portion of the corporation's profits in the form of dividends, and the right to vote.

SHERIFF'S SALE   A court-ordered-and-supervised sale of a debtor's property for the purpose of satisfying a judgment or security interest.

SINE QUA NON   An indispensable precondition which permits something else to exist; a prerequisite. For instance, an offer is a sine qua non to a contract.

SITUS   Location; the place where a thing exists.

SLANDER   Oral defamation.

SOLVENCY   The ability to pay debts as they become due.

SOVEREIGN IMMUNITY   A doctrine of law, which exists in various forms in different jurisdictions, holding that federal, state, and local governments are immune from suit except to the extent that they consent to be sued, usually by legislation.

SPECIAL DAMAGES   Out-of-pocket losses caused by a wrongdoer, such as lost profits. Compare "general damages."

SPECIFICATION   As used in construction, a detailed listing and description of the materials, dimensions, performance capabilities, and so on to be followed in doing the work.

SPECIFIC PERFORMANCE   A type of lawsuit in which the plaintiff, instead of suing for damages, seeks a court order requiring the defendant to perform according to the contract.

SPENDTHRIFT TRUST   A trust which limits the beneficiary's access to the fund held for his benefit, and which restricts the rights of the beneficiary's creditors to attach the fund.

SQUEEZE-OUT   A merger between businesses, effected for the purpose of eliminating the influence and restricting the rights of minority shareholders.

STATE COURT   The system of courts as it exists in each state, usually encompassing a trial court in each county, a middle-level appellate court, and a state supreme court. Compare "Federal Court."

STATUTE   A law passed by a legislature, which courts are bound to interpret and apply.

STATUTE OF FRAUDS   A statute, adopted in various forms in most states, which requires that certain kinds of contracts be evidenced by a writing.

STATUTE OF LIMITATIONS   The period within which a lawsuit must be commenced. There are different statutes of limitations for different kinds of lawsuits.

STAY   A court order which stops proceedings in a lawsuit, pending further order by the court.

STIPULATION   An agreement made among attorneys in a lawsuit.

STOCK RESTRICTION   A restriction, often written on the back of a stock certif-
     icate, which limits the holder's right to transfer the stock to a third person.
STRAW PARTY   A party who acts on behalf of another for the purpose of taking
     title to real estate, in order to conceal the identity of the true purchaser
     of the property.
STRICT LIABILITY   A doctrine of tort law which holds the manufacturer of a
     defective product, and every seller in the chain of distribution to the
     eventual consumer, liable for the damages the product causes to the
     eventual consumer, even if the manufacturer and sellers used the utmost
     care and were in no way negligent.
SUBCHAPTER S   A type of corporation whose profits and losses are, for tax
     purposes, treated as the profits and losses of the individual stockholders.
     This gives the stockholders the tax advantages of a partnership or joint
     venture, while retaining other benefits of the corporate form of doing
     business, such as protection from liability for corporate debts. Also re-
     ferred to as an "S" corporation.
SUBCONTRACTOR   In a construction project, one who contracts with a general
     contractor to do a certain portion of the work which the general contrac-
     tor agreed to do in his contract with the owner.
SUBORDINATION   The act of placing a judgment, lien, or other security inter-
     est in a lower priority, so that another's judgment, lien, or security interest
     is satisfied first—usually accomplished through a contract called a "sub-
     ordination agreement."
SUBPOENA   A command by a court to appear at a certain time and place for
     the purpose of giving testimony or producing documents.
SUBROGATION   A doctrine of law that substitutes one person for another re-
     specting the right to make a claim or enforce a right. The term is most
     often used in an insurance context: when, for example, an insurance
     company pays a claim for property damage to its insured, the doctrine of
     subrogation then gives it the right to step into the shoes of the insured for
     the purpose of suing whoever caused the property damage.
SUBSIDIARY   A corporation most of whose stock is owned by another corpo-
     ration, known as the "parent."
SUCCESSOR   One who takes the place of another, assuming the other's rights
     and liabilities. One can become the successor to another by virtue of a
     will, a contract, a purchase and sale, a corporate acquisition, or various
     other means.
SUMMARY JUDGMENT   A judgment entered in a party's favor upon the filing of
     a motion before trial, based upon there being no real doubt that the party
     would prevail at trial if the trial were held.
SUMMATION   An attorney's final speech to the jury, after all the evidence has
     been presented.
SUMMONS   A document issued by a court upon the commencement of a
     lawsuit and served on the opposing party to notify him of the lawsuit and
     his obligation to appear and defend himself.
SUPERSEDEAS   An appellate court's command to a trial court requiring that it
     suspend efforts to enforce its judgment against a defendant pending the
     appellate court's eventual decision on the defendant's appeal. Without a
     supersedeas, a plaintiff who obtains a judgment can have the trial court
     enforce it against a defendant despite the defendant's appeal.

SURETY Functionally similar to a "guarantor," although there are subtle legal differences: one who agrees to pay money to a third party in the event that the person who owes the money refuses to pay. The obligation of the surety is expressed in a document called a "surety agreement" or "surety bond."

SURVIVORSHIP The right of a joint owner of property to automatically receive the ownership interest of a co-owner of the property upon the co-owner's death. The right of survivorship is important since, if it exists, the interest of the deceased person in the property does not pass to his heirs. Rather, his interest passes to the co-owner.

TEMPORARY RESTRAINING ORDER An injunction, entered on an emergency basis, often designed to preserve the status quo until a court has the opportunity to convene a full hearing.

TENANCY A right to possess real estate pursuant to a lease. The term also refers to an ownership interest in real property. See "joint tenancy," "tenancy in common," and "tenancy by the entireties."

TENANCY BY THE ENTIRETIES An interest usually in real estate, held by a husband and wife as if they were one person, with a right of survivorship so that, upon the death of one, the other becomes the sole owner of the property. Compare "joint tenancy" and "tenancy in common."

TENANCY IN COMMON An interest usually in real estate, in which each tenant in common jointly owns the whole property with the other (as opposed to each owning a divided half of the property). There is no right of survivorship, so that upon the death of a tenant in common, his interest in the property passes to his heirs. Compare "joint tenancy" and "tenancy by the entireties."

TENDER In a contract situation, the act of offering what a party considers to be due to another pursuant to the terms of the contract, such as a tender of full payment.

TESTAMENTARY Pertaining to a will.

TESTATE The state of dying having left a will. Compare "intestate."

TESTIMONY Evidence given by a witness under oath.

THIRD PARTY BENEFICIARY A person who is not a party to a contract, but for whose benefit the contract was made.

THIRD PARTY DEFENDANT A party who is added to a lawsuit by a defendant, on the basis that the party is either liable to the plaintiff or liable to the defendant. In some jurisdictions, termed an "additional defendant."

TIME IS OF THE ESSENCE A contract clause which requires strict adherence, without even minor deviations, from time limits and deadlines in the contract.

TORT A civil wrong, other than breach of contract, for which damages may be recovered.

TORTFEASOR One who commits a tort.

TORTIOUS In the nature of a tort; wrongful.

TRADEMARK A distinctive word, name, symbol, or combination thereof by which a manufacturer or merchant identifies his goods and distinguishes them from goods manufactured or sold by others. A trademark can be registered and protected from use by others.

TRADE SECRET An unpatented formula, process, mechanism, compound, or other confidential matter known only to the owner of a business and those in whom it is necessary to confide it which has commercial value. Trade secrets can frequently be protected from disclosure and use by others.

TRANSCRIPT   The word-for-word copy of a trial, hearing, deposition, or other proceeding, taken down by a court reporter or stenographer. Sometimes referred to as the "notes of testimony."

TREASURY STOCK   Shares of stock that have been issued by a corporation and then reacquired and held by it.

TRESPASS   A tort arising from unlawful interference with or damage to one's person, property, or rights. Also refers to a type of lawsuit generally arising from such matters, referred to as "an action in trespass." Compare "assumpsit."

TRIAL COURT   The court in which the trial was conducted, as opposed to an appellate court.

TRIAL DE NOVO   A new trial, conducted as if there had never been a former trial.

TRUST   An arrangement whereby property, usually called the "res," is transferred to a trustee, to be held for the benefit of a beneficiary, usually pursuant to the terms of a written agreement. There are numerous varieties of trusts.

TYING ARRANGEMENT   An arrangement, frequently illegal under the antitrust laws, in which a seller will sell a product only if the buyer agrees to buy a different product as well.

UCC-1   A form used by a creditor to file in state and local public records evidence of the creditor's security interest in a debtor's personal property. This protects the creditor, since the order of filing establishes the order in which creditors can make a claim against the property in the event of a default by the debtor.

UNAUDITED   A type of accounting service in which information is compiled but not verified for accuracy. See "compilation and review," which is the more current terminology for such accounting services.

UNCONSCIONABLE   Referring to a contract that is grossly one-sided and unreasonably favorable to one party, often through incomprehensible small print. A court can refuse to enforce a contract that is unconscionable.

UNFAIR COMPETITION   A general term referring to various state statutes that prohibit fraudulent, misleading, or deceptive business practices, as where one seller attempts to pass off his goods as being those of another, or where one seller misrepresents the nature and quality of another's goods.

UNIFORM COMMERCIAL CODE   A book-length statute, adopted in all states except Louisiana, intended to regulate and make uniform from state to state commercial transactions involving such matters as sales of goods, commercial paper, security agreements, bank deposits and collections, letters of credit, bulk sales, and investment securities.

UNJUST ENRICHMENT   A legal doctrine which provides that a person cannot retain the benefit of money, property, or services that rightfully belong to another when, in the judgment of a court, it would be inequitable to allow him to do so.

UNLIQUIDATED DAMAGES   Damages that have not yet been determined or calculated in amount.

USURY   Lending practices that violate the amount of interest which may be charged.

VENUE   The particular locality in which a lawsuit may be properly heard by a court.

VERDICT   The decision of a jury.

VICARIOUS LIABILITY   The indirect legal responsibility of one person for the acts of another person. A principal, for example, is vicariously liable for the acts of an agent.

VOIR DIRE   The process by which a jury is selected for a jury trial, involving the questioning of prospective jurors.

WAIVER   The relinquishment of a right or claim. A person can voluntarily waive a right or claim, or a waiver can be implied from a person's actions or conduct.

WARRANTY   A statement respecting the nature or quality of property being sold, made by the seller to induce the sale. Warranties can be either "express," meaning that they arise from the actions of the seller, or "implied," meaning that they arise by operation of law.

WHEREAS   Considering that, or that being the case. Clauses beginning with a "whereas" and appearing at the beginning of a contract document state the factual basis on which the agreement is made.

WIND UP   To terminate and finally resolve the affairs of a corporation or partnership.

WRIT   A court order requiring that an act be performed, or authorizing an officer of the court to perform an act. The two most common writs are the "writ of summons" and the "writ of execution." The writ of summons is employed to commence a lawsuit. The writ of execution is employed to enforce a judgment.

WRONGFUL DISCHARGE   A relatively new and quickly developing tort involving the right of employees to recover damages from employers who terminate their employment, even though they have no employment contracts.

ABOUT THE AUTHOR

Michael G. Trachtman graduated with honors from the Villanova University School of Law, where he also served as an editor of the *Villanova Law Review*. Since founding his own law firm in suburban Philadelphia, he has represented, among other clients, banks, construction companies, manufacturers, sales organizations, software firms, real estate developers, insurance companies, television personalities, sports figures, retailers, engineers, and consulting organizations. The author of numerous published articles, he is a frequent lecturer to the legal and business community, and is regularly retained to teach his "preventive law" techniques to trade associations and companies throughout the country.